Global Commons, Domestic Decisions

American and Comparative Environmental Policy
Sheldon Kamieniecki and Michael E. Kraft, series editors

For a complete list of books in the series, please see pages 293–294.

Global Commons, Domestic Decisions
The Comparative Politics of Climate Change

edited by Kathryn Harrison and Lisa McIntosh Sundstrom

The MIT Press
Cambridge, Massachusetts
London, England

For information about special quantity discounts, please email special_sales@ mitpress.mit.edu

This book was set in Sabon by Toppan Best-set Premedia Limited. Printed and bound in the United States of America.

Library of Congress Cataloging-in-Publication Data
Global commons, domestic decisions : the comparative politics of climate change / edited by Kathryn Harrison and Lisa McIntosh Sundstrom.
    p. cm. — (American and comparative environmental policy)
Includes bibliographical references and index.
ISBN 978-0-262-01426-7 (hardcover : alk. paper) — ISBN 978-0-262-51431-6 (pbk. : alk. paper)
1. Climatic changes—Government policy—International cooperation.
2. Comparative government. I. Harrison, Kathryn, 1958– II. Sundstrom, Lisa McIntosh, 1971–
QC903.G565   2010
363.738′74—dc22

                                                                        2009045669

10 9 8 7 6 5 4 3 2 1

For our children

Contents

Series Foreword

Climate change is often described as the most important environmental problem of the twenty-first century, both because of the magnitude of risks associated with it and the obviously large number of people affected. How governments respond to climate change, both domestically and internationally, also speaks to the broader challenges of confronting third-generation environmental problems. First, these problems are global in scale and therefore require the cooperation of nations that do not necessarily put the well-being of the Earth's population ahead of national interests—essentially posing a worldwide "tragedy of the commons." For example, why should China or the United States cut back sharply on the use of coal if each nation gains little advantage in doing so? Second, the ill-effects (environmental and public health) occur mostly in the future, yet the short-term economic costs of policy actions can be substantial and may adversely affect many powerful interests, such as fossil fuel companies, in addition to creating a burden on the general population. Third, there is almost always considerable scientific uncertainty that can greatly complicate the delicate search for solutions that are broadly acceptable to all interests. Fourth, precisely because they involve long-term and rather complex phenomena, the issues are almost always of low salience to the general public and struggle to gain attention and political support for action, even when polls show an impressive general level of concern. Under these circumstances, how can public policies be advanced both within nations and internationally?

One way to learn about what is possible is to examine what nations have already done using the tools of comparative analysis. Such research can speak to the domestic political factors that affect both national and international willingness to mitigate climate change. By 2009 all developed nations except the United States had endorsed the Kyoto Protocol on climate change, which seeks to reduce industrialized countries' collective emissions to roughly 5 percent below their 1990 levels, and many had adopted and implemented various climate change policies to make those commitments meaningful. Under the Obama administration, the United States finally made a serious effort to approve a national climate change policy, and a diversity of policy actions had already been taken by more than half of the states and more than 950 local governments across the nation. In short, there is now a record that can be examined and assessed to learn more about the politics of climate change policymaking.

Kathryn Harrison and Lisa McIntosh Sundstrom have assembled a team of experienced and talented students of comparative environmental politics to dissect that record in major nations in an effort to assess the progress that has been made and to understand why, to date, it has been so limited. The chapters share a common theoretical framework that points to the role of electoral and political incentives, the normative commitments of policymakers, and the structure and capacity of political institutions as well as the linkage of domestic politics to international policymaking on climate change. This is an opportune time for such a study since nations have already begun negotiations for the post-Kyoto regime that is to take effect in 2012, and future agreements will reflect many of the same forces that the authors describe here.

Earlier versions of some chapters were published in a special issue of *Global Environmental Politics* in November 2007, and they have since been updated and linked to the overall purpose of this volume. The book offers a unique and valuable comparison of the domestic political forces within each nation that affect climate change policymaking and thus provides insights into the conditions under which some countries have been able to adopt innovative and aggressive positions on climate change both domestically and internationally. This is the first study to bring together such analyses of domestic policymaking on climate change in one volume using a common analytic framework. Because the nations and regional governments covered are among the most important players in international climate change policy—the European Union, China, Russia, Japan, Canada, Australia, and the United States—the results should be of interest to a wide audience.

The book illustrates well the goals of the MIT Press series in American and Comparative Environmental Policy. We encourage work that examines a broad range of environmental policy issues. We are particularly interested in volumes that incorporate interdisciplinary research and focus on the linkages between public policy and environmental problems and issues both within the United States and in cross-national settings. We welcome contributions that analyze the policy dimensions of relationships between humans and the environment from either a theoretical or empirical perspective. At a time when environmental policies are increasingly seen as controversial and new approaches are being implemented widely, we especially encourage studies that assess policy successes and failures, evaluate new institutional arrangements and policy tools, and clarify new directions for environmental politics and policy. The books in this series are written for a wide audience that includes academics, policymakers, environmental scientists and professionals, business and labor leaders, environmental activists, and students concerned with environmental issues. We hope they contribute to public understanding of environmental problems, issues, and policies of concern today and also suggest promising actions for the future.

Sheldon Kamieniecki, University California, Santa Cruz
Michael Kraft, University of Wisconsin–Green Bay
American and Comparative Environmental Policy Series Editors

1

Introduction: Global Commons, Domestic Decisions

Kathryn Harrison and Lisa McIntosh Sundstrom

Introduction

Climate change represents a "tragedy of the commons" on a global scale. Like Hardin's hypothetical community of farmers overgrazing the village commons,[1] the nations of the world, and individuals within them, over-exploit the planet's atmosphere because they gain all the material advantages from the activities that contribute to global warming but suffer only a fraction of the environmental costs. In turn, nations and individuals typically are unwilling to reduce their greenhouse gas emissions unilaterally, since in doing so they would pay the full price of abatement but gain only a fraction of the benefits. Indeed, their sacrifices may be futile if other countries or individuals do not exhibit similar restraint.

Despite this formidable challenge, international efforts to address global warming have met with some, albeit limited, success. Under the Framework Convention on Climate Change (FCCC), which took effect in 1994, more than 180 nations committed to a long-term goal of stabilizing greenhouse gas concentrations "at a level that would prevent dangerous anthropogenic interference with the climate system." Although the Convention itself contained only hortatory emissions targets, at the third Conference of Parties to the FCCC (COP 3), agreement was reached on the Kyoto Protocol, in which industrialized countries committed to reducing their collective emissions to roughly 5 percent below 1990 levels by the period 2008 to 2012. Although the United States, which contributes roughly one quarter of global greenhouse gas emissions, withdrew from the treaty in 2001, it was ratified by enough other countries to take effect in 2005.

As the international community looks ahead to a post-Kyoto regime, it is timely to consider what lessons can be learned from experience to date. How can we understand the progress that has been made and why it has been so limited? To date, most political scientists who have studied climate change have done so from the perspective of international relations, with a focus on explaining international agreements based on the interests or ideational orientations of states as unitary actors, without opening the black box of domestic politics.[2] However, when international meetings conclude, actors return to their domestic constituents. The decisions regarding whether or not to ratify international agreements and to adopt national policies to mitigate climate change are in the end domestic political decisions, taken in the context of homegrown interests, national discourses, and domestic political institutions.

In focusing primarily on domestic politics and decisions, with international influences as a critical backdrop, we reverse the lens of previous scholarship. In particular, we seek to understand two potentially distinct outcomes: states' decisions on ratification of the Kyoto Protocol, and the stringency of national climate change abatement policies. Each of the following chapters employs a common theoretical framework that examines the effects on these two outcomes of electoral and political incentives, policymakers' normative commitments, and political institutions, with attention to potential international effects on domestic electoral politics and norms.

Of the highly industrialized countries—the "Annex 1" states that faced binding emissions targets under the Kyoto Protocol—this volume considers the two nations that made decisions not to ratify the Kyoto Protocol before the treaty's entry into force: the United States and Australia (although, notably, Australia ratified the treaty after a change of government in 2007, a development examined by Kate Crowley in chapter 7). We compare those two jurisdictions with four others that did choose to ratify: the European Union (EU), Russia, Japan, and Canada, which are the next largest Annex 1 emitters after the United States. We treat the EU as a single case in the analysis that follows, since EU member states decided jointly on ratification and also coordinated development of climate policies at the EU level. However, in chapter 2 Schreurs and Tiberghien also consider key member states within the EU. To these Annex 1 states, the book compares the largest non-Annex 1 state, China, which looms large not only for its influence among developing countries in international negotiations but also because it recently surpassed the United States as the nation with the greatest greenhouse gas emissions.

To preview our conclusions, we find, first, that the costs of compliance with Kyoto Protocol targets varied significantly among the countries studied and that this tended to play out in the domestic arena, with countries facing more demanding targets encountering stronger domestic opposition to ratification. Thus the United States and Australia, anticipating high costs, declined to ratify, while Russia and China, facing no need to reduce emissions, chose to ratify. It is hardly surprising that anticipated material benefits would lead some countries, and economic actors within them, to embrace the treaty, while material costs would tend to make others reluctant to undertake ratification and mitigation. The question remains, however, why the EU, Japan, Canada, and eventually Australia ratified, despite anticipation of considerable costs.

A normative commitment sufficiently strong to outweigh immediate self-interest can arise from either voters at large or politicians themselves. Protecting the environment tends to be a "motherhood" issue that elicits support in polls in virtually all countries, but limited public attention and thus limited electoral pressure in most countries most of the time. Public support for action to address climate change is widespread but shallow.[3] Faced with the combination of voters' often limited attention to environmental issues and their simultaneous demand for economic growth and low energy prices, it is understandable that politicians in many countries would view polls showing support for the Kyoto Protocol and actions to reduce greenhouse gas emissions with skepticism. Yet when the salience of the environment generally, or climate in particular, increases to the point where it is one of the most prominent issues on the political agenda, politicians' electoral incentives shift significantly. This was influential in EU member states that played an instrumental role in advancing EU-wide positions on climate;[4] in Japan, where the Kyoto Protocol had symbolic significance by virtue of its having originated there; in Australia, where a belated decision to ratify was made after a surge in the salience of climate change on the political agenda; and in Canada, where the reemergence of environmental issues' salience in 2006 prompted a Conservative government to substantially revise its regulatory targets.[5]

In the absence of electoral incentives, however, politicians' own values may carry the day. This was most evident in Canada, where Jean Chretien, the prime minister, made the decision to ratify against political odds. Yet Canada also provides a cautionary tale that politicians' ideational commitments may be fragile in the absence of strong electoral support.

Finally, we find that institutions can dampen or facilitate expression of either ideas or material interests in several important ways. Proportional electoral systems in Europe tended to amplify the voices of a minority of voters for whom climate change has long been a political priority. In contrast, green voters had minimal impact in Canada and the United States, where first-past-the-post electoral systems invite political parties to appeal to the median voter, who has typically been inattentive to environmental issues. In addition, we find that legislative institutions that diffuse authority horizontally, thus creating veto points, make it easier for the status quo, and thus those opposed to ratification and mitigation policies, to prevail. This was most evident in the United States, where the Clinton administration simply did not have the institutional capacity to ratify the Kyoto Protocol in the absence of Senate consent.

Analysis of federalism and, in the EU, multilevel governance offers a complex picture, with the effects of vertical diffusion of authority dependent on interactions of federal institutions with public opinion and the regional distribution of costs and benefits among subnational actors or member states. While a competitive multilevel dynamic prompted EU leadership, and US state governments partially filled a void left by federal government inaction, in Canada federalism has for the most part been an obstacle to both ratification and adoption of domestic mitigation policies.

In this introductory chapter, we provide common background on the international context for the national case studies presented in this volume and review the theoretical framework of the book, developing hypotheses to be tested in light of the case studies that follow. In the final chapter of the book, we compare Kyoto Protocol ratification decisions and domestic climate policies across the case studies in order to draw conclusions about domestic factors that can be expected to advance or obstruct efforts to address climate change in the future, both at the national and international level.

The International Context

In focusing on domestic politics, it is not our intention to ignore the international context. It goes without saying that ratification of the Kyoto Protocol would not be on the domestic political agenda if it were not for prior international negotiations. In this section, we set the stage by reviewing international developments that predate the question of ratification. We later discuss ways in which ongoing international ties shaped domestic debates about ratification and adoption of mitigation measures.

In the case of a common pool resource such as the global climate, a multilateral agreement can play a critical role in facilitating domestic action. Countries that may be unwilling to act unilaterally, both because they do not want to harm the international competitiveness of local producers and because they anticipate that unilateral actions would be of limited environmental benefit, may be more willing to take action if they receive assurance that others will do the same. However, the costs of action depend on the terms of the treaty and may differ among signatory countries, with important implications for domestic political debates.

Several features of the Kyoto Protocol are relevant to assessing and comparing national costs of compliance. First, in recognition of the fact that industrialized countries have much higher per capita emissions than those of the developing world and also have contributed the vast majority of greenhouse gases that have accumulated in the atmosphere to date, the Protocol specified binding emissions reductions targets only for industrialized (Annex 1) countries. While the normative basis for leadership by wealthy countries is indisputable, the inevitable implication is that mitigation measures undertaken by industrialized countries may make them less competitive vis-à-vis developing countries.

Second, the Kyoto Protocol included differentiated targets even among Annex 1 countries, as indicated in table 1.1. The EU accepted a collective

Table 1.1
Comparison of Kyoto Protocol Targets

	Net greenhouse gas emissions in 2008–2012 relative to 1990 base year
China	No obligation
Australia	+8%
Russia	0%
Japan	−6%
Canada	−6%
United States	−7%
EU-15[1]	−8%

Source: UNFCC, http://unfccc.int/kyoto_protocol/items/3145.php.
1. The 15 EU countries that were members before May 1, 2004: Austria, Belgium, Denmark, Finland, France, Germany, Greece, Ireland, Italy, Luxembourg, the Netherlands, Portugal, Spain, Sweden, and the United Kingdom.

target of −8 percent, with individual member states' targets within the EU "bubble" negotiated among EU member states.

Third, the Kyoto Protocol stated that it would not come into force unless ratified by at least fifty-five states that comprised at least 55 percent of Annex 1 countries' 1990 emissions. While the requirement that at least fifty-five states ratify was easily met, since developing countries do not face emissions targets and thus had no reason not to ratify, the second requirement was more challenging, especially after the withdrawal of the United States, which accounted for roughly one-third of Annex 1 1990 emissions. That gave Annex 1 countries with significant emissions, most notably Japan and Russia, greater bargaining power with which to wrest concessions from other states in ongoing negotiations leading up to their ratification decisions.

Finally, the Kyoto Protocol included a number of mechanisms that increased participating states' flexibility in meeting their targets and thus offered the potential to reduce compliance costs. These mechanisms included multiyear averaging, with compliance to be determined based on each country's emissions over a five-year period from 2008 to 2012. A second mechanism was a "basket" of six greenhouse gases, with countries able to trade off deeper reductions in emissions of some gases against lesser reductions, or even increases, in others. Third, the Protocol allowed countries to take into account changes in land use, thereby offsetting emissions either by reducing their rate of land clearing or increasing forest cover. Finally, the Kyoto Protocol included three international flexibility mechanisms: emissions trading among Annex 1 countries, such that a country that exceeded its target could sell its extra credits to another country, thus allowing the latter to meet its target at lower cost; "joint implementation" by Annex 1 countries, such that benefits of a joint project to reduce emissions or increase carbon sinks could be shared, again allowing countries to take advantage of less expensive mitigation opportunities; and the Clean Development Mechanism, through which Annex 1 countries could gain credits toward their target by investing in more cost-effective projects in developing countries. Although inclusion of carbon sinks and international mechanisms were central to the compromise reached at COP 3, critical details concerning what kinds of projects or sinks would "count" and to what degree countries could rely on these flexibility mechanisms remained to be worked out at subsequent conferences of the parties.

Outcomes to Be Explained

Climate policies can be compared on four levels: positions taken in international negotiations; ratification or nonratification of international treaties; adoption of domestic programs to abate climate change (whether or not in response to international treaties); and "street level" implementation of those programs. The first, international negotiations concerning climate change, has been well studied by international relations scholars, while it is premature to assess the last, policy implementation.[6] Our primary focus thus will be the second and third outcomes, ratification of the Kyoto Protocol and adoption of domestic climate policies. While the two may go hand in hand, with leaders both ratifying and adopting aggressive mitigation policies and laggards doing neither, it is also conceivable that some countries may ratify but fail to follow up or adopt activist domestic policies without ratifying.

Comparing ratification outcomes is clear-cut: jurisdictions either ratified the Kyoto Protocol or they did not. The second outcome, domestic abatement policies, is less straightforward. In part this is because abatement programs in most countries remain very much a work in progress. Moreover the range and complexity of climate policies, to say nothing of unrelated policies that nonetheless positively or negatively affect greenhouse gas emissions, present a significant challenge for researchers. As a first step, we compare the extent to which each jurisdiction has relied on an array of policy instruments, arranged below in order from least to most challenging politically.

• Receipt of international funding (for example, via the Clean Development Mechanism)
• Adoption of a climate change mitigation plan
• Adoption of voluntary programs
• Public expenditures on research or subsidies, whether for consumers or business
• Public expenditures on international mechanisms (for example, purchase of international credits or investment in the Clean Development Mechanism or Joint Implementation)
• Regulation of greenhouse gas emissions (with or without trading)
• Adoption of carbon taxes[7]

We consider a policy instrument to be easier to adopt to the extent that it has lower costs and/or diffuses those costs broadly. Instruments such as regulation and taxation, which tend to involve both significant and concentrated costs, are especially challenging politically. Not coincidentally, we also expect them to provide the strongest incentives for individuals or firms to change their behavior.

In seeking to explain the two outcomes of interest, we focus on three broad domestic factors: self-interest, ideas, and political institutions, all of which we define *from the perspective of the policymaker*. Accordingly, the ideas category explores the effects of policymakers' own knowledge and values rather than those of the electorate or other power brokers in a polity. Similarly, we assume that it is in the policymaker's self-interest to stay in power and thus, for democratic contexts, consider electoral incentives as an alternative explanation to ideas. However, although it is in a politician's self-interest to be reelected, one should not necessarily equate the self-interest category with self-interested behavior by the electorate. If voters care enough about addressing climate change, despite personal costs, they may provide sufficient electoral incentives for politicians to act regardless of the politicians' own values. Thus ideas can enter our theoretical framework in two ways, via politicians' values or via the electorate's values.

Self-interest

We begin from an assumption that politicians seek to retain their positions in government. In the case of democracies, this translates to a motive to seek reelection. All else being equal, we hypothesize that the stronger the public demand for action to address climate change in a given country, the more likely that country would be to ratify the Kyoto Protocol and adopt domestic climate change mitigation measures. However, interpretation of public opinion polls with respect to the environment requires some caution. The valence nature of the issue— after all, hardly anyone is in *favor* of global warming!—means that a majority of voters in all countries invariably say that they support action to address global warming. A critical question from a politician's standpoint is thus to what degree the electorate is actually paying attention to the issue, not least because voters inattentive to climate change may be paying closer attention to issues such as energy prices that militate against adoption of effective measures to reduce greenhouse gas emissions. The following chapters thus consider the salience of environmental issues generally and climate change in particular, as expressed by voters' responses to open-ended questions about their political priorities.

When voters at large are not attentive, one can expect politicians to weigh more heavily the voices of interest groups on either side of an issue. The relative influence of those groups will depend on their size, since their members are the voters (and campaign contributors) most likely to take into account the government's actions on the issue come election time. However, since the membership of most interest groups is relatively small, their most important source of influence lies in their claims to speak for and threats to mobilize the electorate at large. When the salience of environmental issues is high, the voices of environmental groups will carry considerable weight. However, when the salience of the environment is low, we anticipate that politicians will be more receptive to members of the business community who claim to speak on behalf of voters' interest in jobs and the economy.

In semidemocratic or authoritarian contexts—Russia and China in this study—where the preferences of the mass citizenry do not exert strong pressure on government leaders, the imperative of reelection does not figure prominently in leaders' efforts to remain in office. Instead, the approval of other key actors, such as industrial managers, ministry bureaucrats, or governing party cadres may be crucial for maintaining power. In addition, the government may feel pressure to maintain or improve economic performance in order to satisfy citizens' basic needs and prevent mass protest that could challenge its rule. To a certain extent, then, we anticipate that the interests of politicians in nondemocratic contexts will resemble the interests of politicians in democracies when electorates are not paying attention to the issue of climate change.

In addition, we expect that the strength and relative influence of political opposition will be greater where there are greater costs of compliance with the Kyoto Protocol and, more generally, of emissions reductions for a given country. Table 1.2, which compares emissions and emissions intensities of the countries examined in this volume, offers preliminary insights into the economic and thus political costs of addressing climate change in different countries.

Not surprisingly, there is considerable variation in per capita emissions across states. To some degree this reflects countries' wealth, with per capita emissions in the one developing country in our study, China, at 4 metric tons per person—a small fraction of the 26 metric tons per year emitted by each resident of Australia and Luxembourg. However, the variation in per capita emissions is significant even among wealthy industrialized countries, with Sweden's per capita emissions less than

Table 1.2
Comparison of Greenhouse Gas Emissions, Emissions Intensities, and Trends in Releases

Country	Kyoto target	Percent change in emissions (without LULUCF), 1990–1997[1]	Share of global emissions (without LULUCF), 2005[2]	Share of annex 1 emissions (without LULUCF), 1990	2005 GHG emissions (without LULUCF), t/person[3]	Emissions intensity relative to GDP (without LULUCF), t/US$GDP[4]
Australia	+8%	10%	1.8%	2.2%	26.0	0.71
Canada	-6%	14%	2.5%	3.0%	23.1	0.66
China[5]	n/a	n/a	16.6%	n/a	3.9	4.16
Japan	-6%	6%	4.5%	6.5%	10.7	0.30
Russia	+0%	-36%	7.1%	16.4%	14.9	2.79
United States	-7%	10%	24.2%	31.1%	24.5	0.58
EU-15	-8%	-2%	14.0%	21.7%	10.9	0.33
Austria	+13%	5%	0.3%	0.4%	11.4	0.31
Belgium	-7.5%	1%	0.5%	0.7%	13.9	0.39
Denmark	-21%	15%	0.2%	0.4%	12.1	0.25
Finland	+0%	7%	0.2%	0.4%	13.3	0.35
France	+0%	1%	1.9%	2.9%	8.9	0.26

Germany	−21%	−12%	3.3%	6.2%	12.1	0.36
Greece	+25%	12%	0.5%	0.6%	12.9	0.49
Ireland	+13%	14%	0.2%	0.3%	17.4	0.35
Italy	−6.5%	2%	1.9%	2.6%	10.0	0.33
Luxembourg	−28%	−27%	0.0%	0.1%	27.2	0.35
Netherlands	−6%	6%	0.7%	1.1%	12.9	0.34
Portugal	+27%	21%	0.3%	0.3%	8.1	0.47
Spain	+15%	15%	1.5%	1.5%	10.9	0.39
Sweden	+4%	1%	0.2%	0.4%	7.4	0.19
UK	−12.5%	−8%	2.2%	3.9%	10.9	0.30

1. From UNFCCC, Times Series Annex 1, http://unfccc.int/ghg_data/ghg_data_unfccc/time_series_annex_i/items/3814.php.

2. Share of global and Annex 1 emissions calculated from UNFCCC, http://unfccc.int/ghg_emissions_data/items/3954.php. Non-Annex 1 (China) data from CAIT, for 2000 (latest available), http://cait.wri.org/cait.php?page=yearly&mode=view.

3. Calculated with emissions data as reported to UN FCCC in 2007 (http://unfccc.int/ghg_emissions_data/items/3954.php); population data from US Census Bureau (http://www.census.gov/ipc/www/idbrank.html). Data for China from 2000.

4. Calculated with 2005 GDP data (millions current US$) from UN Statistics Division, http://unstats.un.org/unsd/snaama/selectionbasicFast.asp. Data for China from 2000.

5. Note that under the UNFCCC, non-Annex 1 countries are not required to report their emissions inventory annually.

one-third those of Canada, Australia, and the United States. To a large extent this reflects geographic factors, including physical size of the country and resulting population dispersion; resource endowments, which largely determine the fuel mix used for energy; and historical development, with "new world" cities built after the advent of streetcars and automobiles tending to be more sprawling than older, European cities. However, past policy decisions, particularly concerning energy paths and pricing, undoubtedly have also had an impact.

A brief summary of the case study countries' emissions profiles highlights these variations. Until recently overtaken by China,[8] the United States has been the country that had contributed the largest share, at roughly one-quarter, of global greenhouse gas emissions. The United States' relatively high per capita emissions, at 24.5 metric tons per person in 2005, reflects, among other factors, its heavy reliance on coal for electricity generation and a relatively fuel-inefficient vehicle fleet.

Although with its relatively small population Canada contributes a minor share of global emissions, in other respects its position is very similar to that of the United States. Blessed by an abundance of fossil fuels and cursed by long distances between population centers, Canada's economy has evolved in a highly greenhouse-gas-intensive manner, led by production of oil and gas both for domestic use and export. The situation in Australia is similar, though with coal production replacing oil and gas, again for both domestic energy and export.

The EU's emissions profile stands in stark contrast to the United States, Canada, and Australia. At 11 metric tons per capita in 2005, carbon emissions per capita are at the low end among industrialized countries. The reasons for such low per capita emissions vary by country within the EU, as do the emissions rates themselves, but European countries generally rely more on nuclear power (France), hydro power (Sweden), and natural gas (UK) rather than coal and petroleum for energy. Moreover, since the region is densely populated, travel distances are shorter than in North America and Australia, homes and vehicles are generally smaller, and public transit is both convenient and heavily used. Existing taxes on energy use, which encourage conservation, are also much higher than in the "new world." Like the EU, Japan also has relatively low per capita carbon emissions, at just under 10 metric tons per capita in 2005, with a relatively energy-efficient economy.

The Russian Federation has emissions levels per capita that lie between these two poles at roughly 15 metric tons in 2005. Russia's emissions profile is characterized by two competing factors. Russia's low per capita income tends to limit emissions. However, its energy-inefficient industrial sector yields emissions that are higher than for comparable facilities in other countries.

The fact that the Kyoto Protocol directed individual countries to reduce their emissions relative to their own 1990 baselines, as opposed to meeting a common per capita target, effectively took into account these accidents of geography and history. In addition, however, countries accepted differentiated targets relative to their 1990 baselines, to be met on average in the five-year commitment period from 2008 to 2012. For each country, the costs of compliance with the Kyoto Protocol would be expected to depend on two factors: the depth of cuts it would need to make, and the marginal costs of those cuts.

The formal Kyoto Protocol target for each country is noted in the second column of table 1.2. The original fifteen members of the EU negotiated as a single unit, committing to an 8 percent reduction relative to 1990. However, as discussed by Schreurs and Tiberghien in chapter 2 and reflected in table 1.2, the EU negotiated differentiated targets for individual member states that range from a 28 percent cut for Luxembourg to a 27 percent increase for Portugal.

The third column in table 1.2 reports each country's emissions in 1997, the year the Kyoto Protocol was negotiated, relative to its 1990 baseline. Russia had already experienced significant emissions reductions as a result of the massive collapse of its economy in 1991, when the Soviet Union was dismantled. Similarly, Germany's emissions declined dramatically in the early 1990s after reunification and the closure of inefficient facilities in the former East Germany. Given the scale of the German economy, Germany alone accounts to a large degree for the modest reduction of EU emissions from 1990 to 1997. In still other cases, most notably the United States, Canada, and Australia, emissions had already increased significantly from 1990 to 1997 as a result of high economic and population growth. To the extent that those "business as usual" trends could be expected to continue in the absence of policy intervention, one would expect the seemingly similar formal targets in the Kyoto Protocol (second column) to be much harder to meet for Canada, Australia, and the United States than for the EU and Russia, with Japan somewhere in between. The question of how far below "business as usual" policymakers anticipated reductions would be necessary at the time they made their ratification decisions is a complex one, considered in greater depth in the chapters that follow. However, all else being equal, we anticipate greater political opposition, and thus a lower likelihood that a country would ratify the Kyoto Protocol, as the necessary cuts relative to a business-as-usual trajectory become deeper.

In theory, the international trading provisions of the Kyoto Protocol would yield a global price for carbon and thus equalize marginal abatement costs in all countries. With full global trading, each country's cost of compliance would simply be proportional to the depth of cuts needed below business as usual. However, to the extent that countries preferred to invest in domestic abatement measures or were constrained internationally by transaction costs or availability of credits, one would expect compliance costs to be a function of domestic abatement costs. Thus, even if two countries committed to equivalent emissions reductions below their business-as-usual trajectories, the anticipated costs would be greater in the country with higher marginal costs of abatement. Of note on this point is the final column of table 1.2, though the results require careful interpretation. High emissions intensity relative to gross domestic product (GDP) can indicate two very different things. In the case of Russia, it indicates highly inefficient operations, which suggest relatively low abatement costs per metric ton, since enterprises within Russia have yet to harvest even the low-hanging fruit of energy conservation. At the limit, some enterprises actually may benefit financially from abatement regardless of environmental considerations. Japan shows the flip side of this, where low emissions intensity per dollar of GDP reflects prior investments in energy efficiency and thus relatively high costs of additional abatement.

On the other hand, emissions intensity also reflects natural resource endowments, which can have very different implications. Next to Russia, Australia and Canada have the highest emissions intensity relative to GDP. While significant energy efficiency gains undoubtedly remain to be realized in both countries, a larger part of the story is the significance of greenhouse-gas-intensive extraction of fossil fuels in both countries. (In contrast, the low emissions intensity of Sweden largely reflects the abundance of hydroelectric potential in that country.) Thus, rather than indicating the ease with which Canada and Australia can reduce their emissions, high emissions intensities reflect the economic significance, and thus political power, of fossil fuel industries that stand to pay the greatest price for emissions abatement in these two countries.

Ideas

Scholars in both international relations and comparative politics in recent years have turned their attention to the impact of ideas. With respect to politicians' ideas, we follow Goldstein and Keohane in distinguishing between causal knowledge (especially science) and principled values or norms.[9] The more convinced a politician is that climate change is real and caused by human activity, the more likely she or he should be to support costly measures to address the problem. However, even if a politician believes the science, the question is how willing she or he is to accept political risks in order to pursue norms of environmental protection.

Not surprisingly, scholars of international relations and comparative politics have adopted different levels of analysis. For international relations scholars, the unit of analysis is often the nation-state, and a critical question is how much a *state*'s behavior is influenced by norms and the state's desire to cultivate a particular identity, even at the expense of its material interest or physical security. Thus Keck and Sikkink emphasize the desire "to belong to a normative community of nations."[10] In contrast, scholars working within a comparative and domestic politics tradition typically focus on the knowledge or values of individual policymakers within the domestic political scene.[11]

A persuasive indicator that norms have a critical influence on actors' decisions is the pursuit of such norms in the face of contrary material interests. In such cases, there is strong evidence of the overriding influence of norms, while it is more difficult to ascertain the influence of particular norms when it is materially costless to comply with them, even though they typically play some role in actors' choices among multiple options.[12] At the level of domestic politics, the question is whether individual policymakers had sufficiently strong *personal* knowledge and commitment that they were willing to accept electoral risk in order to pursue their own values. In other words, did policymakers pursue their "good policy motives,"[13] despite contrary personal interests (for example, in career advancement and wealth)?

Norms of global fairness and responsibility loom large in the ratification and climate policy decisions of industrialized and developing countries. Governments of the global South argue that that they are entitled to pursue economic development without constraints imposed by the industrialized world, since the global North has perpetrated most of the environmental destruction in the world and continues to contribute vastly more greenhouse gas emissions per capita than do poorer countries. This powerful normative claim has been a persistent obstacle to any international treaty that would include binding commitments by all states. Yet even if industrialized countries accept this argument, there are multiple potential conceptual frameworks for assessing responsibility for both past and future emissions, including according to current or historical emissions, capacity to make reductions, and varying definitions of individuals' rights to equal shares of the earth's atmosphere.[14]

Ideological values along a typical left-right spectrum may not be clearly linked to governments' positions on climate change. As Green parties have long argued, protection of the environment is "neither left nor right." However, we expect that such values are likely to play a role in shaping policymakers' preferences in climate policy instruments. Parties on the left would be more willing to pursue the kinds of regulatory or tax interventions that are likely to be most effective in arresting growth of greenhouse gas emissions, while parties on the right would prefer voluntary mechanisms.

Institutions

Many scholars have noted the contingent nature of political institutions, the effects of which often depend on their interaction with other factors.[15] We focus below on two institutional characteristics. The first concerns the ways in which electoral systems express voters' preferences. As noted above, most of the time the average voter is not particularly attentive to environmental issues. However, for a minority group of voters the environment is always their top issue. Proportional electoral systems tend to represent these environmentally concerned voters' interests more closely, often through the emergence of Green parties. Consistent with the correlation between proportional representation and environmental performance reported by Scruggs,[16] we anticipate that jurisdictions with some form of proportional representation (PR)—most notably the EU, with PR in the European Parliament as well as various member states—will face stronger electoral incentives for ratification and adoption of domestic policies at the same level of salience as jurisdictions such as Canada and the United States, which have majoritarian, first-past-the-post electoral systems. In the cases of Japan and Russia, electoral reforms were undertaken during the period of study, thus allowing the authors to consider the effects of electoral change, while Australia has a mixed system with first-past-the-post in the lower house and PR (specifically single transferable vote) in the Senate.

A second institutional characteristic concerns the concentration of authority, though we anticipate less clear-cut effects here. We distinguish between the horizontal concentration or diffusion of authority within a national government and the vertical concentration or diffusion of authority among levels of government within a federation or quasi federation. With respect to the former, concentration of decision making within the hands of an individual or small group of actors, as exists within majoritarian parliamentary systems such as Canada's and the superpresidential system of Russia, can facilitate leadership when key policymakers are personally committed to action.[17] However, concentration of authority can also make it easier for the same actors to decline to act if they do not believe it is the right thing to do. Thus we anticipate the effects of this institutional factor to be contingent on politicians' ideas about ratification of the Kyoto Protocol and adoption of domestic climate change abatement policies.

Institutions may also interact with electoral incentives. Diffuse authority within a national (or subnational) government presents multiple veto points that can be employed to block policy change. Where the status quo is one of inaction, diffusion of authority will tend to make it more difficult for jurisdictions to ratify the Kyoto Protocol and to adopt climate change mitigation policies. Consistent with this, Dolšak found that countries with parliamentary systems were more aggressive in their early climate policies than those with presidential systems.[18] Similarly, Lantis found that leaders in parliamentary systems had greater success in ratifying international treaties than those in presidential systems.[19] We thus expect change to be more difficult in the United States presidential system and the mixed system of the EU than in majoritarian parliamentary systems of Canada, Australia, and Japan. That said, when there are sufficiently strong electoral incentives for action, diffused authority has been known to generate a very different competitive dynamic between branches in the US presidential system, which could in theory occur in the EU as well.[20] Public opinion thus operates like a switch, such that the same institutions deter policy change during normal times but may facilitate change when environmental issues are highly salient.

Federalism is a form of vertical diffusion of authority among levels of government. With the exception of Japan, the jurisdictions under study all involve federal or quasi-federal arrangements, though with important differences among them in the division of powers relevant to climate policy. As with horizontal diffusion of authority, the implications of federalism are likely to depend on the salience of environmental issues with the electorate. Federalism may obstruct national action if subnational governments that have disincentives to take action have an effective veto as a result of decision rules among members of the federation or ownership of key resources. On the other hand, in the face of national inaction, federalism may allow for at least some subnational governments to act, to the extent that there is regional variation in electoral incentives. At the limit, if there is sufficient electoral pressure, competition among states or between states and a national government may emerge in a form of a "race to the top."

Diffusion or concentration of authority may find quite different expression at the policy implementation stage. As noted above, in systems where multiple actors can exercise vetoes, it is likely to be more difficult to achieve agreement on a course of action. However, to the extent that agreement *can* be achieved, diverse actors may insist on more formal reporting and oversight to ensure that their hard-won (and difficult to revisit) compromise is respected. Consistent with this, the US Congress often writes very specific environmental statutes, backed with provisions authorizing "citizen suits," should the executive fail to faithfully execute the statute. In contrast, majoritarian parliamentary systems tend to write discretionary statutes, both to grant the government of the day discretion and because a future government could easily amend unwelcome mandates in any case. While this contrast in policymaking between parliamentary and presidential systems has been noted by other scholars,[21] a similar dynamic may also occur vertically within a federation. In particular, there may be similar pressures, particularly from leading states, to ensure oversight of potential laggard states' follow-through on agreed-upon commitments. To the extent that such agreements have "bite," akin to contractual obligations, they may make it more difficult to backslide on international or national commitments.

Ongoing International Influences

While our primary focus is the influence of domestic politics, we are also interested in the direction and degree of ongoing international influence on domestic politics. Setting aside direct threats of violence or economic boycotts, neither of which is relevant in the context of climate policy, international factors can affect domestic policymakers in two ways—by transforming their ideas or their electoral incentives. With respect to the former, transnational actors of various kinds (whether other states' leaders, international organizations, or transnational networks of nongovernmental organizations) may contribute to shifting the beliefs and values of policymakers or mass publics. Political leaders may be sensitive to their country's international reputation or genuinely convinced by transnational actors' efforts to promote particular norms.

Voters, in turn, may also be persuaded by the evidence or moral arguments presented by transnational actors, thereby affecting domestic politicians' electoral strategies. Transnational advocacy ties that reinforce certain domestic actors' claims may bolster their political influence. Here we anticipate that external environmental networks may strengthen the position of national environmental groups, particularly in less wealthy states.

Material realities of international relations may also influence the balance of opposition and support for ratification and adoption of domestic policies in several ways. Ongoing international negotiations (for instance with respect to side payments) have the potential to sour or sweeten a prior international agreement for a given country. International trade relationships—*economic* rather than *political* globalization—also are likely to be influential, more so in countries with economies open to trade. In particular, business opposition is likely to be enhanced to the extent that a country's key trading partners do not make comparable commitments to reduce emissions.

Summary

In conclusion, with respect to electoral interests, we anticipate that countries will be more likely to ratify where there is greater public support for action and, especially, where voters are more attentive to the issue of climate change. In addition, we expect that opponents of ratification and of domestic mitigation measures will be more influential the greater the costs of compliance in a given country. With respect to ideas, we anticipate that politicians will be more inclined to act the more convinced they are of climate science and the "greener" their personal values, with a possibility that more interventionist left-wing parties may be more inclined to ratify and adopt activist climate policies. Finally, with respect to institutions, we anticipate that proportional electoral systems will increase the likelihood of ratification and of adoption of domestic mitigation measures. However, other institutional effects stemming from varying degrees of horizontal and vertical diffusion of power are likely to be contingent on politicians' normative commitments and electoral incentives in a given country.

Although prior international negotiations set the stage for each jurisdiction to consider ratification, ongoing international influences could shape domestic decisions, through concerns with respect to international reputation, transnational lobbying, changes in terms or the content of the international agreement, and trade vulnerability of key industries.

Without further ado, we turn to individual cases, which reveal the richness and diversity of climate policy debates at the national level and provide us with a wide range of variation in policymakers' electoral interests, ideas, and political institutions. In the final chapter of the book, we compare the case studies in greater detail with regard to these factors and offer conclusions about how they interact to produce different patterns of ratification and policy adoption across cases.

Notes

We are indebted to our collaborators on this volume—Steinar Andresen, Inga Fritzen Buan, Kate Crowley, Gørild Heggelund, Laura Henry, Miranda Schreurs, and Yves Tiberghien—whose work has provided much insight for our introductory and concluding chapters. This project would not have been possible without a grant from the Weyerhaeuser Company Foundation to the United States Studies program at the University of British Columbia. We are also indebted to research assistants Katherine Boothe and Elena Feditchkina, who have provided superb editorial assistance for this volume.

1. Hardin 1968.

2. Paterson 1996; Oberthür and Ott 1999; Grubb, Brack, and Vrolijk 1999; Newell 2005. Cass 2006 explores the effects of international norms on European and US climate policies but is informed by theories of international relations rather than comparative politics. Authors who have employed a comparative politics perspective include Lantis 2006; Busby and Ochs 2005; Zahran et al. 2007; Schreurs 2002; and Dolšak 2001.

3. Haas 2008.

4. Schreurs and Tiberghien, this volume.

5. Harrison, this volume.

6. In the international relations literature, "implementation" refers to adoption of domestic policies to implement treaties, while domestic public policy literature focuses on administration of those domestic policies. Consistent with our primary focus on domestic politics, we adopt the latter usage.

7. While Pigouvian taxes can be a considered a form of regulation (defined broadly as rules backed by a threat of sanctions), we consider them more coercive than either command and control regulation or cap-and-trade programs. In the absence of corresponding tax cuts, a carbon tax will cost those affected more than regulation, since polluters would be required to pay the tax on all releases, even after achieving an optimal level of abatement. Moreover, even if the revenues from the tax are returned via corresponding tax cuts, carbon taxes are likely

to be more challenging politically because taxpayers will be more keenly aware of the costs than the compensating benefits, particularly if they take the form of less pain at tax time.

8. Elisabeth Rosenthal, "China Clearly Overtakes US as Leading Emitter of Climate-Warming Gases," *International Herald Tribune*, 13 June 2008, http://www.iht.com/articles/2008/06/13/business/emit.php.

9. Goldstein and Keohane 1993.

10. Keck and Sikkink 1998, 29.

11. Hall 1993; Schneider and Ingram 1993.

12. March and Olsen 2005; Checkel 2001; Klotz 1995, 13–18.

13. Weaver 1986.

14. Gardiner 2004.

15. Weaver and Rockman 1993.

16. Scruggs 1999.

17. Walsh 2000.

18. Dolšak 2001.

19. Lantis 2006.

20. Jones 1975.

21. Huber and Shipan 2002; McCubbins, Noll, and Weingast 1999.

References

Busby, Josh, and Alexander Ochs. 2005. From Mars and Venus Down to Earth: Understanding the Transatlantic Climate Divide. In *Beyond Kyoto: Meeting the Long-Term Challenge of Climate Change*, ed. David Michels. Washington, DC: Center for Transatlantic Relations, Johns Hopkins University (SAIS).

Cass, Loren R. 2006. *The Failures of American and European Climate Policy: International Norms, Domestic Politics, and Unachievable Commitments.* Albany: SUNY Press.

Checkel, Jeffrey T. 2001. Why Comply? Social Learning and European Identity Change. *International Organization* 55:553–588.

Dolšak, Nives. 2001. Mitigating Global Climate Change: Why Are Some Countries Doing More than Others? *Policy Studies Journal* 29:414–436.

Gardiner, Stephen M. 2004. Ethics and Global Climate Change. *Ethics* 114:555–600.

Goldstein, Judith, and Robert Keohane, eds. 1993. *Ideas and Foreign Policy: Beliefs, Institutions and Political Change.* Ithaca: Cornell University Press.

Grubb, Michael, Duncan Brack, and Christiaan Vrolijk. 1999. *The Kyoto Protocol: A Guide and Assessment.* London: Earthscan/James and James.

Haas, Peter M. 2008. Climate Change Governance after Bali. *Global Environmental Politics* 8 (3):1–7.

Hall, Peter. 1993. Policy Paradigms, Social Learning and the State: The Case of Economic Policy Making in Britain. *Comparative Politics* 25:275–296.

Hardin, Garrett. 1968. The Tragedy of the Commons. *Science* 13:1243–1248.

Huber, John D., and Charles R. Shipan. 2002. *Deliberate Discretion? The Institutional Foundations of Bureaucratic Autonomy.* Cambridge: Cambridge University Press.

Jones, Charles O. 1975. *Clean Air: The Policies and Politics of Pollution Control.* Pittsburgh: University of Pittsburgh Press.

Keck, Margaret, and Kathryn Sikkink. 1998. *Activists beyond Borders: Advocacy Networks in International Politics.* Ithaca: Cornell University Press.

Klotz, Audie. 1995. *Norms in International Relations: The Struggle against Apartheid.* Ithaca: Cornell University Press.

Lantis, Jeffrey S. 2006. The Life and Death of International Treaties: Double-Edged Diplomacy and the Politics of Ratification in Comparative Perspective. *International Politics* 43:24–52.

March, James G., and Johan P. Olsen. 2005. The Institutional Dynamics of International Political Orders. *International Organization* 52:943–969.

McCubbins, Mathew, Roger G. Noll, and Barry Weingast. 1999. The Political Origins of the Administrative Procedures Act. *Journal of Law, Economics and Organization* 15:180–217.

Newell, Peter. 2005. *Climate for Change: Non-State Actors and the Global Politics of the Greenhouse.* Cambridge: Cambridge University Press.

Oberthür, Sebastian, and Herman E. Ott. 2006. *The Kyoto Protocol: International Climate Policy for the 21st Century.* New York: Springer.

Paterson, Matthew. 1996. *Global Warming and Global Politics.* London: Routledge.

Schneider, Anne, and Helen Ingram. 1993. Social Construction of Target Populations: Implications for Politics and Policy. *American Political Science Review* 87:334–347.

Schreurs, Miranda. 2002. *Environmental Politics in Japan, Germany, and the United States.* Cambridge: Cambridge University Press.

Scruggs, Lyle A. 1999. Institutions and Environmental Performance in Seventeen Western Democracies. *British Journal of Political Science* 29:1–31.

Walsh, J. I. 2000. When Do Ideas Matter? Explaining the Successes and Failures of Thatcherite Ideas. *Comparative Political Studies* 33:483–516.

Weaver, R. Kent. 1986. The Politics of Blame Avoidance. *Journal of Public Policy* 6:371–398.

Weaver, R. Kent, and Bert A. Rockman, eds. 1993. *Do Institutions Matter? Government Capabilities in the United States and Beyond.* Washington, DC: Brookings.

Zahran, Sammy, Eunyi Kim, Xi Chen, and Mark Lubell. 2007. Ecological Development and Global Climate Change: A Cross-National Study of Kyoto Protocol Ratification. *Society and Natural Resources* 20:37–55.

2

European Union Leadership in Climate Change: Mitigation through Multilevel Reinforcement

Miranda A. Schreurs and Yves Tiberghien

Introduction

The European Union has positioned itself as the international agenda setter for climate change mitigation. At several critical junctures, the EU and its members have adopted policies and programs that have put it at the forefront of international efforts to address climate change.[1] In the early 1990s several European countries took the lead in establishing voluntary domestic emission reduction targets. In October 1990, reacting to these national developments, the European ministers of energy and the environment announced that the European Community (EC) as a whole would seek to stabilize its joint carbon dioxide emissions at 1990 levels by the turn of the century, a goal that the EU was able to achieve. In 1997, in the months leading up to the Kyoto Protocol negotiations, the EU set the tone for the international negotiations with its proposal that industrialized states commit to reducing their greenhouse gas emissions by 15 percent of 1990 levels by 2010. While in the end the EU committed to a far more modest 8 percent reduction of 1990 greenhouse gas emissions by 2008–2012, the EU put other countries on the defensive, pushing them to go farther than they had said they were willing or able to go.[2]

Another significant instance of EU leadership was its decision to move forward with ratification of the Kyoto Protocol after President George W. Bush made clear on 28 March 2001 that the United States intended to withdraw from the agreement. The US pullout left Europe in a conundrum. The United States accounted for 36.1 percent of the 1990 CO_2 emissions of industrialized countries. The EU as a whole was responsible for a somewhat smaller 24.2 percent. If the Protocol was to survive, the EU would have to convince states representing another 30.8 percent of 1990 industrialized country CO_2 emissions to join it in ratifying the agreement in order to meet the Kyoto Protocol's somewhat arbitrary requirement that 55 percent of industrialized states' 1990 CO_2 emissions be represented by ratifying states in order for the agreement to go into effect. This meant that the EU, at a minimum, would have to convince Japan (responsible for 8.5 percent of 1990 industrialized states' emissions) and Russia (responsible for 17.4 percent) to ratify.

Despite these obstacles, the European Council formally agreed to the Kyoto Protocol on 25 April 2002.[3] The fifteen member states of the EU, represented by Jaume Mata Palou, minister of the environment of Spain (which held the EU presidency at the time), and the European Commission, represented by Margot Wallström, jointly presented their instruments of ratification to the United Nations on 31 May 2002.[4]

In its effort to find cost-effective ways to reduce emissions and despite initial strong resistance from key member states (most noteworthy in this regard Germany), the EU implemented the world's first international CO_2 emissions trading scheme (ETS), modeled on the successful US sulfur dioxide emissions trading system established by the US Clean Air Act Amendments of 1990.[5] Directive 2003/87/EC mandated a system covering approximately 12,000 installations representing just under half of European CO_2 emissions. In 2004, Directive 2004/101/EC was passed to link the Joint Implementation and Clean Development mechanisms of the Kyoto Protocol to the ETS. The ETS went into effect in January 2005. Significant problems surfaced with the design of the first phase of the ETS (2005–2008); as a result, during the development of the second phase (2008–2012) the Commission monitored national allocation plans, demanding that governments be less generous in their allocation of pollution allowances.[6] These policies and programs put the EU well ahead of other major industrialized countries in their mitigation efforts.

In January 2007, with an eye toward the post-Kyoto first commitment period, the European Commission, under a German presidency, published a communiqué calling for limiting mean temperature increases to 2 degrees above preindustrial times.[7] In March 2007 the European Council confirmed Europe's commitment to this approach, announcing that the EU would cut its CO_2 emissions by 20 percent of 1990 levels by 2020, increasing this to 30 percent should other developed countries agree to take action within the framework of an international agreement.[8] The Council also committed to the establishment of a binding target of 20 percent of renewables in the EU's overall total final energy consumption and a binding target of 10 percent for biofuels in the total mix of transportation fuel (gasoline and diesel) consumption by 2020.[9] After the agreement was forged, Tony Blair remarked that Europe now had "a clear leadership position on this crucial issue facing the world."[10] In the negotiations for a post-Kyoto agreement held in Bali, Indonesia, which resulted in the Bali Action Plan, the EU—admittedly unsuccessfully—challenged other industrialized states to accept a 25–40 percent emission reduction target for 2020 relative to 1990 levels as the Intergovernmental Panel on Climate Change suggests will be necessary to maintain global temperatures from rising above 2 degrees Celsius in 2050.[11] In the June preparatory committee meeting for the Copenhagen summit of December 2009, the EU reconfirmed its commitment to a 30% reduction target if other developed countries take comparable action. The United States, in contrast, still awaiting the outcome of domestic legislative debates, offered no firm targets. The EU continued to keep the pressure on the United States, Japan, Australia, and Canada, although the EU's "leadership" was put under question by a group of 40 developing countries that called for 40 percent emissions reductions for the developed countries.[12]

This chapter addresses a series of questions, but behind them all is the overarching puzzle of why the EU has taken on and sustained such a strong leadership role vis-à-vis climate change at so many points in the face of considerable US resistance in the pre-Obama period and at substantial economic cost. Given all that has been said about the weaknesses and failures of EU institutions and the complexity, slowness and indecisiveness of EU decision making, how is it possible that the EU has been able to sustain as much climate change leadership as it has for so long? For the EU, international negotiations entail dealing not only with external actors but also with supranational and national ones. The EU need for internal coordination makes decision making slow and cumbersome. The different interests and perspectives of member states can make finding common ground difficult. While the Treaty of the European Community (Maastricht Treaty) expanded European Community competencies related to the global environment (Article 130r states that community policy on the environment shall contribute to "promoting measures at the international level to deal with regional or world-wide environmental problems" and that community policy shall be based on the "precautionary principle and on the principles that preventive action should be taken"), member states maintain competence on matters of taxation and energy policy.[13] This means that in order to adopt a community-wide carbon tax, for example, all member states must give their consent. This greatly constrains the European Union's ability to coordinate their actions and policies on matters that are central to addressing climate change. It also puts great emphasis on the effectiveness of the EU presidency and the Council Secretariat and its Climate Working Group.[14] Given all of these constraints, what has sustained EU leadership on climate change?

This chapter argues that EU leadership in climate change is the result of a dynamic process of competitive multilevel reinforcement among the different EU political poles within a context of decentralized governance. EU leadership has depended on the actions and commitments of a group of pioneering states and the leadership roles played by the European Parliament (EP) and especially the European Commission. This upward cycle of reinforcing leadership within a quasi-federal system has been triggered by and been dependent on the public's strong support and normative commitment.

Although the EU is now a body of twenty-seven states, it is primarily the fifteen states that comprised the EU prior to 2004 that are at the center of this study. While the new member states have also all ratified the Kyoto Protocol, have their own individual targets (except for Malta and Cyprus), and participate in the EU CO_2 emission trading scheme, they are not part of the EU burden-sharing agreement. This will change for the post-2012 climate change agreement.

The chapter begins with a brief overview of theoretical discussions on leadership, particularly as it pertains to the climate change arena. It then proposes a framework of multilevel mutual leadership reinforcement for explaining how and why the EU has been able to sustain leadership for over a decade's time, culminating in the decisions to ratify the Kyoto Protocol and commit to a unilateral 20 percent reduction in CO_2 emissions relative to 1990 levels by 2020. It concludes by looking to the future and asks whether the EU will be able to be a leader not only in agenda setting but also in implementation of emissions cuts.

The European Union and Climate Change Leadership

At a stakeholder conference launching the second European Climate Change Program in October 2005, Stavros Dimas, commissioner for the environment, explained that with the launching of this program the

European Union was showing its continued commitment to climate change leadership. The program is focused on promoting stakeholder involvement in furthering greenhouse gas emissions reductions in the transportation sector (aviation and vehicles) and through carbon capture and storage, adaptation measures, and the EU emissions trading scheme. Dimas explained, "This is not just leadership for the sake of leadership, or because we think we can fight climate change on our own—we clearly can't. The EU's commitment and success has been an inspiration to our global partners. Without it, it is certain that the Kyoto Protocol would not have entered into force."[15] On a visit to Europe, Al Gore seemed to back up this perspective, arguing that the EU had an "absolutely critical leadership role to play ... [in] helping the world make the changes it must."[16]

European environmental leadership more generally, and climate change leadership more specifically, has attracted considerable scholarly attention. John Vogler suggests that a strengthening of EU institutional capacities has made it possible for the EU to take on environmental leadership, although he cautions that there are still significant limitations to EU autonomy in this realm.[17] Joyeeta Gupta and Michael Grubb have suggested that EU climate change leadership should be viewed from three perspectives: structural, instrumental, and directional.[18] The EU's ability to wield leadership is in part structural; that is, it derives from Europe's substantial political strength in the global order and international respect in the area of environmental protection. It is also partly instrumental: the EU has effectively used its negotiation skills and the instrumental design of regimes to accommodate the different needs of its member states and other country actors. Finally, it has exhibited directional leadership, changing the perceptions of others on climate change mitigation.[19]

Building on this theoretical line of reasoning, Gupta and Lasse Ringius argue that "the EU has been quite successful as an international leader. The Kyoto targets would not have been as ambitious as they are without the EU."[20] They suggest, however, that for the EU to maintain its leadership it will have to enhance its directional leadership (demonstrating through successful implementation efforts that a goal is achievable), instrumental leadership (effectively promoting issue linkage and coalition building to promote mutually beneficial solutions), and structural leadership (crafting incentives for others to cooperate).

In analyzing European environmental policy, Anthony Zito asks why in some, but not all, environmental cases the EU has been able to introduce substantial policy change.[21] He suggests that while intergovernmental bargaining perspectives assume outcomes based on least common denominators—and these are in fact what often result—when "collective entrepreneurship" comes into play, more demanding policies can emerge. He shows how entrepreneurs—a member state or states, the parliament, or the Commission—can pursue policy ideas that can lead to a revision of policy goals, in turn causing a redefinition of actor interests. This can make it possible for actors to move beyond the least common denominator. What is important is not simply ideas, institutions, and interests per se but entrepreneurial opportunism, alliance formation, and persuasiveness. Zito concludes, however, that no set patterns exist for determining whether intergovernmental bargaining or collective entrepreneurship will dominate.

The EU has clearly been a leader in the climate change area along a number of fronts. It has functioned as a classic norm entrepreneur.[22] It has been a powerful backer of the precautionary principle in relation to climate change, heeding the warnings of the International Panel on Climate Change that anthropogenic emissions of greenhouse gases are warming the planet and that this could have serious ecological, health, and climatic effects.[23] It has embraced the notion embodied in the United Nations Framework Convention on Climate Change that the industrialized states have the responsibility to act first given their historic contributions to anthropogenic greenhouse gas emissions.[24] It has defined climate change action as a moral and ethical issue that must transcend narrow economic interests.

Beyond this, the EU has acted as a political entrepreneur[25] actively setting targets, policies, and goals that have become the international standards to which other states have had to react. It has taken the lead in policy innovation, setting examples for others to learn from, and in the politics of persuasion, convincing other states of the importance of joining it in international action.

Focusing on collective entrepreneurship proves useful in exploring the case of EU climate change leadership. Whereas Zito is concerned with particular policy decisions, here we attempt to explain a sustained pattern of policy innovation. What explains the fact that while there have been a few policy failures, such as the inability to establish an EU-wide carbon tax and the excessive allocation by member states of carbon permits to their industries in the first phase of the European ETS, on the whole the EU has continued to be an international policy leader on climate change?

European Institutions and Multilevel Leadership Reinforcement

The EU can be viewed as both an arena for member states to negotiate with one another and an actor in its own right in the international climate change negotiations.[26] It can also be considered a dynamic arena in which, over time, multiple leaders have contributed ideas that have made it possible for the EU to sustain an agenda-setting role internationally.

The open-ended and competitive governance structure of the EU in an issue of shared competence such as the global environment has created multiple and mutually reinforcing opportunities for leadership. This suggests a kind of logic that reverses that of veto points or veto players. In the model of veto players developed by George Tsebelis, the presence of a large number of actors with the capacity to block a decision renders policy change unlikely.[27] In the EU's case, the reverse can also occur.[28] Institutionally, Commission and member states have joint competence in environmental policy; decisions in the EU Council are made by qualified majority voting. Under these circumstances, a positive cycle of competing leadership among different poles can take place.

In the EU climate negotiations, different actors have taken the lead on various occasions. For example, the Dutch played a leadership role when they held the EU presidency in 1992 and 1997, and the Irish did so when they presided over the ratification deal with Russia. The Germans and the British have quite consistently taken on climate change leadership roles within Europe, and have very visibly done so when they have held the Council presidency (2007 and 2005, respectively).[29]

Other member states have reacted to the leaders' initiatives.[30] France, for example, tried to reassert its imprint over EU integration by using the EU Council to advance sustainability legislation. The UK put pressure on Germany to apply more stringent conditions on the allocation of pollution permits to industry under the ETS.[31] In turn, the Commission has asserted itself on a number of occasions and pushed forward climate-wide action and further EU integration. An example has been the Commission's sponsorship of emissions trading. The EP has also demonstrated its relevance by passing resolutions calling for swift European action. Environmental nongovernmental organizations (NGOs) have been able to press their concerns both with the Commission and the Parliament.[32]

This baton passing has continued over the years in a very dynamic and mutually reinforcing way. Under these conditions, multilevel governance has created not just multiple veto points but also numerous leadership points where competitive leadership has been initiated. While it is certainly the case that there are many points where policy proposals can be blocked, the EU's governance structure has opened numerous avenues by which advocates of climate change action have been able to inject their priorities and concerns into policy debate.

Explaining EU Leadership

It is necessary to consider how institutions, interests, and ideas have come together to make it possible for Europe to do what the United States could not—effectively champion the Kyoto Protocol. The EU and the United States are both major economic blocks with entire sectors of the economy that would be heavily affected by mitigation policies. Why was it that in the EU, economic interests (workers, firms, industries) or less environmentally minded and economically developed states did not block the Kyoto Protocol's ratification, as their counterparts succeeded in doing in the United States? Why were European policy entrepreneurs able to develop winning coalitions for policy change when the arguably even stronger environmental community in the United States could not? The stakes were certainly high for European economic interests and they too had numerous ways to express their voice to the EU (through committees of the Commission and lobbying of members of the EP) and at the national level.[33] Why was industrial opposition to Kyoto not stronger?

EU policy toward climate change often has been couched in terms of an ideational agenda, namely the representation of the EU as a different kind of polity—one deeply concerned with international law, institution building, and a normative vision.[34] Through their global policymaking actions, the EU elites seek to increase public support for EU integration.

While these normative arguments have some validity, they fail to explain why supporters of Kyoto were able to trump opponents within Europe. More persuasive is the explanatory power that is provided by a focus on institutions, ideas, and interests and the way entrepreneurs were able to come up with creative policy approaches that made it possible to win acceptance of climate change policies and programs from interests that would otherwise most likely have joined veto blocks.[35] In particular, we look at the divide within European industry and the weakening effect this had on potential veto players; the role of public opinion, Green parties, and NGOs in promoting a precautionary approach to climate change; the adoption of a burden-sharing approach and the possibilities this afforded to win over potential opponents of substantive policy change; the role of national states in shaping community-wide policies; and the influence of the Commission and Parliament on driving community action. Ultimately, a critical structural variable has been the open and multilevel nature of the EU's institutional setup, which enabled a dynamic of competitive leadership reinforcement to take place.

Multilevel Governance and Mutual Reinforcement

The strengthening of European Community environmental capacities has closely paralleled more fundamental treaty-based efforts to strengthen overall European integration and to expand the role and power of Europe in global affairs.[36] Although the EC has been engaged in environmental protection since the early 1970s, it was not until 1986 that the Single European Act added a title on the environment by which the EC's competencies were explicitly extended to the environmental realm. The act called for EC action to "be based on the principles that preventive action should be taken, that environmental damage should be rectified at source, and that the polluter should pay." The 1992 Maastricht Treaty went a step further, making the environment an explicit policy responsibility of the EC, giving the Commission greater powers to represent member states in international organizations and with third parties, and calling upon it to promote measures to deal with regional and worldwide environmental problems.[37] While the principle of subsidiarity assures that many environmental decisions remain at the local and national levels, there has been a steady strengthening of the Community's powers with time.

Treaty revisions have gradually enabled new decision-making processes and altered the rights and responsibilities of the Commission, of the Parliament, and of the Council.[38] In the past, the Council of Ministers of the Environment had to pass decisions unanimously. The Single European Act introduced qualified majority voting within the Council for matters in which the EC has exclusive competence (thus many environmental issues but not energy or taxation questions, which still function on the principle of unanimity). Responding to criticisms of a democratic deficit in European policymaking, the Treaty of Maastricht and the subsequent Treaty of Amsterdam also expanded somewhat the powers of the European Parliament. While the Commission still has the exclusive power to develop proposals and the Council still meets in secret when agreeing on legislation, the Parliament was given codecision authority with the Council in amending Commission proposals and determining whether or not they become law. As a whole, while still not immune to criticisms that a democratic deficit remains, this structure allows for multiple leadership points. Far from creating deadlock, this decentralized multipolar structure has allowed for competitive leadership and mutual reinforcement to take place on climate change.

Interests

European Industry   As is the case in the United States, European industry is divided in its views on precautionary action related to climate change. Also as in the United States, there were certainly industrial voices opposing the Kyoto Protocol. The Centre for the New Europe, a free market think tank that was set up in Brussels in 1993, for example, called on members of the EP to rethink radically the EU's climate change policies beyond 2012. It has argued that curbing greenhouse gas emissions under the Kyoto Protocol will dampen economic growth. The European Sound Climate Policy Coalition, a front organization funded by Exxon Mobil, aimed to coalesce a powerful group of interests against EU support for Kyoto.[39] Industrial lobbies, moreover, managed to gain the support of some key politicians who mainly argued that plans to implement cuts in greenhouse gas emissions pose a severe threat to industry. These included Silvio Berlusconi, prime minister of Italy; Loyola de Palacio, EU commissioner for transport and energy; Charlie McCreevy, EU commissioner for the internal market and services; and Günter Verheugen, EU commission vice president and commissioner for enterprises.

Yet, far more than has been the case in the United States (although there are signs of change there in recent years, as discussed in chapter 3), many European businesses have accepted the Kyoto Protocol framework. Many companies have joined groups such as the Business Council for a Sustainable Energy Future, the European Wind Energy Association, and the International Cogeneration Alliance, which accepted the need for action. Even many fossil fuel firms started to follow the lead of BP, which in 1997 publicly accepted that precautionary action was necessary.[40] In the lead-up to Kyoto, the oil firm Austrian OMV announced its support for the EU's 15 percent reduction target.[41] During 2000–2002, Royal Dutch Shell Group introduced an internal emissions trading scheme. On the whole, in Europe, where corporatist traditions are quite strong, the economic community accepted the need for action as long as it could influence the shape of policies and programs. This scheme worked at both the national and the European levels.

Many firms appeared cognizant of the strong public support for action as well as the high potential for regulatory action within some member states. Several states, such as Denmark, Sweden, the Netherlands, and Norway, had already introduced carbon taxes. Industry also saw the potential to move into new business areas, such as BP's move into solar energy, Royal Dutch Shell Group's development of solar and wind energy, and Austrian OMV's embrace of biofuels. The potential to shape a global carbon ETS also attracted some firms.[42] This does not mean that there were not still intense battles among corporations related to climate mitigation policies. European industry, however, did not work to derail Kyoto in the way that American industry did. To understand why this is so, it is useful to consider the strength of public opinion on climate change matters.

Public Opinion and the Media   Public opinion forms an important necessary condition for the process of mutual reinforcement. Opinion data show a trend of strengthening and widening support for the environment, climate change action, and Kyoto in particular from the early 1990s to the 2000s. As an indicator of the priority put on global environment, 88 percent of Europeans responded that "protecting the environment" should be an EU priority in the 2002 Eurobarometer survey (EU-15), just 3 points below the highest priority, fighting global terrorism.[43] Moreover, this level of support for the environment and expectation of EU action was also consistently high in earlier polls, ranging from 83 to 87 percent between 1997 and 2001 (Eurobarometer, 48, 52, 54, 58).

A sampling of dozens of press reports appearing in European newspapers in the week after Bush's pronouncement that the United States was leaving Kyoto show that the press was highly critical of the US decision. Perhaps not surprisingly, left-leaning newspapers across Europe condemned the US withdrawal. The left-of-center Belgian *Le Soir*, for example, called it "a real scandal" and then asked, "Today, the question is not whether the 15 must continue Kyoto without the United States. ... The real question is will the Europeans be smart and courageous enough to do it?" The center-left Danish *Politiken* lamented that the United States had "in one fell swoop, set back international efforts to address global warming by more than ten years."

Remarkably, many conservative European newspapers criticized the US withdrawal as well. For example, the conservative-leaning Spanish *La Razon* wrote, "The American president is more concerned with the US citizen's standard of living and their energetic spending, than with the future of the planet." The *Irish Times* concluded, "The rest of the world ... has reacted with justifiable anger and outrage." The conservative, populist *Irish Independent* commented, "[Mr. Bush's] stance will be attributed to breathtaking arrogance or his connections with the energy industry, or a combination of the two." The center-right *Berlingske Tidende* of Denmark opined, "It is regrettable that Bush does not support the Kyoto agreement. It is particularly disappointing because it shows that the United States is in the process of running away from its international responsibilities." And, the independent Greek *Kathimerini* wrote, "The White House's presumptuous stance [is] truly unacceptable. ... The fundamental problem lies in the message the White House sends. ... Cynically supporting the interests of specific US industries ... is an extremely negative paradigm for international behaviour."[44]

As suggested by the media responses, European public opinion was strongly behind Kyoto. A Pew Global Attitudes Project poll conducted in August 2001 in the four largest European states and the United States found strong disapproval of the Bush administration's foreign policies in general and especially in relation to the Kyoto Protocol. While 44 percent of US respondents disapproved of Bush's decision to withdraw, almost twice that percentage disapproved in Britain (83 percent), Italy (89 percent), Germany (87 percent), and France (85 percent).[45] Similarly, a Worldwide Fund for Nature (WWF) UK poll conducted in late May and early June 2001 found strong support for EU leadership in bringing the Kyoto Protocol into force even if the United States did not participate. Of respondents in Belgium, 82 percent said that the EU should play a leadership role; 91.3 percent in Spain, 88.7 percent in Italy, and 79.7 percent in the UK agreed. There was also a strong feeling in Belgium, Spain, and the UK (but less so in Italy) that Canada, Japan, and other industrialized states should join the EU in tackling global warming rather than siding with the United States and that their own governments should do more.[46] According to a top official at the Directorate-General for the Environment (DG Environment), climate change is an issue that has reached such a level of social and political acceptability across the EU that it enables (indeed, forces) the EU Commission and national leaders to produce all sorts of measures, including taxes.[47]

Nongovernmental Organizations   There is an active environmental NGO community in Europe.[48] Under the right conditions, NGOs can take advantage of windows of opportunity to induce policy change.[49] The Climate Action Network Europe, the leading NGO network working on climate change, has over 100 members. They have been ardent supporters of climate action.[50] At the EU level, the so-called Green 9 Group of environmental NGOs (BirdLife International, Climate Action Network Europe, European Environmental Bureau, EPH Environmental Network, the European Federation for Transport and Environment, Friends of the Earth Europe, Greenpeace, International Friends of Nature, WWF European Policy Office) has gained advisory status in EU decision making, and all members (except for Greenpeace) receive funding from the Commission do this work.

European NGOs often receive financial support from state governments and the Commission; as a result, they are less dependent on membership contributions. Possibly because of this, they were quicker than their American counterparts to take on climate change campaigns that called for changes not only in corporate but also consumer behavior. American NGOs found themselves having to increasingly depend on European NGOs to help them lobby the US government. A dozen US environmental groups through the US Climate Action Network made the following appeal to the EU in the period after the US withdrawal from Kyoto:

The importance of continued and strengthened EU leadership in addressing climate change for the positioning of the United States cannot be overstated. ... The EU's continued leadership will be essential to maintaining and strengthening the Kyoto Protocol. ... Implementation efforts domestically in the EU provide an important example for US lawmakers and businesses of the feasibility of real action. In addition, EU progress also applies additional pressure on US businesses by highlighting the emissions trading opportunities being missed as well as the loss of market share in reduction technologies and services. The EU's positions and policies have set a tone of urgency while demonstrating feasibility, both of which will continue to be essential for overcoming the significant political barriers for the United States. In fact, a concerted effort on the part of the EU and its member countries to reach out to decision makers and constituencies in the US would be quite beneficial in highlighting the reality and feasibility of actions already taken and commitments made.[51]

European Norms of Social Equity and the Application of Burden Sharing

The EU's ability to push through with the ratification of the Kyoto Protocol depended heavily on the adoption of internal burden-sharing agreements. Burden sharing in the European context is based on European notions of solidarity, Catholic social teachings, and the social democratic notion of social equity. The EU has as one of its goals the promotion of economic and social equality among its member states and regions.

In October 1990 the EC ministers of energy and the environment announced that the EC as a whole would seek to stabilize its joint CO_2 emissions at 1990 levels by the turn of the century. The cohesion countries (Spain, Portugal, Greece), however, demanded that a burden-sharing approach be employed. The basis for their argument was that as less-developed states within Europe, they could not be expected to make cuts in their greenhouse gas emissions comparable to those being proposed by the Netherlands, Germany, Denmark, and Austria.[52] The EC target was, therefore, based on a rough assessment of what the ministers believed could be achieved based on a no-regrets strategy and the targets that had already been established by individual member states, Germany's target being the most important in this regard. The EC stabilization target, moreover, recognized that emissions in Spain, Greece, and Portugal would increase by substantial margins during this time frame and that other member states, such as France, would not be able or willing to reduce their emissions substantially.[53]

Burden sharing was also at the basis of the 1997 negotiating strategy of the EC going into the 1997 Kyoto conference. The European Commission, and in particular DG Environment, played a key role in pushing for an ambitious community-wide target while recognizing the need for differentiation in national targets. The Commission argued that—given the national reduction targets established by Germany, Austria, and Denmark, and the expected emissions reductions to be achieved by the British switch from coal to natural gas—a 10 percent reduction in European emissions could be expected by 2005 regardless of any actions by other member states. They argued that this therefore set a minimum below which the EC could not go under and be taken seriously internationally. After numerous proposals were introduced and debated, Svend Auken, the Danish environment minister, suggested that agreement be established internally on a burden-sharing arrangement that would lead to a 10 percent reduction for the EC, but that a 15 percent external target be proposed. All involved doubted that the final outcome from Kyoto would require the sharper cut. The Danish proposal was accepted. The burden-sharing agreement was renegotiated among member states after the Kyoto Protocol negotiations ended (table 2.1).[54]

Table 2.1
The EU Burden-Sharing Agreement before and after Kyoto: Change in Emission Reduction Targets of Individual EU Member States Going into the 1997 Kyoto Negotiations and after the Kyoto Protocol was Agreed Upon

Member state	1997 targets	1998 targets
Austria	−25%	−13%
Belgium	−10%	−7.5%
Denmark	−25%	−21%
Finland	0%	0%
France	0%	0%
Germany	−25%	−21%
Greece	+30%	+25%
Ireland	+15%	+13%
Italy	−7%	−6.5%
Luxembourg	−30%	−28%
Netherlands	−10%	−6%
Portugal	+40%	+27%
Spain	+17%	+15%
Sweden	+5%	+4%
United Kingdom	−10%	−12.5%

Source: Ringius 1997, 7 and 32.

In Kyoto, the EU committed to an 8 percent reduction relative to 1990 emission levels of a basket of six greenhouse gases.[55] Significantly, only eight member states were expected to reduce their emissions: Austria, Belgium, Denmark, Germany, Italy, Luxembourg, the Netherlands, and the United Kingdom. Other EU member states either pledged to stabilize their emissions (Finland and France) or to work to reduce the rate at which they were growing (Spain, Greece, Portugal, Sweden, and Ireland). Sweden has since changed its position from a target of 4 percent growth in emissions to one of 4 percent emissions reduction by 2010, and 25 percent reduction by 2030. The EU has also negotiated a burden-sharing, or "effort-sharing" or "target-sharing"—the increasingly preferred terms—agreement for its 20 percent renewables goal for 2020 (table 2.2) as well as the 20 percent emission reduction target.

EU leadership was made possible in part because of changing underlying conditions in the three biggest polluter states (Germany, the UK, and Italy) that meant that significant emissions cuts would occur even in business-as-usual scenarios. It would not continue to be possible, however, without EC-wide acceptance of the principle of differentiated

Table 2.2
Distribution of 20% Renewables Target among Member States

Member state	Share of renewables in 2005	Share required by 2020
Austria	23.3%	34%
Belgium	2.2%	13%
Bulgaria	9.4%	16%
Cyprus	2.9%	13%
Czech Republic	6.1%	13%
Denmark	17%	30%
Estonia	18%	25%
Finland	28.5%	38%
France	10.3%	23%
Germany	5.8%	18%
Greece	6.9%	18%
Hungary	4.3%	13%
Ireland	3.1%	16%
Italy	5.2%	17%
Latvia	32.6%	40%
Lithuania	15%	23%
Luxembourg	0.9%	11%
Malta	0%	10%
The Netherlands	2.4%	14%
Poland	7.2%	15%
Portugal	20.5%	31%
Romania	17.8%	24%
Slovak Republic	6.7%	14%
Slovenia	16%	25%
Spain	8.7%	20%
Sweden	39.8%	49%
United Kingdom	1.3%	15%

Source: EurActiv, EU Renewable Energy Policy, 2 August 2007, last updated 28 January 2009.

obligations. The inclusion of a burden-sharing approach has won over states that would otherwise have vetoed targets for EU climate change policy.

The European Commission
At numerous critical points, the Commission and its DG Environment have wielded their agenda-setting power, developing and promoting new

policy ideas and blueprints for agreements or reinforcing other actors' demands. The Commission has pursued three main goals. First, it has sought to respond to public opinion with outcomes, thereby demonstrating its relevance. Second, it has used climate policy as a means to advance EU integration and empower the Commission with new regulatory tools and monitoring powers. Finally, it has used climate change policy to build the EU's overseas identity, especially relative to the United States. As a top official of DG Environment put it, the environment is a great unifying issue for EU integration (an issue of predilection)—everyone expects that the EU must act and must lead.[56] Within the reinforcement model, it is also noteworthy that the Commission is often pushed into a reactive mode by national leaders in key countries or the EP. Thus the Commission must propose ambitious blueprints in order to retain its agenda-setting role.

At the EU Council in Gothenburg, on 15–16 June 2001 the heads of state of member governments called on the Commission to prepare by the end of the year a proposal for the rapid ratification of the Kyoto Protocol by the EC, with the goal of having Kyoto enacted in 2002. The proposal was issued on 23 October 2001 and noted that greenhouse gas emissions in the EU had declined by 4 percent between 1990 and 1999 but were rising in the transportation sector. The proposal concluded that "the EU on the whole is firmly on the road to meeting its targets for 2008–2012."[57] The proposal did note, however, that meeting the targets would require not only new measures in the sectors of transportation, energy, housing, agriculture, households, and research but also the adoption of a system for emissions trading. The Commission thus took the initiative to prepare a separate proposal for the trading of greenhouse gas emissions. This represented a major shift in European attitudes toward emissions trading. When the Kyoto Protocol was initially negotiated, the Clinton administration had been pushing for maximum flexibility in how states reached their Kyoto Protocol targets, including use of joint implementation and emissions trading. The EU (and especially Germany) had opposed this idea, arguing that emissions reductions should primarily be done through domestic policies and measures. Europeans had little real understanding of how emissions trading worked; they were more used to regulatory than market-based approaches to pollution control, and they viewed US calls to permit emissions trading with much skepticism.[58] The idea that a price could be put on pollution was not an idea that was well accepted in social democratic Europe.

Over the course of several years, however, interest in emissions trading began to build in Europe. In 2002 the UK introduced the world's first nationwide scheme for CO_2 emissions trading. The Commission also began to study the possibility of an EU-level system for emissions trading. A March 2000 Commission green paper on emissions trading in the EU helped to initiate greater debate on the potential benefits of an emissions trading system. The October 2001 Commission proposal for Europe to adopt an emissions trading system may have been as much an attempt by Europe to try to win the United States back into the negotiation process as it was a recognition of the potential cost effectiveness of an emissions trading system for reducing CO_2 emissions.

The European Parliament

The European Parliament (EP) has provided another channel for green interests to influence policy outcome. On 5 July 2001 the EP passed a resolution calling on the sixth Conference of the Parties, Part II, "to maintain the central place of the Kyoto Protocol as the driving force in the fight to concentrate attention on, and find ways of combating, climate change" and reiterating "its criticism of the unilateral US decision to reject the Kyoto Protocol as a way forward." The resolution urged "the European Union to take the lead" in crafting a coalition that would ensure entry into force before 2002.[59]

The EP played a key role in January 2005 when it passed a resolution translating the goal of limiting mean global temperature increases to 2 degrees Celsius into concrete targets for industrialized countries. The EU Council adopted these goals in March 2005, responding positively to the EP's leadership.[60]

The EP's proactive role is not surprising given the growing representation of Green parties.[61] After the 1994 EP election, the European Greens held 23 seats (out of 626); after the 1999 elections, 38 (out of 626); after the 2004 elections, 34 (out of 732), and after the 2009 elections, 55 (out of 736).[62] Since the 1999 parliamentary election, the Greens have held onto their position as the fourth largest political group in the EP. They have picked climate change as a strategic issue through which they can gain more legitimacy and power relative to the Council and the Commission.

National Interests and Lead States

The study of interests as a driver of EU climate policy also requires a focus on national interests. In the EU context, countries are in many ways like substate actors in a federal system. Many climate change initiatives have been pioneered by individual states. This chapter focuses on three leading states (Germany, the UK, and the Netherlands), one pivotal state undergoing major change (France), and one initially laggard but increasingly proactive state (Spain). Detailed case analyses are provided in the appendix.

As shown in the appendix, no other countries have been as important to establishing and achieving the EU burden-sharing goals as Germany and the UK, the largest economies in Europe. In 1990 these two countries accounted for approximately 46 percent of the total emissions in the EU.[63] The vast majority of the Community's emission reduction target depends on them. Germany is expected to reduce its emissions by 259 million metric tons of CO_2 equivalent and the UK by 97 million metric tons. Combined, this totals more than the required reduction for the EU-15 as a whole under the Kyoto Protocol (341 million metric tons of CO_2 equivalent). The large reductions expected of Germany and the UK are what made it possible for some other EU member states to increase their emissions.[64] Germany committed to a substantial −21 percent target relative to 1990. It is expected to end up at 5.2 percent below its target with all measures, including carbon sinks and Kyoto flexibility mechanisms, included.[65] As detailed in the case study, Germany's strong leadership can be explained by a combination of strong public opinion support, the presence of a strong Green Party in the governing coalition from 1997 to 2005, and the general acceptance of the need to tackle climate change by the two largest political parties—the Christian Democratic Union and Social Democratic Party.

As for the UK, with existing measures, it is expected to be 6.9 percent below its Kyoto target (and 7.5 percent below with the additional use of the Kyoto flexibility mechanisms and carbon sinks).[66] In absolute terms, the UK overdelivery relative to its 2010 target is expected to reach 53.9 million metric tons of CO_2 equivalent (or 58 million metric tons with the Kyoto flexibility mechanisms and carbon sink effects). This extra emissions reduction will help to balance out the emissions reduction shortfalls that are expected (even with the use of the flexibility mechanisms and carbon sinks) in the cases of Italy, Denmark, and Spain.[67]

France is an interesting comparative case. Its emissions were among the lowest in Europe on a per capita basis in 1990 due to the country's heavy reliance on nuclear energy. Partly as a result, France did not play the role of a leader on climate change early on in the EU. In recent years, however, owing to a strong shift in public opinion and a rapid response by entrepreneurial conservative leaders eager to exploit the new political space, France too has exhibited greater interest in climate change policies and programs.

Spain is emblematic of the problem that faces several EU countries where opinion and electoral incentive are lagging behind the EU's position. Emissions are rising far faster than was expected when Spain signed on to the burden-sharing agreement. Spanish emissions in 2005 were 52.3 percent above 1990 levels, well above the 15 percent rise allowed under the Kyoto Protocol bubble. In Spain, the public has not been as attentive to climate change and NGOs have not received as much support as in northern Europe. A booming economy led to strong support for a pro-growth, conservative agenda. Since the mid-2000s, however, there are signs of a more climate-sensitive politics emerging, with important factors being the political transition to a socialist coalition as well as growing concerns about desertification.

Policy Entrepreneurs and Multilevel Reinforcement

Why did the EU feel so strongly about preserving Kyoto? Why were the Europeans so disapproving of the Bush administration's actions? The US pullout could have provided Europe with an easy way out of a treaty that few states in Europe would find easy to fulfill. As of 2000, many states were already far off their Kyoto targets. Why then was European reaction so strongly opposed to Bush's abandonment of the agreement?

EU leadership has been driven by a combination of factors. While public opinion and the presence of Green parties were certainly important to creating a milieu supportive of action, EU leadership resulted from a process of mutual leadership reinforcement by different actors involved in the EU's process of multilevel governance. The leadership roles played by several member states (especially Germany, the UK, the Netherlands, and Denmark but also Austria, Finland, Luxembourg, and Sweden) were important. This leadership often played out in particularly strong ways at times when these member states held the presidency of the European Council. Perhaps recognizing the importance of this responsibility, member states at times also showed a willing to strategically pass the leadership baton off to the next player. As UK foreign secretary Margaret Beckett said during a speech in Berlin just prior to Germany assuming the dual responsibility of the presidency of the European Union and of the G8, "We are willing to work with you on a concrete proposal [for climate change] to come out of your twin presidencies. ... [W]e will support you. But you must lead. ... The baton has passed to Germany. Please don't drop it."[68]

The Commission has also played a central role. In many ways, the Commission sees climate change as one of the EU's most important and defining issues—and the Kyoto Protocol as a crucial showcase of the EU's willingness and ability to be a foreign policy leader. As a result, the Commission was concerned by research pointing out that many member states were "way off" their EU burden-sharing targets, even though emissions at the end of 2004 were 0.9 percent below 1990 levels. The Commission was well aware that a failure to fulfill Kyoto Protocol obligations could hurt European credibility in any future global environmental negotiations and raise legitimate questions regarding Europe's ability to lead.[69] To remedy the emerging gap between the Kyoto target and reality, a first batch of implementation measures was introduced by the Commission under the European Climate Change Program (ECCP), adopted in June 2001. Subsequently, the Commission pushed several new directives that address, among other things, the promotion of renewables, higher efficiency in heat and power generation, the energy performance of buildings, and emissions trading.[70] By 2006 emissions were 2.7 percent below 1990 levels, a third of the way to the Kyoto Protocol target (table 2.3).

The EP has also been a frequent champion of EU leadership, supported by Green parties and environmental NGOs. In many ways, its role has been reinforcing of the leadership exhibited by key member states and the Commission.

EU leadership on climate change may also have been partly self-serving. It became a wedge issue for the EU, a way for the EU to build coalitional strength with other nations and in the process enhance its strength vis-à-vis the United States.[71] It can also be argued that the EU has not only successfully promoted member state and international cooperation in the obtainment of a collective good, despite high individual costs at times, but also enhanced its own institution-building goals in the process.[72]

The EU institutional setting permitted a process of competitive multilevel entrepreneurship. This has resulted in the EU repeatedly stepping into the lead internationally. Without the role played by various EU institutions and leading nations, it is doubtful that the Community as a whole could have reached an EU-wide stabilization target at 1990 levels by 2000, formulated a 15 percent emissions reduction target going into

Table 2.3

Gap to 2010 Target (Percentage Points Relative to Base Year Emissions) for the EU-15, Based on Data from End 2006

Member state	Kyoto target (%)	Gap to target with existing measures (2006)	Gap to target with additional measures, Kyoto mechanisms, and carbon sinks (2006)	Gap to target with existing measures (2010, projected)	Gap to target with additional measures, Kyoto mechanisms and carbon sinks (2010, projected)
Austria	−13.0	+28.2	+16.0	+30.4	−0.2
Belgium	−7.5	+1.5	−3.3	+3.8	−1.0
Denmark	−21.0	+22.7	+13.3	+18.8	+9.4
Finland	0	+13.1	+10.3	+19.7	−0.6
France	0	−4.0	−4.7	+0.8	−4.2
Germany	−21.0	+2.5	+2.2	−1.5	−5.2
Greece	+25.0	−0.6	−1.7	−1.1	−4.2
Ireland	+13.0	+12.5	+2.3	+9.8	−0.6
Italy	−6.5	+16.4	+7.5	+14.0	+1.9
Luxembourg	−28.0	+29.2	−0.9	+31.2	0
Netherlands	−6.0	+3.4	−2.8	+3.8	−2.4
Portugal	+27.0	+11.3	−6.1	+17.2	−4.3
Spain	+15.0	+34.5	+12.6	+37	+5.5
Sweden	+4.0	−12.9	−15.8	−6.7	−9.7
UK	−12.5	−3.5	−4.0	−6.9	−7.5
EU-15 TTL	−8.0	+5.3	+1.0	+4.4	−3.3

Source: European Environment Agency 2008, compiled from data on pp. 31–40.

Kyoto, worked out an EU burden-sharing agreement of −8 percent, or pushed through ratification. EU institutions were crucial, moreover, to the adoption of two fundamental ideas that have shaped European action on climate change: the precautionary principle and burden sharing.

Yet, as Anthony Zito warns, while "the large number of access points to the EU system favors the position of entrepreneurs in bringing new ideas to the EU agenda ..., the very existence of these access points, makes entrepreneurial efforts later in the policy process that much more difficult. Fertile access points become formidable veto points when opposing status quo interests scramble to challenge a new proposal."[73]

In many ways, the EU's ability to maintain its climate change leadership role in the future will become more difficult, given that in the post-2012 period all EU member states will be expected to participate in any EU-wide climate change agreement. The EU-27 is far more diverse both in economic terms and in terms of environmental capacity and interests. This could make the baton passing more difficult. Moreover, the kind of windfall benefits in greenhouse gas reduction experienced by Germany due to the collapse of the eastern German economy and by the UK due to the transition from coal to natural gas that so greatly facilitated the formation of the EU burden-sharing agreement cannot be expected to reoccur. This suggests that leadership will be harder, but certainly not impossible for Europe to sustain in the future, should it choose to do so.

Conclusion

If the EU succeeds in meeting its burden-sharing target (as seems likely), then it will have achieved something of a moral victory vis-à-vis its skeptics. If the EU fails, cynics are likely to charge that while Europe is good at setting lofty goals, it is poor at implementing them. Regardless of the outcome, the EU has influenced policy change and innovation both at home and internationally through the power of example in the areas of energy efficiency improvements, renewable energy development, emissions trading, energy taxes, and joint implementation. The EU, moreover, will have made a strong case for international cooperation in addressing a serious threat to the planet. The signing and ratification of the Kyoto Protocol has helped to put a variety of new policies and measures in motion. It has also helped to initiate joint projects among developed and transition countries.

In the period leading up to the Copenhagen climate change negotiations in 2009, the EU succeeded again in coalescing around ambitious targets backed by concrete policy measures. Europe pushed considerably harder and earlier than any of its counterparts. Yet Europe's ability to set the agenda has been complicated by the more complex nature of the Copenhagen negotiations. The world's attention is focused on the actions of its two largest greenhouse gas emitters: China and the United States. Industrializing countries being pressured to make their own commitments to slow the growth in business-as-usual emissions are pushing back and demanding compensation and assistance. Moreover, more issues are on the table, including complex discussions regarding an adaptation fund, technology transfer, the Reducing Emissions from Deforestation and Degradation in Developing Countries (REDD) program, a revamped Clean Development Mechanism, an international emissions tradings scheme, and many other matters.

The return of the United States under Barack Obama to the UN-led negotiations has been welcomed by Europe, even though there are differences in approaches between the EU and the United States on such matters as emissions reduction goals and baseline years (1990 versus 2005). Relatively strong signals coming from China suggest that China and the EU have adopted some similar perspectives on several key negotiation points (with both agreeing that the United States is not making strong enough commitments and rejecting the US-proposed 2005 baseline).[74] With more heavyweight players around the table, however, global attention is bound to shift somewhat away from Europe to the United States, China, India, and other major emitting states. For the time being, however, Europe continues to offer many important lessons for other regions of the world on climate change mitigation.

Appendix

Germany

While there are areas where German policy has lagged (most noticeably in relation to the setting of automobile fuel-efficiency standards and autobahn speed limits), Germany has been a leader within Europe in developing policy proposals and goals for reducing dependence on carbon-emitting fuels. Germany was a key player pushing for far-reaching EU goals. In March 1996 Germany called on the EU to bring a 15–20 percent reduction target for 2010 to Kyoto (the EU went instead with a 15 percent reduction target).[75] Germany was strongly behind the EU's decision to move forward with ratification of Kyoto in 2001. By committing to a 40 percent CO_2 emission reduction target for 2020 relative to 1990 levels, Germany became the first country to adopt a concrete midterm greenhouse gas emissions reduction target. Germany's target basically makes it possible for the EU to have a 20 percent reduction target for 2020. What explains this proactive climate politics?

The German case is interesting because the same kind of competitive leadership witnessed among member states and the Commission within the EU has occurred among Germany's political parties and the Environment Ministry. There has been something of a competition among the Christian Democrats, Social Democrats, and the Greens to present themselves as the party of climate change action, and the Environment Ministry, unusually strong relative to the Economics Ministry (when compared with the situation of environmental ministries in most countries), has been able to play an agenda-setting role.

Although competitive party politics and the presence of the Green Party are essential factors explaining German leadership, these are operating with a background of very strong public opinion in favor of action on climate change. For example, in the March 2008 Eurobarometer survey Germans picked climate change as the number one global threat (65 percent versus 57 percent for the EU average). Moreover, 75 percent expected further joint actions from the EU and their government, and 45 percent supported stricter fines (versus 37 percent for the EU average).[76]

Intriguingly, especially when compared to the Republican Party in the United States, the conservative Christian Democratic Union/Christian Social Union has been a strong supporter of German and EU climate change leadership. The biggest difference in the positions of German parties on climate change has been not on *whether* to establish or fulfill them but on *how* to meet emissions reduction targets (for example, whether to include nuclear energy or not).

Chancellor Angela Merkel was Helmut Kohl's environment minister from 1994 to 1998 and helped negotiate the Berlin Mandate and the Kyoto Protocol. She visited Japan in 1997 to persuade its leaders to agree to bold measures.[77] Going into the internal EU negotiations regarding what kind of target to bring to Kyoto, Germany could offer quite a lot to the EU. While Germany was still heavily dependent on coal for its electricity production (in 1997, 55 percent of electricity was produced from coal, 32 percent from nuclear, 9 percent from natural gas, 3 percent from hydroelectric, and 1 percent from oil),[78] as a result of unification and the collapse of the Soviet-style economy in East Germany, Germany had seen its CO_2 emissions drop steeply—approximately 13 percent between 1990 and 1995. Thus Germany was able to make sizeable commitments during the negotiations to form an EU bubble.

The German government agreed to a 25 percent reduction goal when the EU was discussing bringing to Kyoto a 15 percent reduction target for three greenhouse gases.[79] When the Kyoto negotiations resulted in instead an 8 percent reduction goal for six greenhouse gases for the EU as a whole, Germany then agreed within the EU burden-sharing agreement to a 21 percent reduction of these greenhouse gases between 1990 and 2012.

Germany's ability to lead is certainly in part a result of its special domestic situation. Unification in 1990 strongly affected Germany's and by extension the EU's possibilities. While the heavy costs that Germany has had to pay for the environmental cleanup of the former German Democratic Republic are frequently overlooked, the shutdown of many heavily polluting industries strengthened Germany's chances of achieving major emissions cuts. Yet it would be unfair to dismiss the German targets as little more than hot air. According to one estimate, about 50 percent of the German reductions are attributable to wall fall profits; the remainder result from energy efficiency improvements, renewable energy development, and other climate measures. Germany emits one-third less CO_2 per unit of GDP than it did in 1990.[80]

Important policy changes were introduced by the Red-Green coalition that formed after the 1998 elections. In Germany's parliamentary system, with its five main parties, it is almost impossible for any party to obtain a sufficiently large majority to govern alone. This was the case after the 1998 election. The Social Democrats needed a coalition partner, and they turned to Bündnis 90/Die Grünen (the Green Party). The price the Greens demanded for their cooperation was the positions of foreign, health, and environment ministers.

The Greens used their relatively powerful position in the coalition government to push through goals they had long had on their agenda, including ecological tax reform (reducing the tax burden on workers while increasing it on energy consumption), a nuclear phase-out law (a ban on new plants and a phased shut down of existing reactors), a renewable energy law (building on the success of the 1990 Electricity Feed-in Law), and an aggressive climate change policy.[81] These laws were enacted prior to the Bush administration's decision to abandon the Kyoto Protocol. For the Red-Green coalition, there was really little question that the country needed to move ahead with ratification of Kyoto and to work to try to bring the United States back into the agreement. Instead of backtracking, Germany pushed forward. On 19 December 2001, the German government's independent Council of Environment Advisors called on the government to adopt a 40 percent reduction goal for 2020 against 1990 levels (a position the Economics Ministry opposed).[82] The Red-Green coalition eventually did adopt this goal in its National Climate Change Protection Program 2005. The program presented a goal of reducing CO_2 emissions by 40 percent by 2020 if other EU member states agreed to a 30 percent reduction of European emissions over the same time frame.[83]

It is useful to consider the policies introduced by the Red-Green coalition. Based on a polluter-pays principle, the ecological tax reform put a tax on the consumption of electricity and increased taxes on oil and natural gas (but not coal, due to the Social Democrats' strong ties to the coal industry). The decision to phase out nuclear energy—while complicating efforts to reduce reliance on coal and oil—has helped to put support behind bold plans for enhancing renewables. The Renewable Energy Law of 2000 set a target for doubling the share of renewable energy in the electricity market from 5 to 10 percent by 2010. As a result of developments at the EU level (the formation of EU Directive 2001/77/EC) and domestically, this target was subsequently changed to 12.5 percent between 2000 and 2010, 20 percent by 2020 and "around half of energy consumption" by the middle of the century.[84]

Combined, these policies have had a powerful effect on the German energy sector, beginning a shift away from reliance on nuclear and fossil fuels for energy production. With these laws in place, the Red-Green coalition (reelected in 2002) had a strong interest in maintaining a proactive climate change policy.

The policies, moreover, began to have an effect not only on the generation of renewable energy but also on perceptions of climate change policy as an opportunity rather than simply a burden. Germany became a world leader in both wind and photovoltaic power generation. Support for climate change policies increasingly was seen by a wide array of actors as a means of promoting innovation and a technological transformation to a post-carbon economy. This has made pursuit of a progressive climate change policy less divisive.

In November 2005, Angela Merkel became chancellor at the head of a grand coalition between the CDU and SPD. The new coalition maintained the environment and energy legislation introduced by the Red-Green coalition, and also introduced significant new policy goals and programs.[85] In April 2007, also in the run-up to the G-8 summit, the Environment Ministry issued "Climate Agenda 2020," a plan for achieving a 40 percent CO_2 emission reduction without relying on nuclear energy. The plan is a package of measures for increasing the share of renewables in electricity to 27 percent by 2020, doubling combined heat and power, modernizing power plants, and improving energy efficiency by 11 percent.[86] In December 2007 Merkel's cabinet endorsed the comprehensive package.

The September 2009 federal elections brought to power a new coalition between the CDU and the Free Democratic Party. No major changes to Germany's climate programs have been announced, although there is some question whether the coalition partners will attempt to win public approval of a lengthening of the running time of existing nuclear power plants that are scheduled to be shut down by no later than 2020.

United Kingdom

The UK went from being relatively skeptical about EC efforts to forge a leadership role on climate matters to being one of the stronger supporters of the Kyoto Protocol process within Europe. During the negotiations in Kyoto, after the US rejection of the agreement, with the launching of the UK ETS, and most notably in the early stages of the international negotiations of a successor agreement, the UK has played a pivotal agenda setting and international policy-framing role within Europe.

Why did the UK switch from being an obstructionist force within Europe to being at the forefront on climate action? Early British opposition to Commission overtures for harmonization of EC climate action stemmed in part from the fact that the UK's political culture differed from that of the Continent, where German regulatory style and precautionary attitudes held sway. The UK has a more liberal economic tradition than does the Continent: the 2008 Eurobarometer on the UK and the environment found that only 54 percent support EU regulation (compared to 67 percent in the EU as a whole) and only 14 percent support increased taxation.[87] It was also in part due to the interest of the Conservative governments of Margaret Thatcher and John Major, which were closely tied to business. The UK, moreover, has consistently expressed a strong interest in bridging the climate divide between the EU and the United States.[88]

Perhaps not by coincidence, the change to a Labour government in 1997 led by Tony Blair coincided with a more activist climate politics for the UK. To explain the shift in British position as simply based on this change in governing parties, however, would miss the fact that by this time Britain was already well on its way to meeting its target to stabilize emissions by 2000—thanks largely to policies initiated earlier by Margaret Thatcher that spurred the country's switch from heavy reliance on coal to natural gas. This helped make it possible for the UK to agree to take on a sizeable reduction target during the Kyoto negotiations.

When Tony Blair was elected prime minister in May 1997, he campaigned on a pledge to reduce CO_2 levels by 20 percent of 1990 levels by 2010, a commitment that was written into the country's Climate Change Program in February 2000.[89] Since this time, the UK has been relatively consistently among the lead states within Europe on climate change matters.

The decisions of the UK and Germany to work side by side, first in trying to bring the United States back into the Kyoto treaty and, when that failed, in moving forward nonetheless, was certainly important to the Protocol's eventual ratification. In the UK's case, the decision may also have been tied to the unpopularity of Blair's decision to join the "coalition of the willing" in Iraq. As a result, it was important for Blair to show policy leadership in an area where he could prove his "independence" from the United States.

Beyond this, however, genuine interest in playing a leadership role on climate change became increasingly visible as a part of national dialog in the UK about the country's economic future. In the UK, as in Germany, climate change mitigation became linked to the idea of ecological modernization and the notion that a low-carbon society could be technologically more sophisticated, efficient, and competitive.[90]

The UK also saw in climate change the potential to develop new markets. It is noteworthy that while Germany initially resisted the idea of an EU ETS, the UK was the first country worldwide to introduce a (voluntary) national carbon ETS (launched in April 2002). The scheme remained in place until the launch of the European ETS in January 2005. While questions have been raised about the scheme's effectiveness, it did give the UK first mover advantage in learning about emissions trading, a business that has been projected to potentially explode in the future.[91]

A particularly dramatic shift in UK policy was stimulated by the *Stern Review on the Economics of Climate Change* (October 2006). The report concluded that failure to act globally—in other words, a business-as-usual emissions trajectory—"will reduce welfare by an amount equivalent to a reduction in consumption per head of between 5 and 20 percent."[92] On the other hand, it made the point that effective action did not need to be expensive: "The costs for stabilization at 500–550ppm CO_2e were centered on 1 percent of GDP by 2050, with a range of −2 percent to +5 percent of GDP."[93] The report further notes "significant new opportunities across a wide range of industries and services. Markets for low-carbon energy products are likely to be worth at least $500bn per year by 2050, and perhaps much more."[94]

The *Stern Review on the Economics of Climate Change* profoundly affected British, European, and international debates. A year after its release, in November 2007, a climate change bill was introduced in Parliament. One year later Parliament passed the Climate Change Act, which requires that the UK's carbon account be 80 percent below 1990 levels by 2050; moreover, it requires a reduction of at least 26 percent by 2020 (compared with 1990) and periodic carbon budget reviews. This law is the first in the world to make such a long-term target legally binding. It also established a Committee on Climate Change to advise the government on how to achieve this goal.[95]

The UK's policies are having effects. Provisional figures released by the Department of Environment, Forests and Rural Affairs in mid-2009 estimate that the UK's 2008 greenhouse gas emissions were approximately 20 percent below their 1990 levels, well beyond the 12.5 percent reduction target agreed to in Kyoto. Greenhouse gas emissions per gross domestic product (GDP) (purchasing power standard) dropped by 43 percent between 1990 and 2006, putting the UK only slightly behind Sweden, France, and Austria in terms of its strong greenhouse gas intensity performance.[96]

France

France is in the midst of an important political transition with respect to environmental questions and climate change in particular. France was not very active during the Kyoto negotiations. Under the EU bubble, France simply committed to stabilize its emissions at 1990 levels. More recently, however, it has emerged as a new climate change leader within the EU. The arrival of the new France on the EU environmental scene has been crystallized by the activist French presidency of the EU beginning in July 2008, with climate change negotiations positioned as the number one priority for the presidency and a strong push for an EU-wide carbon tax. Domestically, France began in 2007 to take unprecedented regulatory and fiscal steps using a battery of tools available to this strong bureaucratic and developmental state. The French case illustrates the potential effect of state institutions.

France is a relatively small emitter compared to its economic size; it emits less than half the CO_2 levels of Germany.[97] This is largely a consequence of decisions made in the 1970s to become less dependent on energy imports. Fifty-nine nuclear reactors produce 78 percent of the country's electricity and account for the bulk of France's 50 percent energy autonomy.[98] Hydroelectric plants produce another 12 percent of the country's electricity. Owing to this situation and to a less active environmental community,[99] France played a limited role in the international negotiations up to 2005.

Emissions in France in 2006 were 4.0 percent below the 1990 level (table 2.3). With existing measures, France is expected to be 0.8 percent above its Kyoto target, but the use of carbon sinks is currently estimated to put France 4.2 percent below its Kyoto target (ibid.). As of 2007 France was projecting that it would not need to use the Kyoto mechanisms to meet its target. France has made significant progress on the industrial side, particularly with a big drop in nitrous oxide emissions in the chemical industry. As is the case in many other EU countries, it has, however, experienced a significant increase in emissions from the transportation sector (+20 percent from 1990 to 2005).[100]

French industrial interests have been divided over climate change. On the one hand, heavy industry and most manufacturers have lobbied against taxation or strict measures. On the other hand, the powerful nuclear lobby has seen climate mitigation as a great opportunity to expand French nuclear interests in France and abroad. In addition, car manufacturers such as Peugeot and Renault have developed extremely fuel-efficient diesel cars and have pushed for tougher standards on car emissions as a means to gain a competitive edge over larger German automobile manufacturers.

Traditionally, French public opinion has not been a strong force behind environmental issues and climate change. But recent years have seen France converge and even pass the EU average in terms of environmental awareness. Interestingly, the French public is more in favor of direct measures (such as taxation) and EU-wide regulations than the average European. The March 2008 Eurobarometer showed that 59 percent of the French pick climate change as the top environmental concern (compared to the EU average of 57 percent).[101] Of the French respondents, 77 percent prefer EU-level regulations on the environment (compared to the EU average of 67 percent).[102] The French are also more inclined to support fines (41 percent) and green taxes (21 percent) than EU citizens as a whole (36 percent and 14 percent, respectively).

The traditional trust in the state as a pacesetter and coordinator has deep roots in France, going all the way back to Jean-Baptiste Colbert in the seventeenth century. In times of great challenges, the state has institutional resources and the public expects it to lead. That ideational component has played a role in enabling recent top-down leadership.

In all its Kyoto measures, France has resorted to its traditional direct state tools. Initially, the relatively comfortable Kyoto target did not require drastic actions and France was content to rely partly on its earlier investment into the nuclear industry (directed through vigorous industrial policy). In 2007–2008, when France initiated a major acceleration to position itself in a stronger position to influence debate on a post-Kyoto agreement, state institutions responded by resorting to traditional industrial policy measures. The measures unveiled in 2007–2008 include tax credits and penalties on cars, a carbon tax plan, and intrusive regulatory requirements on electricity efficiency in housing (including inspections of all homes by government officials), cars, and transportation planning.

In fall 2009, President Nicolas Sarkozy won approval of his flagship policy, a carbon tax. The carbon tax was set at an initial rate of €17 per metric ton of CO_2 (or €4 cents per liter of gas), a lower level than the €32 recommended by his advisory committee or by the Greens, but still a significant step in a period of economic crisis. His government introduced the bill in September 2009 as part of the 2010 annual budget bill, and the National Assembly approved it on 23 October. The tax is expected to bring €4.8 billion in revenue in 2010, €2.7 billion of which will be handed back to taxpayers through income tax credits.[103] The tax was introduced against the opposition of nearly all parties in parliament: conservatives were reluctant to follow their president due to opposition to tax increases in principle; the socialists opposed it because of its nonredistributive character and thus higher burden on lower classes; and the Greens because they felt it was set too low and lacked accompanying social measures. The media reported that the introduction of the tax caused a drop in the support rating of the president and of the government.

Nevertheless, the carbon tax is the culminating symbol of a changed politics in France. The shift began in 2007 when France began taking a more proactive stance on climate change action. As has been the case with all EU member states who have held the presidency during a major climate change negotiation, the pressure to uphold EU leadership in the climate realm is great. At the G8 meeting in Toyako, Japan, Sarkozy joined forces with Angela Merkel and Gordon Brown in pushing for a concrete emission reduction target. While they did not achieve a commitment to a medium target from the Bush administration, they did get G8 agreement on the importance of a 50 percent emission reduction globally by 2050.

This development in the French stance ran counter to prevailing interest group patterns, the country's poor Green Party representation, and the relative weakness of its NGOs. It also appears all the more puzzling since it emerged as a signature initiative from a pro–United States conservative government that spearheaded the major move toward Kyoto while also reentering the NATO military command and cutting overall taxes. The shift to proactive and powerful regulatory measures in 2007 follows an earlier precursor period under another conservative president, Jacques Chirac, who became a moral activist for the environment and for action to combat climate change after about 2002. His legacy includes enshrining the precautionary principle and a charter for the environment in the constitution, although he did not follow that achievement with concrete implementation measures.

The shift that took place in 2007 was the result of the surprising emergence of climate change as a major issue during the presidential election campaign: Sarkozy used environmental issues to redraw the electoral map and offset his more conservative edges. The shift started in part because a popular (conservative) environmental TV presenter, Nicolas Hulot, threatened to join the presidential election if all candidates did not commit to his "pact" (demanding a carbon tax and a halt to all highway construction, among other things). When opinion polls showed that he could garner 10–12 percent of the vote, most major candidates, especially Sarkozy, signed up to his pact, and Nicolas Hulot duly declined to run as a candidate. He later became a major adviser to the president.

Spain

Spain is part of a group of implementation laggards who are far off their Kyoto commitments under the EU burden-sharing agreement, although Spain has become more aggressive in efforts to slow the growth in greenhouse gas emissions in recent years. Spain is unlikely to be able to meet its Kyoto Protocol target.

Emissions in Spain in 2006 were 34.5 percent above the 1990 level,[104] compared to a Kyoto Protocol target of +15.0 percent by 2010 as part of the EU burden-sharing agreement. Between 1990 and 2005, transportation-related emissions increased by nearly 100 percent.[105] Industrial emissions increased by about 30 percent, the third highest rate of increase in the EU after Greece and Portugal.[106]

As a result of the huge backlog, Spain announced plans to use Kyoto mechanisms—Joint Implementation, the Clean Development Mechanism (CDM), and emissions trading—to the tune of 31.8 million metric tons of CO_2 equivalent (out of a total EU-15 plan of 107.5 million metric tons) for a total budget of €301 million.[107] The bulk of those measures are likely to be CDMs in Latin American countries.

High economic growth drove much of the increase in Spain's greenhouse gas emissions. Spain's economy grew at an average 3.1 percent per year from 1990 to 2006, accelerating after 1997 (5 percent in

2000).[108] Politics also played a key role. The conservative government led by José María Aznar (1996–2004) was openly allied with industrial interests and fostered growth above all. In 2003 and 2004, Loyola de Palacio, the Spanish EU commissioner for transport and energy, who was sent to Brussels by Aznar, openly challenged the EU's commitment to the Kyoto Protocol. She argued that plans to implement cuts in greenhouse gas emissions would pose a severe threat to European industry.

The electoral victory of the Socialists in 2005 resulted in a sharp about-face in Spain's stance on climate change mitigation. The first significant law for the implementation of the Kyoto target and for curbing greenhouse gas emissions was passed in 2005 under the new government of José Luis Rodríguez Zapatero.

Spain has announced its commitment to achieve its Kyoto target.[109] In November 2007 the Cabinet approved Spain's Climate Change Strategy. Spain sees strong potential in renewable energies. It has very rapidly become one of the top three countries in the EU in terms of wind power (along with Denmark and Germany). Solar energy also rose by 90 percent between 2003 and 2005, although Germany outpaced Spain with a rise of 285 percent and there was a crash in the solar market in Spain after government supports were suddenly dropped due to the high demands for solar and concerns about budgetary implications.[110]

The Spanish case is intriguing in part because in recent years the government has shown much stronger concern about reducing the country's emissions. This may well be tied to growing fears among Spain's leadership and public about the implications of climate change—and especially the desertification of the south—for Spain. Opinion polls show that Spanish public opinion is now nearly at the average EU level with respect to climate change. According to the 2008 Eurobarometer on Spain and the environment, 57 percent of the population cite climate change as one of their top five environmental concerns (exactly the EU average), and 71 percent (versus the EU average of 67 percent) support EU regulations as the best tools to deal with it.[111]

Spain is among the most vulnerable of all European states to the effects of climate changes. A 2007 report commissioned by the Zapatero government and conducted by a group of Spanish scientists concluded that if the rise in global greenhouse gas emissions is not substantially curtailed globally, Spain may experience incessant heat waves, desertification across the entire south, extinction of plant and animal species, and a sharp rise in average temperatures. In September 2007 President Zapatero lamented, "For many years Spain did nothing, but now we are going to do everything." He promised that Spain would meet its Kyoto Protocol targets and asked the United Nations "to take the initiative and show its leadership in the climate change battle."[112]

The Netherlands

As a medium-sized economy within the EU, the political and economic influence of the Netherlands is limited. This is the case with other EU member states, such as Austria, Belgium, Denmark, Finland, Luxembourg, and Sweden. Combined, their greenhouse gas emissions in 1990 were less than two-thirds those of Germany. In the area of climate change, however, these states have often formed coalitions in support of aggressive action. Their role in internal negotiations has been crucial.

Early on, the Netherlands, for example, was a particularly strong advocate of climate change action. It was perhaps fortunate coincidence that the Dutch held the presidency of the Council both at the time of the United Nations Conference on Environment and Development negotiations in 1992 and during the EU burden-sharing negotiations in 1997.

In many respects, the Dutch approach is similar to Germany's, with a focus on precautionary action, reliance on voluntary agreements (such as energy efficiency covenants negotiated between the state and industry stipulating energy efficiency improvements), and a consensual decision-making style (known as the polder model in the Netherland's case).[113]

In May 1998 a new coalition government formed. The coalition agreement accepted the importance of the Kyoto agreement and the EU decision on burden sharing (including the 6 percent reduction goal for the Netherlands) but attached a number of conditions to the target, including an allowance that around 50 percent of the reduction total be achieved through international activities.[114]

As of late 2008 the Netherlands are projected to be 3.8 percent above the Kyoto target by 2010.[115] The Dutch government intends to achieve most of the remaining needed emission cuts through CDM projects and the purchase of certified emission reductions, bringing the outcome to 2.4 percent below the Kyoto target. It is quite striking that despite its small size (with a population of roughly 16 million), the Netherlands in August 2008 accounted for 11.2 percent of all registered CDM projects as an investor country (in comparison, the UK accounted for 33.9 percent, Switzerland for 21.85 percent, and Japan for 9.73, percent).[116] Beyond its efforts to implement the Kyoto Protocol, the Dutch government has announced its plans to pursue a 30 percent reduction in greenhouse gas emissions by 2020 relative to 1990 levels.

The Dutch approach to climate change is also tied to the fact that approximately two-thirds of the country's population lives below sea level. For the Netherlands, a rise in sea level is a serious concern. Although the Dutch have the world's most sophisticated system of dikes to hold back the sea, Hurricane Katrina sent shivers throughout the country. In September 2007 the Netherlands announced a new commission to begin preparing water defenses that would serve through the year 2200.[117]

Notes

The authors would like to acknowledge the generous support of the Weyerhaeuser Company Foundation and the able research assistantship of Vanessa Meadu.

1. Harris 2007.

2. The shift in the target was in part an accession on the part of the EU to the demand of the US that a larger basket of greenhouse gas emissions be included. The EU's 15 percent target was in relation to three greenhouse gases, while the 8 percent target covered six greenhouse gases.

3. Council Decision 2002/358/EC of 25 April 2002, http://www.climnet.org/EUenergy/ratification/EUCOM01579_en.pdf.

4. European Commission, "EU Unanimously Ratifies Kyoto Protocol to Combat Climate Change," 30 May 2002, EC02–108EN, http://europa-eu-un.org/articles/en/article_1419_en.htm; "European Union Ratifies the Kyoto Protocol," 31 May 2002, Brussels.

5. Peeters and Deketelaere 2006.

6. Skjæseth and Wettestad 2008.

7. European Commission, "Limiting Global Climate Change to 2 Degrees Celsius," MEMO/07/16, Brussels, 10 January 2007.

8. "Europe to Cut Greenhouse Gases 20 Percent by 2020," *Environment News Service*, 8 March 2007, http://www.ens-newswire.com/ens/mar2007/2007-03-08-04.asp; Germany 2007—Presidency of the European Council, "The Spring European Council: Integrated Climate Protection and Energy Policy, Progress on the Lisbon Strategy," 12 March 2007, http://www.eu2007.de/en/News/Press_Releases/March/0312AAER.html.

9. Council of the European Union, Presidency Conclusions, 7224/1/07 Rev 1, Concl 1, Brussels 8/9 March 2007.

10. "EU Agrees Renewable Energy Target," *BBC News*, 9 March 2007, http://news.bbc.co.uk/2/hi/europe/6433503.stm.

11. "EU Pressures US to Reach Climate Consensus in Bali," *DW-World.de*, 13 December 2007.

12. EurAktiv, EU, "US Criticized for Low Profile in Bonn Talks," *EurAktiv*, 16 June 2009.

13. Bomberg 1998, 38–40.

14. We wish to thank an anonymous reviewer for suggesting this point.

15. Stavros Dimas, "Developing the European Climate Change Programme," Stakeholder conference launching the Second European Climate Change Programme, Brussels, 24 October 2005, Europa, SPEECH/05/635.

16. Quoted in Stephen Castle, "Gore Calls on EU to Take Critical Role in Cutting Greenhouse Gas Emissions," *Independent*, 8 March 2007, http://www.independent.co.uk/environment/climate_change/article2338373.ece.

17. Vogler 1999.

18. Gupta and Grubb 2000.

19. Ibid.

20. Gupta and Ringius 2001, 294.

21. Zito 2000.

22. Ellickson 2001; Hechter and Opp 2001; Lightfoot and Burchell 2005; Manners 2000, 2002; Cass 2006.

23. Intergovernmental Panel on Climate Change 2007.

24. Cass 2006.

25. Downs 1957; Kingdon 1984; Tiberghien 2007.

26. Liberatore 1997; Vogler 1999; Vogler and Bretherton 2006.

27. Tsebelis 2002.

28. Zito 2000.

29. Tallberg 2006.

30. A similar phenomenon is noted by Jordan, Wurzel, Zito, and Brückner (2003) in their study of the transfer of new environmental policy instruments.

31. Roger Harrabin, "Germany to Spark 'Climate Crisis,'" *BBC News*, 27 June 2006, http://news.bbc.co.uk/1/hi/sci/tech/5121334.stm.

32. McAdam, McCarthy, and Zald 1996; McAdam, Tarrow, and Tilly 2001.

33. Michaelowa 1998.

34. Manners 2000; Reid 2004; Rifkin 2004.

35. Zito 2000.

36. Sbragia 2002.

37. Hildebrand 2002; Wilkinson 2002; Axelrod, Vig, and Schreurs 2004.

38. Gualini 2004; Hooghe and Marks 2001.

39. *Independent*, http://news.independent.co.uk/environment/article331768.ece.

40. Pew Center on Global Climate Change, Business Environmental Leadership Council, http://www.pewclimate.org/companies_leading_the_way_belc/.

41. Kirsty Hamilton, "The Oil Industry and Climate Change," *A Greenpeace Briefing*, August 1998, Amsterdam: Greenpeace International.

42. Markussen and Svendsen 2005.

43. Eurobarometer 58, Autumn 2002, http://ec.europa.eu/public_opinion/archives/eb/eb58/eb58_en.pdf.

44. Irene Marr, ed., "US State Department Round Up of International Press Stories on US Withdrawal from the Kyoto Protocol," http://www.climnet.org/news/bushroundup.html.

45. Pew Research Center for the People and the Press, "Bush Unpopular in Europe, Seen as Unilateralist," *Pew Global Attitudes Project*, 15 August 2001, http://pewglobal.org/reports/print.php?PageID=39.

46. WWF UK, "British Public Supports the Kyoto Protocol," 12 June 2001, http://www.wwf.org.uk/news/n_0000000292.asp.

47. Tiberghien's interview, Brussels, 16 June 2005.

48. Andresen and Gulbrandsen 2004.

49. McAdam, McCarthy, and Zald 1996; McAdam, Tarrow, and Tilly 2001.

50. Climate Action Network Europe, http://www.climnet.org/index.htm.

51. Lee Hay Browns, US CAN Coordinator, http://circa.europa.eu/Public/irc/env/action_climat/library?l=/uscan_consultation/_EN_1.0_&a=d.

52. Ringius 1997, 8.

53. Huber and Liberatore 2001.

54. The changes in position between the 1997 and the 1998 commitments suggest that several states had to accept sharper relative cuts (for example, Portugal, Denmark, Germany, the UK) while others came off with lighter, but with still substantial burdens (for example, Austria, the Netherlands).

55. Significantly, the 1990 baseline was to become a major point of contention between the United States and Europe, with the former declaring that the 1990 baseline favored European states ability to meet their Kyoto target due to the collapse of the East German economy.

56. Tiberghien's interview at the EU Commission, 16 June 2005.

57. Commission of the European Communities 2001.

58. Damro and Luaces Méndez 2003; Jordan, Wurzel, Zito, and Brückner 2003.

59. European Parliament, Bonn Conference on Climate Change, B5–0473/2001, European Parliament resolution on the European Union's strategy for the Bonn Conference on Climate Change (COP 6, part 2), Official Journal of the European Communities, 14 March 2002, pp. C 65/E/380–2, http://europa.eu.int/eur-lex/pri/en/oj/dat/2002/ce065/ce06520020314en03800382.pdf.

60. Hassi, Satu, "EU Leadership or Another Planet?," *Parliament Magazine*, 31 May 2005, 55–56.

61. Schreurs and Papadakis 2007.

62. European Parliament: European Greens, http://www.greens-efa.org/cms/default/rubrik/6/6648.history@en.htm.

63. Gummer and Moreland 2002.

64. European Environment Agency 2008.

65. European Environment Agency 2008.

66. Ibid., 39.

67. Ibid., 40.

68. Speech by Margaret Beckett made at the British Embassy in Berlin, 24 October 2006, http://www.britischebotschaft.de/en/news/items/061024.htm.

69. On this point see Skodvin and Andresen 2006.

70. European Environment Agency 2006, 34–35.

71. Rifkin 2004.

72. Frohlich, Oppenheimer, and Young 1971.

73. Zito 2000, 172.

74. Discussion with Franz-Josef Schafhausen, Berlin, 23 June 2009.

75. Oberthür and Ott 1999, 116.

76. Eurobarometer (Attitudes of Europeans toward the Environment), March 2008, Germany.

77. Schreurs's attendance at meeting with Angela Merkel in Germany Embassy in Japan, 1997.

78. World Bank Development Indicators, 2000.

79. Hatch 2007.

80. Ziesing 2006; Weidner and Mez 2008.

81. European Greens: National Elections, http://www.europeangreens.org/info/archive/results.nat.archive.html.

82. "Government Advisors Call for 40 percent Reduction in Carbon Dioxide Emissions," *Environment Information Note 2.02*, 7 January 2002, http://britischebotschaft.de/en/embassz/environment/pdf/env-note_02-02.pdf.

83. Federal Ministry for the Environment 2005.

84. Bundesministerium für Umwelt, Naturschutz und Reaktorsicherheit, Indicative Target of the Federal Republic of Germany for the Consumption of Electricity Produced from Renewable Energy Sources in 2010 and Measures to Achieve this Target, Report from the Federal Republic of Germany pursuant to Article 3 para. 2 of EU Directive 2001/77/EC.

85. Schreurs 2002.

86. Bundesumweltministerium, Klimaagenda 2020: Der Umbau der Industriegesellschaft, Berlin, April 2007.

87. EU Commission. 2008. Eurobarometer: Attitudes of European Citizens Toward the Environment. Results for the United Kingdom (March), 2.

88. Cass 2007.

89. Gummer and Moreland 2002, 22.

90. Jänicke 2004.

91. ENVIROS Consulting Ltd. Appraisal of Years 1–4 of the UK Emissions Trading Scheme, December 2006, http://www.defra.gov.uk/environment/climatechange/trading/uk/pdf/ukets1-4yr-appraisal.pdf.

92. Stern 2006.

93. Ibid., xiv.

94. Ibid., xvi.

95. Department for Environment, Food and Rural Affairs, Climate Change Bill, www.defra.gov.uk/environment/climatechange/uk/index.htm; United Kingdom Parliament, Climate Change Act 2008, Chapter 27.

96. European Environment Agency 2008, 25.

97. As of 1990, French total GHG emissions in CO_2 equivalents were 564 million metric tons, compared to 1,228 million in Germany and 771 million in the UK, an economy of smaller size than France (Commission of the European Communities 2007).

98. International Atomic Energy Agency, Energy and Environment Data Reference Bank, http://www.iaea.org/inis/aws/eedrb/data/FR-npsh.html.

99. Valantin 2005, 139.

100. Ibid., Annex on France, 4.

101. EU Commission. 2008. Eurobarometer: Attitudes of European Citizens Toward the Environment. Results for France (March), 2.

102. Ibid., 3.

103. Claire Guelaud, "Les députés font entrer la taxe carbone dans la fiscalité française," *Le Monde*, 27 October 2009.

104. Commission of the European Communities 2007, 5.

105. European Environment Agency 2007, 77.

106. Ibid., 82.

107. Commission of the European Communities 2007, 15.

108. OECD, author's calculations.

109. Ibid., 12.

110. Commission of the European Communities 2007, 70.

111. EU Commission. 2008. Eurobarometer: Attitudes of European Citizens Toward the Environment. Results for Spain (March), 2–4.

112. "Zapatero Asks UN to Lead Climate Change Battle," *Olive Press*, 27 September 2007.

113. Fisher 2004.

114. Ministry of Housing, Spatial Planning and the Environment, Directorate Climate Change and Industry, Third Netherlands' National Communication on Climate Change Policies, Prepared for the Conference of the Parties under the Framework Convention on Climate Change, October 2001.

115. European Environment Agency 2008, 31–40.

116. Clean Development Mechanism Web site, http://cdm.unfccc.int.

117. "Dutch to Draft 200-Year Plan against Warming," *Associated Press,* 11 September 2007.

References

Andresen, Steinar, and Lars H. Gulbrandsen. 2004. NGO Influence in the Implementation of the Kyoto Protocol: Compliance, Flexibility Mechanisms, and Sinks. *Global Environmental Politics* 4 (4):54–75.

Axelrod, Regina, Norman J. Vig, and Miranda A. Schreurs. 2004. The European Union as an Environmental Governance System. In *The Global Environment: Institutions, Law and Policy*, ed. Norman Vig and Regina S. Axelrod, 200–225. Washington, DC: Congressional Quarterly Press.

Bomberg, Elizabeth. 1998. *Green Parties and Politics in the European Union.* London: Routledge.

Cass, Loren R. 2006. *The Failures of American and European Climate Policy.* Albany: State University of New York Press.

Cass, Loren R. 2007. The Indispensable Awkward Partner: The United Kingdom in European Climate Policy. In Harris 2007, 63–86.

Commission of the European Communities. 2001. Proposal for a Council Decision: Concerning the Conclusion, on Behalf of the European Community, of the Kyoto Protocol to the United Nations Framework Convention on Climate Change and the Joint Fulfillment of Commitments Thereunder. COM (2001) 579 (23 October).

Commission of the European Communities. 2007. Commission Staff Working Document: Accompanying document (SEC [2007] 1576) to Communication from the Commission; Progress towards Achieving the Kyoto Objectives. COM (2007) 757 (27 November).

Damro, Chad, and Pilar Luaces Méndez. 2003. Emissions Trading at Kyoto: From EU Resistance to Union Innovation. *Environmental Politics* 12 (2):71–94.

Downs, Anthony. 1957. *An Economic Theory of Democracy.* New York: Harper.

Ellickson, Robert C. 2001. The Market for Social Norms. *American Law and Economics Review* 3 (1):1–49.

European Environment Agency. 2006. *Greenhouse Gas Emission Trends and Projections in Europe 2006.* http://reports.eea.europa.eu/eea_report_2006_9/en/eea_report_9_2006.pdf.

European Environment Agency. 2007. *Greenhouse Gas Emission Trends and Projections in Europe 2007: Tracking Progress towards Kyoto Targets.* EEA Report 5/2007.

European Environment Agency. 2008. *Greenhouse Gas Emission Trends and Projections in Europe 2008: Tracking Progress towards Kyoto Targets.* EEA Report 5/2008.

Federal Ministry for the Environment. 2005. *Nature Conservation and Nuclear Safety, General Information: Climate Protection.* http://www.bmu.de/english/climate/general_information/doc/4311.php.

Fisher, Dana. 2004. *National Governance and the Global Climate Change Regime.* Lanham, MD: Rowman and Littlefield.

Frohlich, Norman, Joe Oppenheimer, and Oran Young. 1971. *Political Leadership and Collective Goods.* Princeton: Princeton University Press.

Gualini, Enrico. 2004. *Multi-Level Governance and Institutional Change: The Europeanization of Regional Policy in Italy.* Aldershot, UK: Ashgate.

Gummer, John, and Robert Moreland. 2002. European Union: A Review of Five National Programs. In *Climate Change: Science, Strategies, and Solutions,* ed. Eileen Claussen, Vicki Arroyo Cochran, and Debra P. Davis, 88–115. Leiden: Brill Academic Publishers.

Gupta, Joyeeta, and Michael Grubb. 2000. Climate Change, Leadership and the EU. In *Climate Change and European Leadership: A Sustainable Role for Europe?,* ed. Joyeeta Gupta and Michael Grubb. Dordrecht: Kluwer Academic.

Gupta, Joyeeta, and Lasse Ringius. 2001. Climate Leadership: Reconciling Ambition and Reality. *International Environmental Agreements* 1:281–299.

Harris, Paul G. 2007. *Europe and Global Climate Change: Politics, Foreign Policy and Regional Cooperation.* Cheltenham, UK: Edward Elgar.

Hatch, Michael T. 2007. The Politics of Global Warming in Germany: Domestic Sources of Environmental Foreign Policy. In *Europe and Global Climate Change: Politics, Foreign Policy and Regional Cooperation,* ed. Paul G. Harris, 41–62. Cheltenham, UK: Edward Elgar.

Hechter, Michael, and Karl-Dieter Opp. 2001. *Social Norms.* New York: Russell Sage Foundation.

Hildebrand, Philipp M. 2002. The European Community's Environmental Policy, 1957–"1992": From Incidental Measures to an International Regime. In *Environmental Policy in the European Union,* ed. Andrew Jordan, 13–36. London: Earthscan.

Hooghe, Liesbet, and Gary Marks. 2001. *Multi-Level Governance and European Integration.* Lanham, MD: Rowman and Littlefield.

Huber, Michael, and Angela Liberatore. 2001. A Regional Approach to the Management of Global Environmental Risks: The Case of the European Community. In *Learning to Manage Global Environmental Risks,* vol. 1, *A Comparative History of Social Responses to Climate Change, Ozone Depletion, and Acid Rain,* ed. Social Learning Group, 295–322. Cambridge, MA: MIT Press.

Intergovernmental Panel on Climate Change. 2007. *Climate Change 2007: Synthesis Report.* Contribution of Working Groups I, II, and III to the Fourth

Assessment Report of the Intergovernmental Panel on Climate Change (Core Writing Team, R. K. Pachauri and A. Reisinger, eds.). Geneva: IPCC.

Jänicke, Martin. 2004. Industrial Transformation Between Ecological Modernisation and Structural Change. In *Governance for Industrial Transformation: Proceedings of the 2003 Berlin Conference on the Human Dimensions of Global Environmental Change*, ed. Klaus Jacob, Manfred Binder, and Anna Wieczorek, 201–217. Berlin: Environmental Policy Research Centre.

Jordan, Andrew, Rüdiger Wurzel, Anthony R. Zito, and Lars Brückner. 2003. European Governance and the Transfer of "New" Environmental Policy Instruments. *Public Administration* 8:555–574.

Kingdon, John W. 1984. *Agendas, Alternatives, and Public Policies*. Boston: Little, Brown.

Liberatore, Angela. 1997. The European Union: Bridging Domestic and International Environmental Policy-Making. In *The Internationalization of Environmental Protection*, ed. Miranda A. Schreurs and Elizabeth Economy, 188–212. Cambridge: Cambridge University Press.

Lightfoot, Simon, and Jon Burchell. 2005. The European Union and the World Summit on Sustainable Development: Normative Power Europe in Action? *Journal of Common Market Studies* 43:75–95.

Manners, Ian. 2000. *Substance and Symbolism: An Anatomy of Cooperation in the New Europe*. Aldershot, UK: Ashgate.

Manners, Ian. 2002. Normative Power Europe: A Contradiction in Terms? *Journal of Common Market Studies* 40:235–258.

Markussen, Peter, and Gert Tinggaard Svendsen. 2005. Industry Lobbying and the Political Economy of GHG Trade in the European Union. *Energy Policy* 33:245–255.

McAdam, Doug, John D. McCarthy, and Mayer N. Zald. 1996. *Comparative Perspectives on Social Movements: Political Opportunities, Mobilizing Structures, and Cultural Framings*. Cambridge: Cambridge University Press.

McAdam, Doug, Sidney G. Tarrow, and Charles Tilly. 2001. *Dynamics of Contention*. New York: Cambridge University Press.

Michaelowa, Axel. 1998. Impact of Interest Groups on EU Climate Policy. *European Environment* 8 (5):152–160.

Oberthür, Sebastian, and Hermann Ott. 1999. *The Kyoto Protocol: International Climate Policy for the 21st Century*. Berlin: Springer Verlag.

Peeters, Marjan, and Kurt Deketelaere. 2006. *EU Climate Change Policy: The Challenge of New Regulatory Initiatives*. Cheltenham, UK: Edward Elgar.

Reid, T. R. 2004. *The United States of Europe: The New Superpower and the End of American Supremacy*. New York: Penguin Press.

Rifkin, Jeremy. 2004. *The European Dream: How Europe's Vision of the Future Is Quietly Eclipsing the American Dream*. New York: Jeremy P. Tarcher/Penguin.

Ringius, Laase. 1997. *Differentiation, Leaders and Fairness: Negotiating Climate Commitments in the European Community. CICERO Report.* Oslo: University of Oslo.

Sbragia, Alberta. 2002. Institution-Building from Below and Above: The European Community in Global Environmental Politics. In *Environmental Policy in the European Union*, ed. A. Jordan. London: Earthscan.

Schreurs, Miranda A. 2002. *Environmental Politics in Japan, Germany, and the United States.* Cambridge: Cambridge University Press.

Schreurs, Miranda, and Elim Papadakis. 2007. *Historical Dictionary of Green Movements.* Lanham, MD: Scarecrow Press.

Skjæseth, Jon Birger, and Jørgen Wettestad. 2008. *EU Emissions Trading: Initiation, Decision-Making and Implementation.* Aldershot, UK: Ashgate.

Stern, Nicolas. 2006. *The Stern Review Report on the Economics of Climate Change.* London: Office of Climate Change. http://www.occ.gov.uk/activities/ stern.htm.

Tallberg, Jonas. 2006. *Leadership and Negotiation in the European Union.* New York: Cambridge University Press.

Tiberghien, Yves. 2007. *Entrepreneurial States: Reforming Corporate Governance in France, Japan, and Korea.* Ithaca: Cornell University Press.

Tsebelis, George. 2002. *Veto Players: How Political Institutions Work.* Princeton: Princeton University Press.

Valantin, Jean-Michel. 2005. *Menaces climatiques sur l'ordre mondial.* Paris: Lignes de repères.

Vogler, John. 1999. The European Union as an Actor in International Environmental Politics. *Environmental Politics* 8 (3):24–48.

Vogler, John, and Charlotte Bretherton. 2006. The European Union as a Protagonist to the United States on Climate Change. *International Studies Perspectives* 7:1–22.

Weidner, Helmut, and Lutz Mez. 2008. German Climate Change Policy: A Success Story with Some Flaws. *Journal of Environment and Development* 17 (4):356–378.

Wilkinson, David. 2002. Maastricht and the Environment: The Implications for the EC's Environmental Policy of the Treaty on the European Union. In *Environmental Policy in the European Union*, ed. Andrew Jordan, 37–52. London: Earthscan.

Ziesing, Hans Jochen. 2006. Kohlendioxidemissionen in Deutschland im Jahr 2005 deutlich gesunken. *DIW-Wochenbericht*, no. 12, 153–162. (CO_2 emissions decreased significantly in 2005 in Germany, in DIW Weekly Report).

Zito, Anthony. 2000. *Creating Environmental Policy in the European Union.* New York: St. Martin's Press.

3

The United States as Outlier: Economic and Institutional Challenges to US Climate Policy

Kathryn Harrison

Introduction

Until recently overtaken by China, the United States was the largest single contributor to global warming, accounting for almost one-quarter of global greenhouse gas emissions. The magnitude of the US contribution reflects not only the scale of its economy but also per capita emissions that were second highest (after Australia) among industrialized countries.[1] However, while clearly a significant part of the problem, to date the United States has not been part of the solution. At the international level, President George W. Bush confirmed in 2001 that the United States would not ratify the Kyoto Protocol. With Australia's belated ratification in 2007, the United States was isolated as the only advanced industrialized country to decline to ratify. At the domestic level, the US federal government has adopted relatively weak climate policies, relying on voluntary programs and modest government expenditures on research. Not surprisingly, in response US emissions have continued to increase, if at a rate lower that its population and economic growth.

This chapter argues that US resistance to action at both the international and domestic levels is explained by electoral disincentives, reinforced by the United States' distinctive political institutions. With respect to the former, the emissions intensity of the US economy, combined with a relatively demanding target under the Kyoto Protocol, provoked formidable business opposition both to ratification and adoption of domestic regulations. Although American voters have generally indicated support for ratification of the Kyoto Protocol and adoption of domestic mitigation measures when asked, that has not been a sufficient counterweight to business opposition given the electorate's limited attention to climate change.

US political institutions have amplified electoral disincentives to action in three ways. First, weak party discipline renders members of Congress especially responsive to local economic interests that stand to pay the price for regulatory efforts. Second, a lack of party accountability that flows from weak party discipline has facilitated a strategy of questioning climate science to a much larger degree than witnessed in other jurisdictions. Finally, the separation of powers allowed the US Senate, motivated to protect the competitiveness of US business, to block ratification of the Kyoto Protocol, despite President Clinton's support for the treaty.

That said, significant shifts in US climate policy are under way. Although the diffusion of authority among US legislative institutions remains an obstacle to climate policy, other political institutions are simultaneously facilitating policy change. Within US federalism, an increasing number of state governments have filled the void left by the federal government with relatively aggressive policies to control greenhouse gas emissions.[2] In addition, advocates of federal regulation have enjoyed recent successes in the courts, thus placing increasing pressure on the federal executive to act. Finally, the Democratic Party's victory in both houses of Congress in the 2006 midterm elections prompted an increase in congressional attention to climate change, while the election of a Democratic president, Barack Obama, presents an opportunity for concerted action on climate change not seen for almost fifteen years.

Electoral Incentives

The United States accepted the most challenging target during the Kyoto Protocol negotiations. Although its nominal target of a 7 percent reduction below 1990 levels by the 2008 to 2012 commitment period was comparable to that of its major trading partners in Europe (−8 percent), Japan (−6 percent) and Canada (−6 percent), growth of the US population and economy meant that the United States anticipated that it would need to make a 31 percent a reduction to its business-as-usual emissions in 2010 in order to comply with its Kyoto Protocol target.[3] As discussed in chapter 9, that represented a much deeper cut relative to emissions projections for 2010 than the targets undertaken by the European Union (−3 percent to −9 percent) or Japan (−12 percent), though only slightly greater than Canada (−29 percent).

In response, the US business community, led by trade associations including the American Petroleum Institute, the US Chamber of Commerce and the National Association of Manufacturers, as well as the cross-sectoral Global Climate Coalition, presented strong and united opposition to ratification of the Kyoto Protocol, arguing that "the science was unproven, reductions could be economically ruinous, trade competitiveness could be damaged, fuel costs could skyrocket and countless jobs would be eliminated."[4] While some sectors, such as oil and coal, effectively are in the business of producing greenhouse gases, others rely heavily on energy derived from inexpensive fossil fuels. As a result, American business argued that ratification would hinder the competitiveness of the US economy. Although the business community may have closer ties to the Republican Party, they were often joined by the Democrats' traditional allies in the labor movement, who were fearful of job losses. Such fears were reinforced by the Global Climate Coalition's estimate (later cited by the Bush administration) that the Kyoto Protocol would result in the loss of 4.9 million American jobs.[5]

In addition, right-wing think tanks, in many cases funded by the same firms and trade associations, sponsored studies and advertisements that strategically questioned the validity of climate science by increasing the visibility of the handful of remaining climate change skeptics in the scientific community.[6] Opponents of ratification and mitigation measures also emphasized the potential impacts on US consumers. The effects of even modest costs on prices would be significant in percentage terms, given the low energy prices US consumers have historically enjoyed. Indeed, the contemporary American dream is to a large degree predicated on low energy prices, which have made possible sprawling houses in remote suburbs to which residents commute in gas-guzzling minivans and SUVs. Gary Bryner notes that in the United States "cheap energy is a widely held political mantra that causes politicians and citizens alike to fear policies on climate change or any other issue that might threaten to raise energy prices."[7]

While the US business community "circled the wagons" to present a united front in the lead-up to and initial aftermath of the Kyoto negotiations, in recent years divisions have begun to emerge both between and within sectors.[8] As early as 1998, BP and Shell both withdrew from the Global Climate Coalition (GCC). They were followed over the next two years by Ford, Daimler Chrysler, GM, and Texaco, prompting the GCC thereafter to limit its membership to trade associations rather than individual firms. The Coalition disbanded entirely after claiming victory when the United States withdrew from the Kyoto Protocol in 2001. More recently some firms have joined in coalitions with environmental groups and think tanks in actually calling for government regulation. Examples include the Pew Center on Global Climate Change's Business Environmental Leadership Council and Environmental Defense Fund's partnerships with individual firms. In 2007 members of the US Climate Action Partnership, including environmental groups Environmental Defense Fund and the Natural Resources Defense Council as well as firms such as Shell, BP, General Motors, and Xerox, "call[ed] on the federal government to quickly enact strong national legislation to require significant reductions of greenhouse gas emissions."[9] In 2009 several prominent firms, including Apple and PG&E, left the US Chamber of Commerce in protest over its opposition to climate change legislation.[10]

One can speculate about possible motives for the waning opposition of at least some firms. First, even if regulation entails significant costs, relatively green firms may still benefit if their competitors incur greater costs than they do. Second, if firms anticipate that legislation is inevitable, they may adopt a more conciliatory position in order to influence the magnitude and distribution of abatement costs. Finally, as discussed below, in recent years many US state governments have moved ahead of the federal government on climate change, potentially prompting firms operating in "green states" to lobby for comparable national standards to level the playing field faced by competitors in "brown states." Similarly, firms selling regulated products in multiple states may prefer national, or even international, standards. Whatever the rationale, the emergence of business support has lent credibility to the argument that action to address climate change need not harm employment and competitiveness, thus "prying open a window of opportunity for national policy change."[11] That said, it would be a mistake to conclude that on balance the US business community now embraces action to address climate change. Business opposition remains formidable. In 2008, the National Association of Manufacturers described the leading Senate bill calling for reductions in greenhouse gas emissions as "economic disarmament" while television advertisements sponsored by the Chamber of Commerce depicted it as a fundamental threat to the American way of life.[12]

On the other side of the policy debate, US environmental groups are well established and respected, and enjoy influence via the courts unparalleled in other jurisdictions considered in this volume. However, environmentalists' influence with politicians turns largely on the credibility of their claim to speak for the electorate at large, and support for that claim has been mixed. US public opinion with respect to the environment in general, and climate change in particular, has been characterized by a high level of support for action but low levels of attention.[13] As indicated by figure 3.1, Gallup polls have reported that a majority of Americans express either a "great deal" or "fair amount" of concern for global warming since 1997.[14] With respect to the Kyoto Protocol in particular, Michael Lisowski reports that 61 percent of Americans polled in early 2001 supported ratification.[15] Similarly, after President Bush announced the United States' withdrawal from the Protocol, PSRA/Pew Research Center polls found that 47–51 percent of respondents disapproved of the president's decision, almost twice the 25–32 percent who approved.[16]

An intriguing side from these polls, however, is that American voters have tended to perceive the "fairness" of mitigation efforts in a remarkably self-interested way. In 1997, 73 percent of respondents expressed support for the statement, "The same energy regulations to reduce global warming should apply to all countries around the world," compared to just 21 percent who agreed that "there should be strict energy regulations for the United States and other advanced countries, and less strict regulations for Third World countries that have not yet achieved economic development."[17] Little had changed by 2001, when 67 percent agreed that "every country, rich or poor, should make the same changes now in order to limit future global warming, no matter how much of the

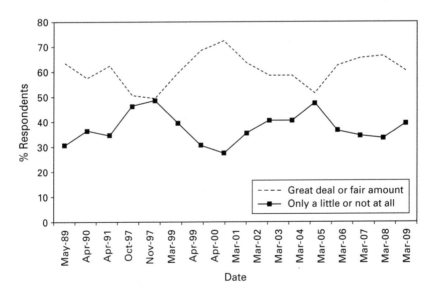

Figure 3.1
How much do Americans worry about global warming? *Source:* Gallup USA.

pollution they created originally" compared to 24 percent who felt that "since poorer countries did not cause much pollution, they should not have to bear as much of the burden in dealing with global warming."[18] While respondents were undoubtedly primed by the arguments of opponents of US participation in the Kyoto Protocol, it is nonetheless striking that those arguments should resonate so strongly even when respondents were reminded of their relative privilege and disproportionate contribution to the problem.

While close-ended questions reveal that Americans support actions to protect the environment, open-ended questions suggest that they are not paying much attention. As indicated in figure 3.2, Gallup reports that the percentage of Americans volunteering the environment as the "most important problem" facing their country fluctuated between 0 and 5 percent from 1995 to mid-2008, a small fraction compared to those

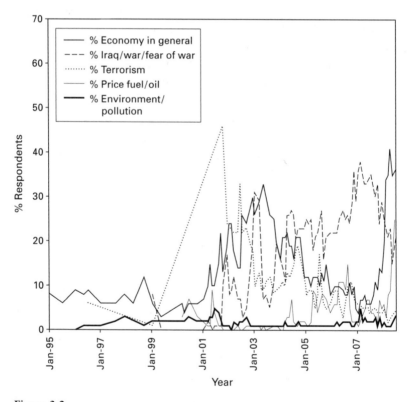

Figure 3.2
Salience of environment versus other issues, January 1995–June 2008. *Source:* Gallup USA.

identifying issues such as terrorism, the economy, the Iraq war, and, more recently, the price of gasoline as more important.[19] Consistent with this, three years after the United States withdrew from the Kyoto Protocol, 42 percent of Americans still believed President Bush *supported* the treaty and fewer than half of Americans (48 percent) were aware of the President's opposition to the Protocol.[20] Indeed, PSRA/Newsweek polls found that voter approval of President Bush's environmental record *improved* over the course of 2001 (even before September 11), the year he announced US withdrawal from the treaty, and a plurality of voters continued to approve of the president's environmental record until 2005.[21] As recently as 2007, a CNN/ORC poll found that climate change ranked eighth of ten issues on which respondents were asked to indicate their priorities for Congress and the president.[22]

In contrast to recent trends in public attention to the environment in Canada, Australia, and Japan, there has been no surge apparent in the salience of environmental issues in the United States since 2005. In the wake of Hurricane Katrina, Al Gore's documentary *An Inconvenient Truth*, and the Fourth Assessment Report of the Intergovernmental Panel on Climate Change (IPCC; see Intergovernmental Panel on Climate Change 2007), there has been an increase in coverage of climate change, though figure 3.3 suggests that that coverage may be more pronounced in national media than in local outlets. However, figures 3.2 and 3.4 suggest that increased media coverage has not had the same impact on the salience of environmental issues in the United States as in neighboring Canada (discussed in chapter 6). Indeed, figure 3.4 indicates that Americans have been *less* willing to pay a price for environmental protection since the economy took a turn for the worse mid-decade.

That support was further dampened with the onset of an economic recession in late 2008. In March 2009, a majority of Americans indicated that economic growth should be given priority even at the expense of the environment, for the first time since Gallup began asking that question in 1984 (figure 3.4). Consistent with this, the Pew Research Center reports that the fraction of Americans who agreed that there is "solid evidence the earth is warming," which had been steady at 77 percent in 2006 and 2007, declined to 71 percent by April 2008 and 57 percent by October 2009. Over the same period, the fraction indicating to Pew pollsters that global warming is "very" or "somewhat" serious declined from 79 percent to 65 percent.[23]

It is possible that the "most important problem" question is simply too crude to capture movements in US public opinion, albeit less pro-

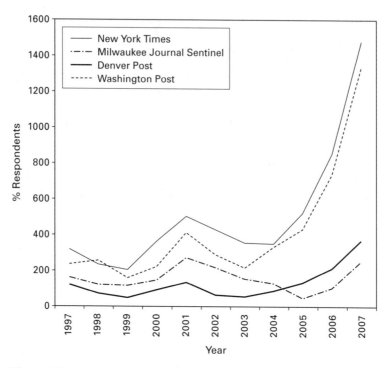

Figure 3.3
Trends in media coverage of "climate change," "global warming," or "greenhouse effect." The key words appear anywhere in the story or headline. *Source:* Factiva.

nounced ones than in other jurisdictions, in light of the confounding effect in the United States of the Iraq war. That said, voters remain keenly aware of the price of gasoline and the state of the economy, factors that tend to undermine support for meaningful actions to address climate change.

Policymakers' Ideas

Regardless of electoral incentives or disincentives, politicians may choose to follow their own ideas. An individual policymaker's commitment to action to address climate change action rests on two ideas: a causal belief that climate change is both real and caused by human activities and a principled belief that his or her country has a responsibility to help mitigate the problem.[24]

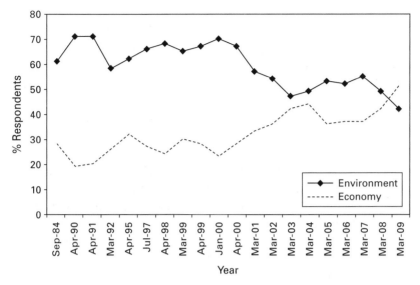

Figure 3.4
Americans' priorities: Environment versus economy. Respondents were asked which statement they most agreed with: "protection of the environment should be given priority, even at the risk of curbing economic growth" or "economic growth should be given priority, even if the environment suffers to some extent." *Source:* Gallup USA.

With respect to the former, US climate scientists have made major contributions to the scientific literature on climate change and also have played prominent roles within the IPCC. Although American policymakers thus have had access to the same scientific advice as their counterparts in other jurisdictions, there has nonetheless been a much higher level of *political* debate about climate science in the United States than in other countries. The question remains, however, whether a larger fraction of policymakers in the United States than elsewhere really do not believe the scientific evidence or have consciously embraced a political approach of strategically challenging climate science. It is telling that a 2007 poll of members of Congress found that 95 percent of Democrats agreed while 84 percent of Republicans disagreed with the statement, "It's been proven beyond a reasonable doubt that the Earth is warming because of man-made problems."[25] It is hard to imagine that party affiliation alone could have such a stark impact on *causal* beliefs, suggesting that partisan differences result from a combination of political ideology and self-interested support for partners in partisan electoral coalitions. Moreover, there is evidence that this ideological cleavage is spilling over to the electorate at large. Despite increasingly strong consensus in the scientific community, the gap between Republican and Democratic voters is growing on questions related to the validity of climate science.[26]

With respect to ideology, one would expect the center-right Republican Party to be less supportive of regulatory intervention in the economy than the center-left Democratic Party. Consistent with this is the contrast between President Bill Clinton and Vice President Al Gore and President George W. Bush and Vice President Dick Cheney. Whereas Gore wrote a book on climate change, Bush was a former Texas oilman and his vice president was formerly CEO of the world's largest oilfield support company. Equally marked is the contrast between former Republican chair of the Senate Committee on Environment and Public Works, James Inhofe, who represents oil-rich Oklahoma, and the current Democratic chair of the same committee, Barbara Boxer of California, perhaps the most environmentally progressive state.

That said, on the issue of climate change the Democratic Party leadership is considerably to the left of the party's congressional rank and file. While new leadership in Congress since the 2006 elections has yielded pronounced differences in the political agenda,[27] it remains a challenge to muster sufficient support from either moderate Democrats or moderate Republicans to pass climate legislation.

Political Institutions

To understand the reasons, we turn to political institutions. US legislative institutions, with their distinctive checks and balances, are characterized by a diffusion of authority that has deterred action on climate change in three distinct ways.

First, the separation of powers means that passage of US climate legislation requires approval by three distinct actors: the House, the Senate, and the president, each acting independently of the others. Indeed, filibuster rules and the threat of a presidential veto mean that supermajorities may be required in one or both houses of Congress. This means that advocates of policy change need to build a broader coalition than do interests who seek to block change. While this benefited environmentalists in rebuffing Republican efforts to weaken US environmental laws passed at the height of environmental concern in the 1970s, more recently business opponents have successfully blocked passage of even modest programs to address climate change.[28] In the case of the

Kyoto Protocol, the implications of the separation of powers were quite specific and, as it turned out, insurmountable: to ratify an international treaty, the Constitution requires that the president obtain support from two-thirds of the Senate, which was not forthcoming.

A second aspect of US legislative institutions concerns the implications of fixed elections for the strength of opposition to policies to address climate change. Without the confidence requirement of a parliamentary system, US senators and representatives are less constrained by party discipline and thus not only free but to a large degree *expected* to defend the economic interests of their local constituents, regardless of party affiliation. In the case of climate change, this is exacerbated by the regional nature of the US economy, not least given the presence of two senators from each state, large and small. While the oil industry may be staunchly supported by Republican senators from Texas and Alaska, the interests of coal are defended in the Senate by both Republicans from Wyoming and Democrats from West Virginia, while Democrats from Michigan look out for the auto industry.

The flip side of weak party discipline is that US political parties are less accountable for their members' statements. This has influenced US climate policy in a third way—by facilitating a strategy of questioning climate science.[29] Not only are the parties not expected to answer for their members' at times outrageous statements concerning climate science, but it may actually be in the interests of the Republican Party in particular, given its antipathy to the Kyoto Protocol, to allow its "loose canons" to speak out, if only to legitimize less extreme statements about scientific uncertainty.

While the diffusion of authority in US legislative institutions has, to date, been an obstacle, there is one respect in which it can *facilitate* policy change. Although the separation of powers makes it harder for the US government to pass any legislation, when the various actors do achieve sufficient consensus for action, they tend to lock in their compromises to prevent future backsliding on commitments. Thus, since the 1970s the US Congress has tended to pass "action-forcing" environmental statutes, which combine nondiscretionary mandates for the executive backed by deadlines and "citizen suit provisions" that authorize anyone to sue the federal government should it fail to meet those obligations. US environmental law and policy are thus characterized by much higher involvement of the courts than in other countries.[30] In practice, virtually every regulatory decision—and nondecision—is contested in court. The nondiscretionary wording of statutes written decades before climate change emerged as a political issue is an increasingly important resource for US environmentalists.

The diffusion of authority via federalism is increasingly relevant to US climate policy. In the context of federal government inaction to date, a growing number of state governments have elected to take unilateral action.[31] That said, not all states are taking action, and a battle over preemption looms as Congress turns its attention to national legislation.

Negotiating the Kyoto Protocol

The UN Framework Convention on Climate Change (FCCC) proposed stabilization of national emissions at the 1990 level by the year 2000. The fact that the goal was nonbinding reflected the influence of the United States, which under President George H. W. Bush had opposed inclusion of any binding "targets and timetables."[32] Having won that concession, the United States readily ratified the FCCC just three months after the Earth Summit in Rio.

Soon thereafter, Democratic President Bill Clinton assumed office with a vice president, Al Gore, who had built his public reputation on environmental issues. That the Clinton White House did not have a greater impact on US climate policy is attributable in no small part to congressional resistance. Clinton reiterated his support for the FCCC target on Earth Day 1993.[33] Thereafter, the administration proposed a broad-ranging BTU tax on fossil fuels as an energy conservation measure. Lamont Hempel reports that

Congress, bowing to pressure from the fossil fuel lobby and energy-intensive industries, not only discarded the broad-based tax proposal in favor of a much narrower gasoline tax but also reduced the tax rate by about 50 percent (to 4.3 cents per gallon). Framing the energy tax proposal as a large, new, and additional burden on the economy—an economy designed to run on cheap energy—ensured congressional opponents a victory in terms of public opinion.[34]

It is noteworthy that the administration's proposal failed even though the Democrats at the time controlled both the Senate and House. On the heels of the failed BTU tax, the administration's Climate Change Action Plan, released in October 1993, relied exclusively on voluntary programs that did not require legislative action.

By the mid-1990s, it was clear that the United States, like most other FCCC signatories, would not meet the goal of stabilization at 1990 levels by 2000. In response, the United States and its allies conceded at the first

Conference of the Parties to the FCCC (COP 1) to negotiate binding targets for industrialized countries. However, opposition from US business and labor strengthened with the approach of the critical meeting in Kyoto at which those targets were to be finalized. The Global Climate Coalition, described by Loren Lutzenhiser as "a *Who's Who* of American manufacturers,"[35] spent $13 million on a print and broadcast media campaign arguing that energy prices could rise by 20 percent and urging the president not to "rush into an unwise and unfirm United Nations agreement that's bad for America."[36] The coalition found a receptive audience not only in the business-friendly Republican Party,[37] which had won control of both houses of Congress in the 1994 midterm elections, but also with Democrats concerned about the potential effects of a climate agreement on employers in their constituencies—oil in Louisiana, coal in West Virginia, and automobiles in Michigan.[38] At the same time, the science of climate change had been increasingly challenged by the Republican Congress. Riley E. McCright and Aaron M. Dunlap document that the fraction of scientists testifying at congressional hearings who sided with the views of the IPCC declined from 100 percent at the time of the Earth Summit in Rio in 1992 to 50 percent, evenly balanced with climate change skeptics, in the lead-up to COP 3,[39] despite an increasingly strong consensus having emerged within the scientific community.

In July 1997, just months before the Kyoto meeting, the Senate drew a line in the sand by unanimously passing the Byrd-Hagel resolution, which stated that the Senate would not ratify any international treaty that, first, "would mandate new commitments to limit or reduce greenhouse gas emissions for the Annex I Parties, unless the protocol or other agreement also mandates new specific scheduled commitments to limit or reduce greenhouse gas emissions for Developing Country Parties within the same compliance period"; or, second, "would result in serious harm to the economy of the United States."[40]

Such a strong display of bipartisanship is rare in the US Congress, suggesting at minimum a White House decision not to pressure Democrats to oppose a politically popular resolution.[41] In any case, that the Senate was on record as opposing ratification of any treaty that did not include binding commitments for developing countries would present a formidable obstacle for the administration in years to come.

The Clinton administration announced in late October 1997 that it would seek an agreement in COP 3 in Kyoto to return emissions to 1990 levels by 2010 with unspecified reductions thereafter—a far cry from the

European Union's call for a 15 percent reduction below 1990 emissions. The administration also indicated that it would seek "meaningful participation" from developing countries, the latter prompted by the Byrd-Hagel resolution but seemingly incompatible with COP 1's call for leadership in the first round from industrialized countries.

The deep divide between the United States and the EU was not confined to emissions targets. The JUSCANZ coalition (Japan, United States, Canada, Australia, New Zealand) also sought inclusion in the agreement of various flexibility mechanisms, including international emissions trading and credit for carbon sinks, which the EU strongly opposed. US negotiators considered the EU's opposition to trading to be hypocritical in light of its own "bubble" agreement, which effectively traded deeper commitments in some EU countries with lighter commitments by others. In response, the JUSCANZ group joined with potential trading partners, Russia and the Ukraine, to form a new "umbrella group," with common interests in both differentiated targets and international trading.

The arrival in Kyoto of Vice President Al Gore and his direction to the US delegation "to show increased negotiating flexibility" was critical to breaking the impasse between the negotiating blocs.[42] Former Under Secretary of State Stuart Eizenstat reflected at the conclusion of the Kyoto meeting that "the Vice President's visit clearly changed the entire atmosphere and direction of the talks." Eizenstat also stressed the level of engagement of the president and vice president, noting that President Clinton "personally signed off on each percentage point that was offered."[43]

Even then, negotiations between the two blocs were contentious, with agreement reached only after a marathon 24-hour negotiating session. Eizenstat recalled:

It was very dramatic, because even after all these negotiations, we didn't have an agreement coming into the last plenary meeting, and there was no time for further negotiation. The translators had left and you could hear construction in the background getting ready for some trade show that was coming in. And the chairman of the COP, Estrada, was a real hero in this. ... We had worked for about five days straight with maybe two hours of sleep each night. When he came to our delegation, a lot of my people were laying on the ground sleeping, others were resting against the wall sleeping. ... Estrada called three or four of us back, our team, the EU team, I can't remember who else, and said we can't not get an agreement. And we basically hammered out the language in the green room behind the stage. And we came back and announced it.[44]

That backstage agreement essentially split the difference between the reductions proposed by the EU and the United States, with resulting targets for the EU, the United States, and Canada of −8 percent, −7 percent, and −6 percent, respectively, relative to 1990 levels to be achieved by 2008 to 2012. While the United States moved significantly from its opening commitment of stabilization, the EU conceded to the umbrella group's demands for differentiated targets, flexibility in the form of international emissions trading, credits for land use changes and forestry practices, averaging over a multiyear target, and inclusion of a "basket" of six greenhouse gases rather than the three sought by the EU.

The formal targets in the Kyoto Protocol do not necessarily reflect the magnitude of effort required to achieve them, however. Going into the Kyoto meeting, the United States anticipated significantly greater emissions growth by 2010 than did the EU, not least because of higher population growth.[45] Seemingly comparable formal targets in the Kyoto Protocol thus demanded deeper cuts below the business-as-usual trajectory, and presumably higher costs as a result, for the United States than for the EU. Why, then, did the United States agree to what in retrospect seems like a rather bad deal? Interviews with members of the US team point to three factors.

The first is a strong normative commitment to addressing climate change, despite anticipated economic and political costs. A senior White House staff member, Gene Sperling, recounted a private conversation with Vice President Gore that occurred before the Kyoto meeting:

I told him that I admired him for going [to Kyoto] ... but I also told him how easy it would be for somebody to translate this into kind of a crass political TV ad against him someday for raising energy taxes. And I remember he ... looked down at me; I'm 5′5″ or 5′6″ and he's about almost a foot taller than me and he looked down at me and he said ... I really appreciate the fact that you're— you're looking out for my interests and then he kind of put his hand to his heart and he just said but this is core for me—this is just core; this is just who I am. I've got to do this.[46]

With respect to the president, Sperling similarly reflected, "I can still remember ... President Clinton saying in very strong terms that ... there was no way that he wanted his—his and Vice President Gore's— legacy to be that the US was the holdout on the Kyoto agreement."[47] A member of the "principals group" that coordinated the US position recalled, "We were all thinking of this as a moral issue."[48]

When asked why the United States would accept a deeper commitment below business as usual, a member of the US delegation in Kyoto explained, "The VP was going to have a deal, no matter what."[49] Indeed, one US negotiator reflected that Vice President Gore's public statement in Kyoto was "terrible ... [it] undercut the negotiating team. You don't set it up in advance to say we're going to give away the store."[50]

A second factor explaining the disparity in cuts below business as usual is that at least some US negotiators curiously seem to have been focused on targets relative to 1990 rather than 2010. The following statement by Eizenstat suggests that although he was keenly aware of the imperative to remain competitive with key trading partners, he was preoccupied with the formal targets in the agreement rather than their implications relative to projected emissions:

For us, from a competitiveness standpoint, it was not only the absolute reduction, it was the relative reduction. ... Our feeling was that if we could be in the ball-park with Japan and the EU, we couldn't be politically criticized for putting our industries at a competitive disadvantage relative to our major competitors. ... [With Japan at −6 and the EU at −8] that seemed like a really good deal to us. We were actually making less of a reduction than the EU, about the same as Japan, so our industries would not be at a competitive disadvantage.[51]

The third factor that accounts for the disparity between US and EU commitments relative to business as usual is the nature of the grand compromise between the EU and umbrella blocs: the United States conceded to undertake a deeper reduction than it had originally proposed,[52] and in turn the EU conceded to the various flexibility mechanisms proposed by the umbrella group. A member of the US team explained that "it felt like a give," but the result was that the EU gained materially relative to the United States—both because it relaxed its original 15 percent reduction commitment to roughly match that of the United States and because it too stood to benefit from the various Kyoto Protocol flexibility mechanisms. Thus, the nature of the central compromise in Kyoto, between US material interests and EU norms, had the effect of *increasing* the disparity in costs between these two jurisdictions.

The Aftermath of COP 3

The ideas that influenced the administration in the Kyoto negotiations clearly did not resonate with the US business community, labor, and their congressional allies. Vice President Gore welcomed the weary US negotiating team home from Kyoto with a reception at the White House, in which he told his staff, "I need all your help. We now have to make this work. And I commit I will do it." In contrast, the morning after the Kyoto agreement was announced, "Republican Congressional leaders held a news conference declaring the Protocol 'dead on arrival' in the

US Senate."[53] Lest there be any doubt that the Kyoto Protocol did not satisfy the terms of the Byrd-Hagel resolution calling for binding commitments from developing countries, a fact acknowledged by Stuart Eizenstat at the close of the meeting in Japan,[54] the Senate passed another resolution affirming that the Kyoto agreement did not satisfy the provisions of the Byrd-Hagel Resolution.[55]

In the face of Senate resistance, the president committed not to "submit the Kyoto Protocol to the Senate for advice and consent until key developing countries agreed to participate meaningfully."[56] The administration continued negotiations with developing countries in an unsuccessful effort to convince one or more to accept binding targets under the Kyoto Protocol. In addition to satisfying the Senate's concerns about differential impacts on industrialized and developing countries, there was another reason for the White House's commitment to "meaningful participation" by developing countries: potential savings for the United States through emissions trading with developing nations. Although often depicted as a demand for emissions *cuts* from the developing world, the administration only sought to convince key developing countries to commit to curtail their emissions *growth* below current projections. Developing countries' acceptance of a business-as-usual baseline would have had the effect of authorizing emissions trading between developing and industrialized nations, a prospect that the administration anticipated would reduce US compliance costs by as much as 60 percent compared with trading only among Annex 1 countries.[57]

More generally, the administration projected an 87 percent reduction in compliance costs relative to a scenario in which all reductions would have to be achieved within the United States. The assumption of international trading thus allowed the White House to report more palatable projected costs of compliance to a hostile Congress: $14 to $23 per ton of *carbon* (not the higher cost per ton of CO_2, typically reported by other jurisdictions), or $7–12 billion per year, just 0.1 percent of GDP.[58] Indeed, the administration's economic analysis did not even include a projection of costs without trading, nor did it make explicit the expectation that 75–80 percent of the United States' reductions would be achieved overseas.[59] A former staff member who helped prepare Council of Economic Advisors chair Janet Yellin for her congressional testimony recalled that it was "very clear that the administration didn't want Janet to say how many permits would come from abroad."[60]

Significant savings would come from trading not only with developing countries but also with post-Soviet umbrella group partners—Russia and the Ukraine. The umbrella group thus continued to press for maximum flexibility in interpretation of the provisions of the Protocol concerning emissions trading as well as sinks and land use changes. Although the United States was in a strong bargaining position, since it accounted for 36 percent of 1990 Annex 1 emissions and the Protocol could not come into force until it was ratified by countries comprising at least 55 percent of Annex 1 1990 emissions, it nonetheless was rebuffed on each of these issues by the EU.

In the meantime, Congress defeated "virtually every budget item and bill that so much as mention[ed] the possibility of climate change."[61] Congress also attached anti–climate change policy provisions to other bills to tie the administration's hands,[62] including riders that prohibited any effort to review corporate average fuel efficiency standards for automobiles.[63] E. B. Skolnikoff reflects that "efforts by the Clinton administration to promote mild policies that would make sense even without the threat of global warming ... [were] attacked as 'end-runs' around the Kyoto Protocol ratification process."[64]

Some have questioned whether the administration was ever really committed to ratification, since it did not even submit the Kyoto Protocol to the Senate.[65] Moreover, although the EPA's legal counsel under President Clinton issued an opinion that authority to regulate CO_2 emissions could be found within the Clean Air Act, the agency declined to exercise that existing authority. Indeed, it "put on ice" a request by a small environmental group to regulate greenhouse gas emissions from motor vehicles.[66] Former Clinton administration officials pointed to three reasons for the administration's inaction. First, it was abundantly clear that the Senate would not ratify the Kyoto Protocol, and there were also clear signals that any regulatory proposals by the administration would prompt even more restrictive riders from Congress to limit the EPA's actions. As Eizenstat insisted, "We didn't negotiate [the Kyoto Protocol] just to walk away from it. ... But it would have been a huge political fight to get two thirds in the Senate. With 95 to 0 [on the Byrd-Hagel Resolution] they'd given us a pretty strong signal of where they stood."[67] Second, the administration was to some degree distracted by the unrelated presidential impeachment scandal throughout 1998. Finally, there was hope that a second chance would be forthcoming under a Gore presidency after the 2000 election.

Despite that, climate change and other environmental issues played surprisingly little role in the election campaign, apparently in response to Vice President Gore's advisors' view that the Kyoto Protocol was a political liability.[68] Moreover, the Republican candidate, George W. Bush, undercut his opponent to some degree by committing during the campaign to mandating CO_2 reductions from electric utilities, which account for roughly 40 percent of US greenhouse gases.[69] Before the presidential election, mired in recounts and litigation, could be resolved, the sixth Conference of the Parties took place in The Hague in November 2000. Faced with a very real possibility of a Bush presidency, the Clinton administration "launched a last-minute push to resolve in two weeks a host of issues that had been left unsettled for three years."[70] However, they were again rebuffed by the EU. Vice President Gore, who had been so influential in breaking the deadlock in Kyoto, remained at home, preoccupied with his own battle for the presidency.[71]

The US Withdrawal from Kyoto

The Supreme Court's declaration of George W. Bush's victory heralded a dramatic change in the White House's perspective on climate change, though less so in actual US climate policy. In March 2001, just two months after his inauguration, President Bush wrote a letter to four Republican senators restating his opposition to the Kyoto Protocol and repudiating his earlier pledge to regulate emissions. In his letter to the senators, the president offered three arguments for the United States' withdrawal from the Kyoto Protocol.[72] First, the president opposed "the Kyoto Protocol because it exempts 80 percent of the world, including major population centers such as China and India, from compliance." Second, he emphasized the potential for "serious harm to the US economy," particularly in light of the United States' reliance on coal for more than half of its electricity. Third, he cited "the incomplete state of scientific knowledge of the causes of, and solutions to, global climate change." In reversing his campaign pledge, the president undermined his newly appointed EPA administrator, Christine Todd Whitman, who just days before had reiterated the administration's commitment to cap emissions from power plants to her G8 counterparts.[73] The president explained, "I will not accept a plan that will harm our economy and hurt American workers. Because first things first are the people who live in America. That's my priority."[74]

The extent of scientific uncertainty concerning anthropogenic causes of climate change was a recurring theme in the Bush White House. When the president announced that the United States would not ratify the Kyoto Protocol, he asked the National Academy of Sciences to review the state of climate science. The Academy's report subsequently affirmed the conclusion of the second IPCC assessment that "there is new and stronger evidence that most of the warming observed over the last 50 years is attributable to human activities."[75] However, the report also concluded that "a causal linkage between the buildup of greenhouse gases in the atmosphere and the observed climate changes during the 20th century cannot be unequivocally established," a statement that White House and the Republican leadership selectively cited time and again.[76]

The White House's selective citations and the Republican congressional leaders' efforts to give equal time to the minority perspective of skeptical scientists suggest a deliberate strategy to "manufacture uncertainty."[77] Indeed, a leaked memo sent to all House Republican press secretaries in advance of the 2002 congressional election by a party strategist stated, "You need to continue to make the lack of scientific uncertainty a primary issue in the debate. ... The scientific debate is closing but not yet closed. There is still a window of opportunity to challenge the science."[78] In 2003 an internal EPA memo was leaked to the press in which EPA staff complained of heavy-handed White House editing of the climate chapter of EPA's *Report on the Environment* to the extent that the text "no longer reflect[ed] scientific consensus on climate change."[79] When it later came to light that the White House editor was Philip A. Cooney, a lawyer with no scientific credentials whose previous job had been as a lobbyist for the American Petroleum Institute, Cooney promptly resigned and accepted a position with ExxonMobil, the company leading the charge against greenhouse gas abatement in the United States.[80] The White House's emphasis on the uncertainty of climate science paled, however, in comparison to statements by influential Republican members of the Congress, particularly the chair of the Senate Committee on Environment and Public Works from 2002 to 2006, James Inhofe, who likened global warming to "the greatest hoax ever perpetrated on the American people"[81] and attributed climate change to a plot by weather channels to increase viewership.[82]

In announcing the US withdrawal from the Kyoto Protocol, the White House promised that the United States would develop its own plan. David Victor has described the resulting plan, released in late 2002, as "a series of voluntary measures and underfunded technology programs designed mainly to give the appearance of a credible response."[83] The administration's plan called for a reduction in greenhouse gas *intensity* relative to GDP by 18 percent by 2008–2012, little more than the projected business-as-usual reduction in intensity of 14 percent over the same period,[84] with the additional reductions to be achieved through a package of "relatively painless and ineffective policies" similar to those pursued by the Clinton administration.[85] Since the rate of GDP growth was expected to exceed the reduction in intensity, the plan, even if successful, was expected to yield a 12 percent *increase* in greenhouse gas emissions over the decade.[86]

Although the United States declined to ratify the Kyoto Protocol, it remains a signatory to the Framework Convention on Climate Change and thus continued to participate in international meetings concerning the Convention. At the same time, however, the Bush administration sought to substitute international climate partnerships of its own creation rather for those within the purview of UN institutions. The United States launched the Asia-Pacific Partnership on Clean Development and Climate in 2006, along with Japan, Australia, China, India, and South Korea. In contrast to the binding targets and timetables of the Kyoto Protocol, the goal of the Asia-Pacific Partnership is "to accelerate the development and deployment of clean energy technologies" through voluntary public-private partnerships.[87]

Toward the end of his second term, President Bush launched negotiations with sixteen "major economies" that collectively contribute over 80 percent of global greenhouse gas emissions. As with the Asia-Pacific Partnership, however, the United States advocated countries setting their own voluntary goals, rather than submitting to binding targets via an international treaty. In response, even many of the foreign government officials that attended meetings at the White House expressed skepticism.[88] Despite these efforts to forge international partnerships, at COP 13 in Bali the United States was "isolated as never before."[89] The United States ultimately agreed to proceed with negotiations to achieve "deep cuts" in emissions, with a goal of achieving a post-Kyoto agreement at the Copenhagen meeting in December 2009.

"A New Chapter"

Much has changed in US climate policy since 2005, with further changes poised on the horizon. The devastation wrought by Hurricane Katrina increased attention to the extreme weather events predicted to occur as a result of climate change. The UK's Stern report (Stern 2007) received prominent coverage in the United States in 2006, counteracting to some degree powerful voices decrying the costs of action with a message about the even greater costs of inaction. Former vice president Al Gore's documentary *An Inconvenient Truth* enjoyed surprising box office success in 2006 and received an Academy Award the following year. Finally, the message of the scientific community gained in prominence with the IPCC's release of its Fourth Assessment and the awarding of the 2007 Nobel Peace Prize jointly to Al Gore and the IPCC.

Although, as noted above, movement in US public opinion polls has been muted in response to these developments, changes in US interest group politics are evident. Coalitions of strange bedfellows have emerged, including not only the environmentalist-business alliances noted above but also coalitions between environmentalists and traditionally conservative evangelical Christians concerned about stewardship of "God's world"[90] as well as between environmentalists and military hawks concerned about energy security.

The Bush White House responded to these developments modestly at best. The president first addressed the problem of climate change in his 2007 State of the Union address, calling for a 20 percent reduction in automobile emissions over a decade, though it was little noted that the reduction was relative to projected rather than current emissions and thus still would entail an increase in emissions from motor vehicles relative to 2007. In early 2008 the administration announced a new target to stabilize US emissions by 2025 but continued to oppose mandatory actions either internationally or domestically.

There has been much greater activity on other fronts, however. Barry Rabe has documented the tremendous innovation occurring in US climate policy at the state level.[91] In a replay of a dynamic David Vogel has dubbed "the California effect,"[92] states have followed California's lead in setting ambitious medium-term emissions targets—a return to 1990 emissions by 2020 in California's case.[93] More importantly, state governments have adopted concrete measures to move toward those targets. Twenty-five states have renewable energy mandates, eighteen have proposed hard caps on emissions from industry,[94] and nineteen—comprising over half the US population—committed to more stringent motor vehicle emissions standards, prompting the Obama administration in 2009 to raise the bar nationally (discussed below).[95]

The last is the result of a special provision in the Clean Air Act, which in recognition of historical air quality challenges faced in the Los Angeles basin authorizes only the state of California to depart from national emission standards for motor vehicles, and then only with approval of the EPA. However, if California is granted such a waiver, all other states then have the option of matching California's standards. In 2004 California promulgated a regulation requiring that greenhouse gas emissions from motor vehicles be reduced by 30 percent by 2016. Although California petitioned EPA for a waiver in December 2005, and even sued in pursuit of a response, the agency did not respond until December 2007, at which time it denied a waiver, the first time in over fifty such petitions. In addition to its efforts to regulate tailpipe emissions, however, in April 2009 California finalized a "low carbon fuel standard" based on life cycle greenhouse gas emissions of fuels from different sources, which some sixteen states have already committed to match.

State governments also have collaborated in establishing regional cap and trade systems. The first of those was the Regional Greenhouse Gas Initiative, through which ten Northeastern and mid-Atlantic states agreed to cap greenhouse gas emissions from power plants at 2009 levels by 2015 and thereafter to achieve a 10 percent reduction by 2018.[96] On the other coast, the Western Climate Initiative involves seven states and four Canadian provinces that have committed to a broader goal of a 15 percent reduction in 2005 emissions from all sources by 2020. In the face of federal inaction, state leaders thus have moved unilaterally, in so doing prompting many, if not all, other states to match their actions, and generating pressure from at least some in the business community for federal action to "level the playing field." *with Brown states.*

A second arena of increasing importance, one unique to the US context, is the courts. Cases launched years ago by environmental advocates are now beginning to bear fruit. The most important concerned a lawsuit launched by a coalition of states, cities, and environmental groups challenging the Bush administration's refusal to regulate greenhouse gases from motor vehicles under the Clean Air Act.[97] In April 2007 the Supreme Court rejected the administration's arguments that it did not have authority to regulate greenhouse gases under the act, directing EPA to issue a finding on whether greenhouse gases endanger public health or welfare, as required to authorize regulatory actions under the act.[98] While a clear victory for proponents of policy change, at the urging of White House officials[99] the EPA administrator declined to publish the "endangerment finding" and draft tailpipe regulations as recommended by his own EPA staff. Instead, in July 2008 the EPA published an "advance notice of proposed rulemaking" that was little more than a request for public comment on a broad range of possible actions.

A final source of potential change is the partisan shift in both Congress and the White House. Since the Democrats seized majorities in both houses in the 2006 midterm election there has been renewed congressional attention to climate change. In contrast to a Democratic Congress's obstruction of early Clinton White House's initiatives and their Republican successors' support for the Bush White House, the new Democratic leadership challenged the Bush administration's position on climate change at every turn. Oversight hearings laid bare the administration's manipulation of science[100] and White House interference in the EPA's decision concerning California's proposed motor vehicle standards.[101] In 2007 Congress passed legislation to amend fuel economy standards for the first time in thirty-two years.

The election in November 2008 of a Democratic president and simultaneous strengthening of the Democratic Party's majorities in both houses of Congress signaled more dramatic changes in US climate policy. The Obama-Biden platform proposed reengagement with international negotiations concerning climate change, increases in motor vehicle fuel economy standards, a target of 25 percent renewable energy by 2025, and a national cap-and-trade program with goals of returning US emissions to 1990 levels by 2020. Efforts to achieve each of these goals have been put in motion in the first six months of the new administration, despite the onset of the worst economic crisis since the Great Depression.

Within days of the election, President-elect Obama signaled a departure from the Bush administration in stating, "The science is beyond dispute and the facts are clear. ... My presidency will mark a new chapter in America's leadership on climate change."[102] That statement was reinforced after the inauguration by a presidential memorandum directing staff to "guarantee scientific integrity" in executive branch decisions.[103] With respect to international engagement, Secretary of State Hillary Clinton declared, "We are back in the game."[104] The new US negotiating team under the FCCC was warmly welcomed in Bonn in the spring of 2009. The administration has focused in particular on seeking a post-2012 agreement with China, though the gap in positions between China and the United States remains formidable.[105]

The Obama administration moved quickly on automobile emissions. Within days of the inauguration, the president directed the EPA to reconsider the Bush administration's rejection of California's request for a Clean Air Act waiver in order to issue tailpipe standards for greenhouse gases. However, even before the public comment period on EPA's proposed California waiver ended, the president announced that the administration would pass national standards to match California's. In making the announcement, the president was joined at the White House by supportive representatives of state governments, environmental groups, and, remarkably, the automobile industry. Although the industry had fought California's tailpipe standards at every turn, two factors contributed to the turnaround. First, the foregone conclusion that EPA would approve California's request for a waiver presented the costly prospect of two different emissions standards for motor vehicles sold within the United States. Second, by the spring of 2009 the US auto industry was dependent on the federal government for its survival. Although the economic crisis strengthened other sectors' opposition to regulation of greenhouse gas emissions, the US government's investments in bailing out domestic auto manufacturers gave it significant leverage over the future direction of the industry.[106] (Similarly, the call for economic stimulus prompted President Obama to include a $15 billion per year investment in renewable energy in his 2009 budget proposal.) As anticipated, EPA granted the California waiver in June, and also followed up on the president's announcement with publication of a 1,200-page draft federal regulation for motor vehicle emissions in September 2009.[107]

Significant steps have also been taken toward regulation of other sources. The 2007 Supreme Court decision directed the EPA to determine whether greenhouse gas emissions from motor vehicles "may reasonably be anticipated" to endanger public health or welfare, a finding that would then trigger regulation of tailpipe emissions. The EPA published a draft finding in April 2009, concluding that the possibility of harm to public health and welfare was "compelling and, indeed, overwhelming."[108] The administration's announced commitment to new federal motor vehicle emission standards, even before the public comment period ended on the "endangerment finding," rendered an eventual finding of endangerment a foregone conclusion.

Less clear, however, is whether a determination of endangerment under one section of the act will automatically trigger regulation of stationary sources under other sections of the act. Written with less pervasive pollutants in mind, the new source review provisions of the Clean Air Act require permits for sources as small as 250 tons per year, which would be far-reaching indeed in the case of greenhouse gas emissions. In September 2009, the EPA published a proposal that sought to limit application of the Act to the roughly 14,000 stationary sources emitting at least 25,000 tons annually. While the proposal is supported by major environmental groups, industry groups have challenged the legality of using regulation to tailor application of the Act only to large sources.

Although it may seem surprising that industry would oppose a strategy to *limit* application of greenhouse gas regulations, success in forcing application to hundreds of thousands of small sources as well would underscore the impracticality of regulating greenhouse gases under the Clean Air Act.[109]

The inflexibility of the Clean Air Act as a vehicle for regulation of greenhouse gas emissions prompted President Obama to call on Congress to pass legislation to establish a more cost-effective national cap-and-trade program, even while his administration maintained pressure on Congress by forging ahead with a regulatory strategy for mobile and stationary sources alike.[110] Changes in congressional leadership have facilitated action. Most noteworthy is the successful challenge, following the 2008 elections, of John Dingell for the chair of the House Energy and Commerce Committee by Henry Waxman, a long-serving representative from a wealthy and green district in Los Angeles. Dingell, a member of Congress from suburban Detroit since 1955 who had been either chair or ranking minority member of the committee since 1981, is literally "married to General Motors," since his wife is a member of GM's founding family and until 2009 was also a senior executive in the company.[111] Waxman's challenge pitted rustbelt and fiscally conservative Democrats against greener, and often junior, members of the caucus. When the latter prevailed, leadership on climate change shifted from the Senate to the House.

Waxman and his new Environment and Public Works Subcommittee chair, Edward Markey, introduced a cap-and-trade bill seeking to cut emissions to 20 percent below 2005 levels by 2020. After weeks of horse trading to win votes through allocation of emissions permits, the resulting 1,400-page bill promised free initial allocation of 85 percent of allowances, retroactive offsets for farmers, deletion of the low-carbon fuel standard, and a relaxed target of a 17 percent reduction. The bill passed the House by a narrow 219–212 margin in June 2009.

Senate passage of a climate change bill is far from assured. Although senators Boxer and Kerry introduced a similar bill in October 2009, it is considered to be assured of just 31 votes. In order to achieve a filibuster-proof 60 votes, concessions are sure to be demanded on permit allocation, tariffs to protect industry competitiveness, nuclear power, and offshore drilling.[112] With extensive debate still to come in the Senate, it is virtually impossible that the US will pass legislation before the Copenhagen meeting in December 2009, to a large degree tying the hands of US negotiators.

Discussion

The two outcomes to be explained in the US case to date are quite consistent: the United States has both declined to ratify the Kyoto Protocol and (at the federal level) has yet to adopt more politically challenging domestic policies, such as regulations or taxes. The strongest explanation for both lies in the electoral interests of policymakers. The prospect of relatively deep cuts under the Kyoto Protocol prompted formidable opposition from both the business community and organized labor. Although environmentalists may have found a sympathetic ear in the Clinton White House, voters' inattention to climate change limited the environmental community's influence with members of Congress. Fearful of the effects of mitigation on the greenhouse-gas-intensive American way of life, Congress blocked action to address climate change again and again.

This volume considers ideas in two forms, causal knowledge and principled norms. With respect to the former, questions concerning the scientific basis for action have been especially prominent in US debates about climate policy. However, the lengths to which critics have gone to highlight scientific uncertainty and the degree to which interpretations of science coincide with party affiliation suggest a conscious political strategy to challenge climate science rather than genuine disagreement about causal knowledge.

With respect to norms, there was a strong commitment to addressing climate change at the very highest levels in the Clinton administration. In particular, Vice President Gore's values to a large degree explain the United States' original consent to the Kyoto Protocol in the face of significant political obstacles. However, in the end, the depth of Vice President Gore's commitment was not sufficiently widely shared to carry the day, and the United States neither ratified the agreement nor adopted the kinds of domestic policies needed to ensure reduction of its greenhouse gas emissions.

Partisan effects may indicate political ideology, although it is difficult to know to what degree partisan differences are a result of ideology as opposed to electoral coalitions. Certainly there have been pronounced differences between the Republican and Democratic parties' positions on climate change, exemplified at the limit by the contrast between Al Gore's receipt of a Nobel Prize for his work on climate change and President George W. Bush's depiction of the Kyoto Protocol as a threat to the American way of life. It would be a mistake, however, to overstate the impacts of partisanship, since differences have been more pronounced among the leadership than among the rank and file of Congress. It bears emphasis that President Clinton's proposal for a BTU tax was rebuffed by a Democratically controlled Congress, while opposition to ratification of the Kyoto Protocol was exceptionally bipartisan.

The diffusion of authority by US political institutions has amplified the political challenges of addressing climate change in three ways. First, while much has been made of the Bush administration's announcement that the United States would not ratify the Kyoto Protocol, Vice President Dick Cheney has accurately observed, "Kyoto was a dead proposition before we ever arrived in Washington."[113] As a result of the separation of powers, it was the US Senate, not George W. Bush, that was responsible for the United States' nonratification of the Kyoto Protocol.

The explanation for why Democrats in Congress would diverge from their party leader in the White House, Bill Clinton, lies in a second institutional factor. The weakness of party discipline flowing from fixed elections has rendered members of Congress especially responsive to local economic interests, regardless of party, and given the greenhouse gas intensiveness of the US economy, many such interests stand to lose from serious efforts to address climate change. While other sectors will undoubtedly benefit in the long term, for the most part the relevant enterprises do not yet exist and thus do not have equally strong champions in Congress. Finally, the weakness of party discipline, and thus of party accountability, has facilitated the Republican Party's strategy of challenging climate science.

The discussion thus far has focused primarily on domestic factors. However, international factors can influence both the ideas debated and the balance of interests in domestic debates. The United States influenced international norms through its insistence on emissions trading, a policy instrument with which it had significantly more experience than did other parties to international negotiations in 1997. However, another international norm, that of differentiated responsibility, received remarkably little attention in a domestic debate that framed questions of fairness relative to the status quo. Indeed, Congressional representatives from both parties stressed the *unfairness* of a US commitment to reductions in the absence of a matching commitment from developing countries, an argument that resonated strongly with the American public.

With respect to international influences on domestic interests, US environmentalists worked closely with their counterparts from other countries at international meetings and arguably exerted some influence in countries such as Russia (discussed in chapter 4). However, transnational ties do not appear to have strengthened environmentalists' influence in the United States. Nor is there any evidence that President Bush was swayed either by foreign government officials or by huge crowds protesting his rejection of the Kyoto Protocol on his first European visit in 2002. However, while *political* globalization thus had limited impact on US domestic decisions, *economic* globalization clearly strengthened opposition to ratification. Competitiveness with developing countries was central to both the Senate's Byrd-Hagel resolution and President Bush's justification for US withdrawal from the Kyoto Protocol.

Looking Ahead

While the US story to date is far from encouraging, shifts in each of the explanatory variables point toward significant change. First, although political institutions primarily have been an obstructive force to date in US climate policy, more recently federalism has enabled policy innovation by state governments, while the courts are playing an increasingly important role in prodding the federal government.

Second, there are signs of shifting electoral incentives, particularly in the emergence of prominent business advocates of mitigation measures. The increase in media attention to climate change may have prompted an increase in public attention and concern in some quarters, although evidence from public opinion polls is far from clear-cut. It is thus an open question whether the Democratic leadership's enthusiasm for addressing climate change reflects partisan ideology or a response to new electoral incentives.

That said, Democrats' persistence in pursuing climate change legislation in the face of a deep economic recession indicates a fundamental shift in the principled ideas of the congressional leadership. A similar shift is evident in the White House where, despite an economic crisis that has devastated the US auto industry, President Obama has forged ahead with regulation of motor vehicle greenhouse gas emissions. It will be President Obama who concludes international negotiations of a post-2012 treaty on behalf of the United States. Time will tell whether it enjoys a more successful fate in the United States than the Kyoto Protocol.

Notes

1. If one also takes into account land use change and forestry, the United States ranks third after Australia and Canada. Emissions data are from US Environmental Protection Agency 2008 and, for comparison, Canada's and Australia's equivalent submissions to the FCCC for 2006, with population data from the US Census Bureau.

2. Rabe 2004.

3. US Department of State 2002.

4. Carpenter 2001, 214.

5. As cited in Blanchard 2007.

6. McCright and Dunlap 2003; Jacques, Dunlap, and Freeman 2008.

7. Bryner 2008, 328.

8. Carpenter 2001.

9. United States Climate Action Partnership, 2007, http://www.us-cap.org.

10. Michael Burnham and Anne C. Mulkern, "Enviros Waging 'Orchestrated Pressure Campaign' —US Chamber CEO," *E&E News*, 8 October 2009.

11. Selin and VanDeveer 2007, 21.

12. *New York Times*, 2 June 2008.

13. Dunlap and Scarce 1991.

14. A brief exception occurred in the fall of 1997, during the business opposition's media campaign in the lead-up to COP 3, when the combined total fell to 49 percent.

15. Lisowski 2002, 114.

16. AEI 2008, 53.

17. Ibid., 47.

18. Ibid., 50.

19. Quarterly Gallup Poll (1995–2000) and monthly Gallup Poll (2001–2008), via Roper Center iPoll.

20. Program on International Policy Attitudes/Knowledge Networks 2004.

21. AEI 2008, 6–7.

22. Ibid., 43.

23. Pew Research Center for People and the Press, "Fewer Americans See Solid Evidence of Global Warming," 22 October 2009.

24. Selin and VanDeveer 2007, 16.

25. *National Journal*, 2 March 2007, 6.

26. Dunlap and McCright 2008.

27. Cox and McCubbins (2005) argue that although party leaders have limited control over their members' votes, they have a greater impact on the legislative agenda.

28. Bryner 2008.

29. A general statement of this argument can be found in Fiorina 1980.

30. Kagan 2002.

31. Rabe 2004.

32. Hempel 2002, 308.

33. *New York Times*, 22 April 1993, A1.

34. Hempel 2002, 319.

35. Lutzenhiser 2001, 514.

36. Lopez 2003, 295.

37. Skolnikoff 1999, 20.

38. Sussman 2004.

39. McCright and Dunlap 2003.

40. S. Res 98, 105th Congress (1997).

41. In confidential interviews with the author, two former US officials speculated that the White House sought to render less significant a resolution it could not hope to block by dismissing it as uncontroversial.

42. Oberthür and Ott 1999.

43. Eizenstat 1997.

44. Author's interview with Stuart Eizenstat, 2006.

45. In 1997 the United States anticipated a 29 percent increase in US emissions and a 20 percent increase in Western Europe's emissions between 1990 and 2010 (Energy Information Administration 1997). The EU itself projected even lower emissions growth, with an increase in CO_2 emissions of between −11.5 percent and 17 percent over the same period (European Union 1996). These analyses project a disparity in emissions growth of between 9 and 40 percent.

46. America Abroad Media 2007.

47. Ibid.

48. Author's confidential interview with White House official, 2007.

49. Author's confidential interview with White House official, 2006.

50. Author's interview with Jonathan Pershing, 2006.

51. Author's interview with Stuart Eizenstat, 2006.

52. The US concession was not as deep as it might seem since the flexibility gains were considered equivalent to a 4 percent cut (1 percent for the expanded basket of gases, 3 percent for carbon sinks). See Eizenstat in US Congress 1998, 57; and White House Council of Economic Advisors 1998, 22.

53. Wirth 2002, 72.

54. Eizenstat 1997.

55. S. Res 86, 105th congress, Report no. 105–170.

56. White House Council of Economic Advisors 1998, 2.

57. US Congress 1998, 297.

58. White House Council of Economic Advisors 1998.

59. That figure can be found, however, in documents that the administration sent to Congress following congressional hearings. US Congress 1998.

60. Author's interview with Joe Aldy, 2006.

61. Claussen 2001.

62. Steurer 2003.

63. Lutzenhiser 2001, 512.

64. Skolnikoff 1999, 20.

65. Wirth 2002.

66. The Bush administration's reversal of the former EPA counsel view and denial of that petition by the International Center for Technology Assessment was the basis for the 2007 Supreme Court decision discussed below.

67. Author's interview with Stuart Eizenstat, 2006.

68. Wirth 2002, 73.

69. Whitman 2005.

70. Wirth 2002.

71. Jacoby and Reiner 2001, 301.

72. Text of letter from the president to senators Hegel, Helms, Craig, and Roberts, Office of the Press Secretary, 13 March 2001, http://www.whitehouse.gov/news/releases/2001/03/20010314.html.

73. Whitman 2005.

74. *Los Angeles Times*, 30 March 2001.

75. National Academy of Sciences 2001.

76. Mooney 2005, 92.

77. Ibid., 82.

78. Luntz Research Companies (ND).

79. Issue Paper: White House Edits to Climate Section of EPA's Report on the Environment, 29 April 2003; also *New York Times*, 19 June 2003.

80. Kolbert 2006; also *New York Times*, 8 June 2005.

81. Climate Change Update, *Senate Floor Statement by US Sen. James M. Inhofe*, 4 January 2005, http://inhofe.senate.gov/pressreleases/climateupdate.htm.

82. *Mother Jones*, 1 May 2007.

83. Victor 2004, 130.

84. Ibid.

85. Aldy 2004.

86. Kolbert 2006, 159.

87. Asia-Pacific Partnership on Clean Development and Climate, www.asiapacificpartnership.org.

88. John Heilprin, "Bush Seeks to Change US Image on Global Warming among Major Polluters," *Associated Press*, 28 September 2007.

89. Christoff 2008, 470.

90. Evangelical Climate Initiative, "A Christian Call to Action on Climate," http://christiansandclimate.org/.

91. Rabe 2004, 2007.

92. Vogel 1995.

93. "A Look at Emissions Targets," Pew Center on Global Climate Change, http://www.pewclimate.org/what_s_being_done/targets.

94. *New York Times*, 20 March 2008.

95. *Environment and Energy Daily*, 20 May 2008.

96. Regional Greenhouse Gas Initiative, http://www.rggi.org/about.htm.

97. Other cases of note include lawsuits by the auto industry against both Vermont and California, arguing (unsuccessfully) that state governments do not have authority to regulate greenhouse gas emissions from motor vehicles, a common law case in which the state of California is seeking damages from the auto industry, a suit seeking injunctive relief against electric utilities under common law, a case that forced the administration to release (four years late) a report on the impacts of climate change mandated by law, a case seeking EPA regulation of the airline industry, and litigation concerning listing of polar bears under the Endangered Species Act. With respect to the last of these, although litigants won a decision forcing the administration to render a decision by May 2008, the administration declared the act an inappropriate vehicle to protect the species from the effects of global warming, a decision that prompted a further legal challenge.

98. Massachusetts v. Environmental Protection Agency, 549 U.S. 497 (2007), [1].

99. Letter from Jason Kestrel Burnett to the Honorable Barbara Boxer, Chairman, Committee on Environment and Public Works, US Senate, 6 July 2008.

100. House Committee on Oversight and Government Reform 2007.

101. *New York Times*, 25 June 2008.

102. Brian Knowlton, "Obama Promises Action on Climate Change," *New York Times*, 18 November 2008.

103. Barack Obama, "Memorandum for the Heads of Executive Branch Departments and Agencies. Subject: Scientific Integrity," 9 March 2009.

104. John M. Broder, "Clinton Says U.S. Is Ready to Lead on Climate." *New York Times*, 28 April 2009.

105. John M. Broder and Jonathan Ansfield, "China and U.S. Seek a Truce on Greenhouse Gases." *New York Times*, 8 June 2009.

106. John M. Broder, "Obama to Toughen Rules on Emissions and Mileage." *New York Times*, 19 May 2009. Also John M. Broder, Micheline Maynard, "As Political Winds Shift, Detroit Charts New Course." *New York Times*, 20 May 2009.

107. Federal Register, vol. 74, no. 186, 28 September 2009, 49454.

108. Federal Register, vol. 74, no. 78, 24 April 2009, 18904.

109. Robin Bravender and Darren Samulesohn, "As Hill Debate Flounders, EPA Plows Ahead on Emissions Rules," Greenwire, 10 September 2009 (http://www.eenews.net/gw/).

110. The president called for a reduction to 14 percent below 2005 by 2020 with 100 percent auction of permits, thus raising the prospect of $645 billion in federal government revenues over 10 years.

111. John M. Broder, "A Power Duo, Dingells Battle on Two Fronts," *New York Times*, 16 November 2008.

112. Darren Samuelsohn, "On Road to 60, Senate Swells with Fence Sitters," Environment and Energy Daily, 20 October 2009 (http://www.eenews.net/eed/).

113. Kahn 2003, 564.

References

Aldy, J. E. 2004. Saving the Planet Cost-Effectively: The Role of Economic Analysis in Climate Change Mitigation Policy. In *Painting the White House Green: Rationalizing Environmental Policy Inside the Executive Office of the President*, ed. R. Lutter and J. F. Shogren. Washington, DC: Resources for the Future.

America Abroad Media. 2007. *Feeling the Heat: The Global Politics of Climate Change*. April 2007, program transcript.

American Enterprise Institute. 2008. Polls on the Environment and Global Warming. 18 April, www.aei.org/publicopinion11.

Blanchard, Odile. 2007. The Bush Administration's Climate Proposal: Rhetoric and Reality? Unpublished manuscript, http://ideas.repec.org/p/hal/journl/halshs-00199616_v1.html.

Bryner, Gary. 2008. Failure and Opportunities: Environmental Groups in US Climate Change Policy. *Environmental Politics* 17:319–336.

Carpenter, Chad. 2001. Business, Green Groups and the Media: The Role of Non-Governmental Organizations in the Climate Change Debate. *International Affairs* 77:313–328.

Christoff, Peter. 2008. The Bali Roadmap: Climate Change, COP 13 and Beyond. *Environmental Politics* 17:466–472.

Claussen, Eileen. 2001. Global Environmental Governance: Issues for the New Administration. *Environment* 43:29–34.

Cox, Gary W., and Matthew Daniel McCubbins. 2005. *Setting the Agenda: Responsible Party Government in the US House of Representatives*. Cambridge: Cambridge University Press.

Dunlap, Riley E., and Aaron M. McCright. 2008. Widening Gap: Republican and Democratic Views on Climate Change. *Environment* 50 (5):26–35.

Dunlap, Riley E., and R. Scarce. 1991. Poll Trends: Environmental Problems and Protection. *Public Opinion Quarterly* 55:651–672.

Eizenstat, Stuart. 1997. Statement at Press Conference. 11 December, http://www.state.gov/www/global/oes/ 971211_eizen_cop.html.

Energy Information Administration. 1997. *International Energy Outlook 1997*. Washington, DC: Department of Energy.

European Union, Directorate General for Energy. 1996. European Energy to 2020: A Scenario Approach.

Fiorina, Morris P. 1980. The Decline of Collective Responsibility in American Politics. *Daedalus* 109 (Summer):25–45.

Hempel, Lamont C. 2002. Climate Policy on the Installment Plan. In *Environmental Policy*, ed. Norman J. Vig and Michael E. Kraft. Washington, DC: CQ Press.

House Committee on Oversight and Government Reform, US Congress. 2007. Political Interference with Climate Change Science under the Bush Administration.

Intergovernmental Panel on Climate Change. 2007. *Climate Change 2007: Synthesis Report*. Geneva: Intergovernmental Panel on Climate Change.

Jacoby, Henry D., and David M. Reiner. 2001. Getting Climate Policy on Track after The Hague. *International Affairs* 77:297–312.

Jacques, Peter J., Riley E. Dunlap, and Mark Freeman. 2008. The Organization of Denial: Conservative Think Tanks and Environmental Skepticism. *Environmental Politics* 17:349–385.

Kagan, Robert A. 2002. *Adversarial Legalism: The American Way of Law*. Cambridge, MA: Harvard University Press.

Kahn, G. 2003. The Fate of the Kyoto Protocol under the Bush Administration. *Berkeley Journal of International Law* 21:548–571.

Kolbert, Elizabeth. 2006. *Field Notes from a Catastrophe*. London: Bloomsbury.

Lisowski, Michael. 2002. Playing the Two-Level Game: US President Bush's Decision to Repudiate the Kyoto Protocol. *Environmental Politics* 11 (4):101–119.

Lopez, Todd M. 2003. A Look at Climate Change and the Evolution of the Kyoto Protocol. *Natural Resources Journal* 43:285–312.

Luntz Research Companies. n.d. The Environment: A Cleaner, Safer, Healthier America.

Lutzenhiser, Loren. 2001. The Contours of US Climate Non-Policy. *Society and Natural Resources* 14:511–523.

McCright, Aaron M., and Riley E. Dunlap. 2003. Defeating Kyoto: The Conservative Movement's Impact on US Climate Change Policy. *Social Problems* 50:348–373.

Mooney, Chris. 2005. *The Republican War on Science.* New York: Basic Books.

National Academy of Sciences. 2001. *Climate Change Science: An Analysis of Some Key Questions.* Washington, DC: National Academy Press.

Oberthür, Sebastian, and Herman Ott. 1999. *The Kyoto Protocol: International Climate Policy for the 21st Century.* New York: Springer.

Program on International Policy Attitudes/Knowledge Networks. 2004. Americans on Climate Change, 25 June, http://www.pipa.org/OnlineReports/ClimateChange/ ClimateChange04_Jun04/ClimateChange_June04_rpt.pdf.

Rabe, Barry G. 2004. *Statehouse and Greenhouse: The Emerging Politics of American Climate Change Policy.* Washington, DC: Brookings.

Rabe, Barry G. 2007. Beyond Kyoto: Climate Change Policy in Multilevel Governance Systems. *Governance* 20:423–444.

Selin, Henrik, and Stacy D. VanDeveer. 2007. Political Science and Prediction: What's Next for U.S. Climate Change Policy? *Review of Policy Research* 24 (1):1–27.

Skolnikoff, E. B. 1999. The Role of Science on Policy: The Climate Change Debate in the United States. *Environment* 41 (5):16–20 and 42–45.

Stern, Nicholas. 2007. *The Economics of Climate Change: The Stern Review.* Cambridge: Cambridge University Press.

Steurer, Reinhard. 2003. The US's Retreat from the Kyoto Protocol: An Account of a Policy Change and Its Implications for Future Climate Policy. *European Environment* 13:344–360.

Sussman, G. 2004. The USA and Global Environmental Policy: Domestic Constraints on Effective Leadership. *International Political Science Review* 25:349–369.

US Congress. 1998. *Hearing before the Subcommittee on Energy and Power of the Committee on Commerce, House of Representatives, One Hundred Fifth Congress, 2d Session,* 4 March, Serial 105–108.

US Department of State. 2002. *U.S. Climate Action Report.* Washington, DC, May.

US Environmental Protection Agency. 2008. *Inventory of U.S. Greenhouse Gas Emissions and Sinks: 1990–2006.* Washington, DC: US Environmental Protection Agency.

Victor, David. 2004. *The Collapse of the Kyoto Protocol and the Struggle to Slow Global Warming.* Princeton: Princeton University Press.

Vogel, David. 1995. *Trading Up: Consumer and Environmental Regulation in a Global Economy.* Cambridge, MA: Harvard University Press.

White House Council of Economic Advisors et al. 1998. The Kyoto Protocol and the President's Policies to Address Climate Change: Administration Economic Analysis. Washington, DC, July.

Whitman, Christine T. 2005. *It's My Party Too: The Battle for the Heart of the GOP and the Future of America*. Toronto: Penguin.

Wirth, Timothy. 2002. Hot Air over Kyoto: The United States and the Politics of Global Warming. *Harvard International Review* 23 (4):72–77.

4

Russia and the Kyoto Protocol: From Hot Air to Implementation?

Laura A. Henry and Lisa McIntosh Sundstrom

Introduction

On 5 November 2004, the Russian Federation ratified the Kyoto Protocol. Since the treaty required the participation of states responsible for at least 55 percent of Annex 1 greenhouse gases, Russia's ratification tipped the scales, and the Protocol went into effect on 15 February 2005. At first glance, it is surprising that Russia turned out to be the key ratifying state of the Kyoto Protocol. The Russian government has spent the last fifteen years focused on economic recovery and development, and environmental regulation and treaties have been low on its list of priorities. Russia has become the world's largest exporter of natural gas, the second largest oil exporter, and the third largest energy consumer.[1] Russia's continued economic growth significantly depends on the demand for carbon-based fuel.

Yet for close analysts of the Kyoto Protocol and Russia, there were clear incentives for Russia's participation. Russia experienced massive industrial decline in the immediate aftermath of the Soviet Union's collapse in 1991. Since 1990 is the benchmark year for emissions limits under the Kyoto Protocol, Russia has considerable room to *increase* emissions prior to 2012 before it will exceed its Kyoto emissions targets. Moreover, Russia can sell its excess credits or attract investment designed to further reduce emissions. The real puzzle is why Russia took so long to ratify the treaty since, to outside observers, its potential for material gains (or at least negligible costs) from ratification seemed clear. In addition, Russia's initial ambivalence about ratification has led to relatively slow domestic implementation of the Protocol, both in terms of fulfilling its reporting requirements and of developing a strategic climate policy.

There were a number of reasons for Russia's delay. First, there was significant pessimism regarding the consequences of the Kyoto Protocol among some prominent Russian scientists, who doubted the link between carbon emissions and climate change, and economists, who argued that Russia would have to limit its economic growth to avoid exceeding Kyoto emissions limits before 2012 and that direct material benefits from the Protocol might not be as great as expected. Second, once the United States announced its decision not to ratify, Russia, responsible for 17.4 percent of 1990 Annex 1 emissions, became the only state with sufficient emissions to bring the Protocol into effect, and it therefore held a crucial diplomatic bargaining chip. As a result of these two factors, President Vladimir Putin had incentives to delay a decision until he had, first, clarified the balance of evidence regarding causes of climate change and economic consequences of ratification and, second, secured significant rewards from international partners on other issues in exchange for ratification, while still elevating Russia's image as a cooperative partner in international affairs. These international factors explain why Putin, who in Russia's highly centralized system retained a great degree of autonomy in foreign affairs, made numerous contradictory statements relating to Kyoto prior to ratification and why he allowed Kyoto critics close to his administration to continue their negative public statements for so long. Putin wished to maintain a sense of uncertainty about the likelihood of Russia's ratification in order to obtain inducements from other Kyoto-ratifying states.

In contrast to the significant role of international factors in encouraging Russia's ratification of the Kyoto Protocol, implementation of the agreement is a largely domestic process, which generally occurs after the wave of international interest and pressure has subsided. Unlike most other Annex 1 states, Russia needs to do very little to comply with the Protocol given that its emissions are well below 1990 levels. Yet Russia's active participation in Kyoto's flexibility mechanisms would contribute to the overall success of the agreement in bringing about emissions reductions and providing a means for other Annex 1 states to meet their emissions targets through flexibility mechanisms.

The Russian case indicates that international partners can offer incentives for states to implement the Protocol through financial and technological investments and the environmental benefits that may result, but ultimately implementation depends primarily on buy-in from domestic actors. Implementation of real emissions reduction measures proceeds effectively if government officials and institutions see that implementation enhances their institutional authority and become invested in their role as climate policy implementers; if private-sector actors see themselves as potential beneficiaries from Kyoto's flexibility mechanisms and lobby for implementation; and if the public in general, and environmental organizations in particular, become increasingly concerned about climate change and demand political action. These dynamics play out not only in the case of Russian implementation but in some other cases examined in this book, especially Canada. Based on the ratification process, in Russia one might expect that bureaucratic politics and influential firms from the natural resource sector would play a disproportionate role in determining the speed and quality of implementation. Yet institutional instability, the broader economic climate, and the necessity of maintaining good relations with the executive branch also strongly influence the behavior of these actors.

As mentioned in the introductory chapter to this volume, while many scholars have examined states' decisions on ratification of the Kyoto Protocol from an international relations perspective, analysis from theoretical perspectives in the field of comparative politics has been largely absent. While the Russian government's ratification decision did rest significantly on international factors (particularly bargaining over side payments and development of a positive reputation as neoliberal institutionalists would expect), domestic configurations of policymakers' ideas, electoral and economic interests, and political institutions played a role in determining Russia's response to international pressures. These domestic factors are even more crucial in determining the course of policy responses to the Kyoto treaty following ratification. This chapter weighs the significance of Russian domestic institutions, interests, and ideas (both causal and normative)—and international influences on them—to determine which factors have most significantly affected the nation's ratification and implementation path and how these factors have interacted with one another at various stages.

We find that a highly centralized institutional decision-making process provided a filter through which economic interests and foreign policy concerns were weighed to produce a decision in favor of ratification. In the implementation process, the consequences of ratification without generating buy-in from many domestic actors combined with frequent bureaucratic reorganization and low capacity have made the work of setting up the requisite systems to take advantage of Kyoto implementation mechanisms proceed much more slowly than in many other ratifying states.

The Politics of Ratification

In the 1990s Russian representatives to climate change negotiations seemed more concerned about negotiating favorable terms for their participation in any international agreement than forestalling climate change. The Russian delegation argued that transitional economies should be allowed "a certain degree of flexibility" in meeting their emissions targets.[2] Russia and Ukraine also insisted on the 1990 level of carbon emissions as their shared binding target, even though the two countries' greenhouse gas emissions had dropped substantially in the following decade due to the collapse of Soviet-era industries.[3]

Despite the long delay in Russia's final decision to ratify Kyoto, there were a number of material factors in favor of ratification from the Protocol's conclusion in 1997. Russia's emissions fell by an estimated 30 percent between 1990 and 2000, meaning that in practice Russia could increase significantly its carbon dioxide emissions without violating the letter of the agreement.[4] The great scope for further emissions reductions by Russia's inefficient industrial sectors makes Russia the largest potential seller of emissions credits on the international market. Early estimates of Russia's potential annual income from the sale of its carbon emissions, prior to the US decision not to ratify, ranged from US\$4 billion to \$35 billion annually.[5] In addition, Russia seemed a likely beneficiary of Kyoto's Joint Implementation (JI) program, in which states can earn emissions credits by investing in reducing emissions or enhancing removal by carbon sinks in other states.

In April 2002 President Putin announced that Russia soon would move forward on the Kyoto Protocol, leading many observers to expect that Russia would ratify in time for the World Summit on Sustainable Development in Johannesburg in September 2002.[6] Yet Russia did not do so. In order to understand the delay, we need to take a closer look at the debate over the Protocol inside Russia, paying particular attention to the ways in which ideas, domestic interests, and institutions intersected with international factors.

Ideas

A significant battle of scientific and economic ideas framed the domestic debate for and against ratification. Most climate scientists, ecologists, and environmental economists in Russia agreed that ratification was advisable because greenhouse gas emissions contribute to global warming and Russia's expected economic growth and carbon intensity trends would not cause the country to exceed the allowable emissions threshold under the treaty, which meant that ratification had little or no economic cost for Russia. In fact, many economists projected that Russia would benefit from Kyoto through treaty mechanisms that would encourage international partners to pay for the modernization of Russia's industrial and energy sectors.[7]

Yet the director of the Russian Academy of Sciences' Global Climate and Ecology Institute, Yuri Izrael, and the president's chief economic adviser, Andrei Illarionov, were two powerful dissenters from these claims. Izrael questioned the causal relationship between climate change and anthropogenic emissions and the potential effectiveness of the Kyoto Protocol in addressing the problem.[8] He went so far as to ask Putin to revoke his signing of the Protocol and continued his opposition to the agreement even after Russia ratified.[9] Izrael's views did not represent the entire scientific community, however. In fact, in reaction to his position, more than 250 members of the Academy of Sciences signed a petition in 2003 supporting Kyoto ratification.[10]

In the two years prior to the ratification decision, Illarionov developed an economic model projecting that Russia's GDP was likely to double over the next decade and that the country would then necessarily exceed its 1990 greenhouse gas emission levels. In the prestigious Russian journal *Voprosy ekonomiki* (Problems of Economics), Illarionov argued that "ratification of the Kyoto Protocol will force Russia's economic actors to face a dilemma: either acquisition of emissions quotas on the external market, or a necessary slowdown (cessation) of economic activity."[11] Elsewhere, Illarionov also pointed out that Russia's burden was unfair, noting that "Russia, which now actually accounts for just 6 percent of greenhouse gas emissions, will have to implement reductions while China, which accounts for 13 percent, has no obligations and the United States, which accounts for almost a third, has rejected them altogether."[12] Critics of Illarionov argued that he did not take into account the declining carbon intensity of Russia's economy and pointed out that there is no direct relationship between economic growth and intensity of carbon usage.[13] In 1999 Russian industries produced 3.8 times more greenhouse gases than the leading European countries per dollar of GDP when measured at purchasing power parity, a number that will decline as industries adopt more energy-efficient production techniques.[14] In a report directly responding to Illarionov's IEA paper, economists at the Environmental Defense Fund estimated that even if Russia experienced robust economic growth with a doubling of GDP by 2012, it would only reach 86 percent of its Kyoto-allowed carbon emissions, and that there was a zero probability that Russia would exceed its Kyoto target.[15] World Bank economists similarly cast doubt on the Illarionov model.[16] In spite of these critiques, Illarionov continued to object vociferously to the Kyoto Protocol even after Russia's decision to ratify.[17]

Interests

Press coverage of Russia's debate over the Kyoto Protocol was dominated by the pronouncements of Izrael and Illarionov. Many scientists publishing in the largest state-owned Russian newspaper, *Rossiiskaya gazeta* (widely perceived as publishing views agreeable to the government), expressed considerable skepticism that the effects of global warming in Russia would be disastrous and frequently argued that climate fluctuations were cyclical.[18] These opponents, although few in number, were formidable due to their senior positions and access to key decision makers. Many of those involved in the debate interpreted Illarionov's remarks as representative of President Putin's position. In 2003, partly as a result of the arguments of these vocal critics, the Kyoto decision process slowed down significantly.

In spite of the high-profile opposition to Kyoto, however, a number of interest groups worked in support of the Protocol. Nongovernmental organizations such as the World Wildlife Fund Russia (WWF Russia), Greenpeace Russia, the Center for Russian Environmental Policy, Eco-Accord, the Russian Regional Environmental Center, and others countered arguments against the Protocol, reaching out to government officials and the general public. For example, Aleksei Kokorin of WWF Russia notes that his organization published more than one hundred articles in favor of Kyoto ratification in addition to participating in numerous radio and television interviews. At various times WWF Russia strategically employed up to fifteen contractors who also held positions inside government ministries to write reports on the legal and ecological implications of Kyoto, which could then be passed on to the relevant government officials. Greenpeace Russia established a joint Web page entitled "Kyoto, yes!" for supporters to post publications and announce Kyoto-related events.[19] Nongovernmental organizations (NGOs) also sponsored independent research. Yuri Safonov, an economist at the Moscow Higher School of Economics and affiliate of the Environmental Defense Fund and the Russian Regional Environmental Center, explains that he and his colleagues presented research in many venues "showing that there is no serious reason to doubt that Russia would fulfill its commitments on Kyoto and there is no situation under which Russia would not get benefits."[20]

In addition to fighting the domestic "information war," NGOs cooperated with their international allies. In October 2003 Greenpeace Russia, with the help of Greenpeace International, gathered approximately ten thousand signatures from around the world endorsing a letter asking President Putin to ratify the Kyoto Protocol. The letter was delivered to the president's office and to Russian embassies in more than thirty countries on Putin's birthday. Also in 2003 the Center for Russian Environmental Policy, in conjunction with the US-based Environmental Defense Fund, organized the Social Forum on Climate Change. The Social Forum was designed to coincide with President Putin's World Conference on Climate Change and to address the economic, environmental, and social benefits of the Kyoto Protocol. Ultimately, more than 250 people from 33 countries attending the Social Forum produced a final statement affirming the reality of anthropogenic global warming and advocating Russia's ratification of the Kyoto Protocol.[21]

Yet despite the advocacy of environmental NGOs, the Russian public remained largely unengaged in the debate over ratification. In general, environmental organizations are not well known by the Russian public. A 2005 survey by the Public Opinion Foundation found that even in Moscow, site of the most recognized and active green NGOs, only 33 percent of respondents were aware of the existence of environmental organizations in the city.[22] In addition, in June 2005 the polling agency ROMIR, in a survey of 1,500 Russians across the federation, found that the environment ranked ninth in an open question about respondents' current concerns.[23] Knowledge of the Kyoto Protocol also appeared to be low. A 2003 survey arranged by Greenpeace Russia and executed by the organization Popular Initiative, including 1,000 citizens from 18 Russian oblasts, found that 80.7 percent of respondents had never heard of the Kyoto Protocol and 73.7 percent did not know whether Russia's ratification of it would help to resolve the problem of climate change.[24] Vladimir Zakharov, of the Center for Russian Environmental Policy, argues that ignorance is not the same as opposition, however, suggesting that "the population ... knows little about [Kyoto]. ... But when people find out about it, they say: that is a good thing."[25] Many Kyoto supporters attribute the public's ambivalence to the negative media coverage of the issue. Several pro-Kyoto activists estimated that 80 percent of the news coverage was either negative or incorrect.[26]

Some of Russia's most powerful business interests were allies of the Kyoto supporters, which contrasts with many other advanced industrialized democracies, such as the United States, Canada, and Australia, where energy and natural resource sectors in particular have been opposed to Kyoto. Certain businesses and oil companies opposed ratification.[27] Norilsk Nickel purportedly feared heightened environmental standards for industry in the Arctic. Oil companies, such as Yukos, were understandably concerned that Kyoto requirements would reduce demand for their products and place further restrictions on their activities. Indeed, according to some observers, the international conglomerate ExxonMobil was a strong lobbyist against Russia's ratification.[28] Yet firms such as United Energy System (RAO UES), Russian Aluminum, Gazprom, the service sector giant Sistema, Siberian Ural Aluminum, and the Russian Union of Industrialists and Entrepreneurs supported ratification and acknowledged the potential advantages of the Protocol. The most notable representative of business interests was the National Carbon Union (NCU), a coalition of Russian economic actors who formed a nonprofit advocacy organization after participating in a working group under the Russian president's economic directorate in 2002.[29] The NCU's members, responsible for more than one-third of Russia's greenhouse gases, advocated market mechanisms for emissions reductions, including a domestic emissions trading program, and sought to attract foreign investment through participation in JI projects. According to its leader, Stepan Dudarev, the NCU supplied the Ministry for Economic Development and Trade with research materials related to Kyoto ratification and implementation.[30] Oleg Pluzhnikov, former head of the environmental economics division at the ministry, agrees that business pressure played a positive role in the ratification process, noting that businesses independently arranged projects with potential investors, demonstrating their desire to take advantage of the Kyoto Protocol's flexibility mechanisms.[31]

Institutions

During the debate over ratification, various Russian ministries and the Federal Service on Hydrometeorology and Environment Monitoring (Rosgidromet) weighed in on the question of whether or not to ratify the Kyoto Protocol. The Ministry of Energy (merged into the Ministry of Industry and Energy in March 2004 before regaining ministerial autonomy in 2008) was apparently in favor of ratification throughout most of the process. This ministry saw Kyoto's JI mechanisms as a route to greater energy efficiency and modernization of energy infrastructure. Yet one former bureaucrat from the Ministry of Energy stated that opinion within the ministry had swung against ratification just prior to Putin's decision to ratify.[32] The Ministry of Natural Resources was reportedly most consistently concerned about constraints on the exploitation of natural resources, and the Ministry for Economic Development and Trade cooled toward ratification in 2002, when it appeared that bureaucratic authority to manage the implementation mechanisms might go to the Ministry of Energy.[33] Rosgidromet, although subsumed under the Ministry of Natural Resources, had led the Russian delegation to the negotiations over Kyoto and generally remained positively oriented toward ratification, despite its insistence that more funding would be necessary for it to implement the treaty obligations.[34] One Ministry for Economic Development and Trade insider recounts that at first an active debate occurred among ministries resulting in a rough balance of opinion; then, however, Illarionov's public statements led government officials to fall silent or adopt a more negative position on the issue of Kyoto ratification. Once Putin announced his intention to ratify the Protocol during the fall of 2004, suddenly the ministries were almost unanimous in their support. In the post-ratification setting, it became difficult to find a ministry spokesperson who would claim that his or her ministry had ever wavered on the question of ratification.

Two parliamentary committees within the lower house of parliament, the State Duma, were responsible for the question of Kyoto ratification—the Foreign Affairs and Ecology committees. Alexander Kosarikov, the deputy chairman of the Ecology Committee, calls these two bodies the "initiators" of ratification, although he also acknowledges that some committee members feared that the Kyoto Protocol was part of an international strategy to place pressure on Russian industry.[35] Members reportedly also soured on ratification following the United States' refusal to ratify.[36] The Federation Council, the upper house of parliament, was not a vocal participant in the debate over ratification. For the most part, regional governments did not play a significant role in Kyoto ratification, although in June 2003 the state advisory council, composed of Russia's regional governors, formally supported ratification.[37]

Yet in Russia's political system, these bureaucratic battles among ministries, parliamentary debates, and regional interests were less important to the decision to ratify than the overwhelming power of the executive branch of government. In practice, Russia has a superpresidential system, with ultimate decision-making power in the hands of the executive. The party that supports the Kremlin and the president, United Russia, dominates the Duma; as a rule, bills that the president endorses pass quickly and unchallenged through the upper house and with debate but little delay in the lower house.[38] Thus, although approval by the State Duma and Federation Council was formally required, because of his institutional power it was Vladimir Putin's decision alone that would determine the outcome of the ratification debate. His was an exceptionally powerful position compared to other heads of state of Annex 1 countries engaged in ratification debates.

The Decision to Ratify

Throughout the debate over Kyoto, President Putin's position on the issue was ambiguous. The presidentially appointed prime minister, Mikhail Kasyanov, declared in a cabinet meeting in April 2002 that Russia should ratify Kyoto and then announced officially at the Johannesburg World Summit on Sustainable Development in September 2002 that Russia would indeed ratify.[39] At the 2003 World Conference on Climate Change, more than a year after Kasyanov's announcement, Putin argued that Russia should be "reluctant to make decisions [about the Protocol] just on financial considerations. We should be guided primarily by more noble ideas rather than the consideration of mundane, quick economic benefit."[40] Yet at the same meeting Putin joked that, under conditions of global warming, "We'll need to spend less money on fur coats and grain harvests will increase," though Putin also acknowledged the danger of increased droughts and floods.[41] This ambiguity was disconcerting to Protocol supporters, given President Putin's high level of decision-making autonomy.

Which aspects of the debate influenced President Putin? With authority concentrated in the executive and loyalty highly prized within the presidential administration, the details remain somewhat opaque. Yet it seems clear that the decision, as well as the delay, were primarily influenced by international incentives in other policy areas and broader concerns for Russia's reputation rather than anticipated benefits from Kyoto itself.

Many potential material benefits did weigh in favor of ratification: the possibility of selling carbon credits for profit on the international market; the modernization of industry that Russia could gain free of charge from international partners via Kyoto's joint implementation and green investment mechanisms; and public health benefits from reduced pollutants and particulate matter from a refurbished industrial sector. It does not seem to be the case, however, that the Protocol's economic benefits were the primary factor behind the eventual decision to ratify Kyoto.[42] Expected earnings from the sale of emissions credits plummeted with the US decision not to ratify Kyoto. In 2004 a Cambridge Economic Policy Associates report argued that Russia's potential income from emissions trading was likely to range from US$150 million to $2 billion annually, much less than Russia had expected prior to US rejection of the Protocol.[43] Viktor Danilov-Danilian, the former head of the State Committee on Ecology and current head of the Russian Academy of Sciences' Institute of Water Problems, argued, "The money that could be earned thanks to the Kyoto Protocol through selling allowances and receiving investments in Joint Implementation projects is of no interest to the authorities."[44] Safonov agreed that the economic benefits of the Kyoto Protocol appear small when weighed against revenue from other sources, in particular from the petroleum sector.

Indeed, concerns about Russia's progress on other foreign trade issues and the country's international image appear to have played the primary role in the decision to ratify. While domestic attention may not have been focused on the question of Kyoto ratification, international actors took a keen interest in Russia's decision. The European Union was the most active international advocate of the Protocol and European leaders personally pressured Putin to ratify Kyoto. For example, in September 2003, Jacques Chirac urged Putin to move forward on the Kyoto Protocol and suggested that such a decision would lead to the "enhanced legitimacy" of Russia-European partnerships.[45] Nongovernmental organizations circumvented superpresidential politics inside Russia by promoting third-party pressure on Putin. WWF Russia used its contacts in European WWF offices to encourage European environmentalists to push leaders, including Schroeder and Chirac, to press Putin on Kyoto's ratification, arguing that "if you don't ask Putin to carefully consider the Kyoto Protocol, as a friend, then he may soon decide against ratification."[46] Kokorin stresses the importance of this transnational networking and third-party influence on Putin by concluding that "it is simply the case that without WWF International we would never have been able to achieve our goal."[47] Safonov agrees that an important factor was "the international image of ... Russia and Putin himself. ... European leaders—I would say world leaders except Bush—always were talking about Kyoto and calling and writing to Putin [asking] why we don't ratify."[48]

Although Putin later adopted a more independent and at times confrontational foreign policy, several observers who watched the debate
closely argued that at that time Putin was using ratification as a way to
signal his unity with "the world community," "European politics," or
"Western values."[49] There is some evidence for this view from a statement of German Gref, the Russian minister of economic development
and trade, who said shortly prior to ratification that the Kremlin viewed
the step mainly as a symbolic gesture to improve Russia's international
image.[50] The decision not only symbolized Russia's cooperative stance
as an international partner but more specifically signaled strategic distancing from the United States and a closer alliance with Europe. Thus
some delay in the final decision likely came from tensions in Russian
foreign policy between these two sets of alliances. Natalia Olefirenko of
Greenpeace Russia notes that Putin began to backpedal on ratification
after meeting with President Bush in 2003, not wishing "to terminate
these relations [with the US]."[51] Duma deputy Kosarikov concluded that
the main reason for ratification was "Putin's desire not to lose contact,
not to move away from a common European politics."[52]

However, Russia's concern with its international image was not merely
a selfless desire to develop its "European" identity. Had that concern
dominated, Putin would have made his decision to ratify much earlier
out of a basic normative impulse. Instead his concerns about Russia's
image were reinforced by the opportunity for a side payment for Kyoto
ratification, unrelated to the Protocol itself. This opportunity helps to
explain why the government delayed ratification for two years beyond
President Putin's initial announcement of his intention to ratify. During
negotiations with the EU, Russia seems to have identified a concession
clearly within its national interest that tipped the scales in favor of Kyoto
ratification: the EU's agreement to support Russian membership in the
World Trade Organization. While the linkage of these two issues was
never formally acknowledged by either side, many observers and Russian
and Western media sources remarked on the simultaneity of the announcements.[53] Some Russian government officials publicly linked the two
issues. In May 2004 Sergei Yastrzhembsky, Russia's envoy to the EU,
stated that ratification would depend on the condition that Russia's
"interests are welcomed and satisfied in different spheres ... for example,
the WTO."[54] Putin himself denied that there was a formal bargain struck
but stated that the WTO concession was helpful: "The EU's willingness
to accommodate our interests during the negotiations will affect Russia's
attitude to the Kyoto question in a positive way. We are going to speed

up the pace of our preparations leading to the country's eventual ratification of the protocol."[55] Alexander Golub provides supporting evidence that the two issues were related, noting that the Environmental Defense Fund acted as a go-between in the negotiations, suggesting to the European Commission that Russia might be willing to ratify the Protocol if the EU retracted its earlier insistence that Russia increase its domestic natural gas prices to world market levels as a condition for WTO admission.[56] The nature of the debate over the potential costs of ratification changed after the May 2004 EU Summit linked the WTO and Kyoto as well. As Vladimir Kotov argues, "The economic benefits for Russia from WTO entry exceed by several-fold its potential losses from surpassing the Kyoto [emissions] targets."[57]

Some observers believe that Putin was largely in favor of ratification all along but allowed the debate to continue in order to gain as many benefits as possible from other states that had ratified Kyoto, as well as to assure himself that the anti-Kyoto forces were wrong in their cataclysmic predictions about economic constraints imposed by the treaty. Indeed, Wilson Rowe argues that ascertaining economic implications, rather than reconciling scientific opinions, hindered ratification.[58] According to Aleksei Kokorin of WWF Russia, "It's not as if the man slept and then suddenly awoke. He simply acted very slowly, without hurrying. Listening unfortunately to the voices of Kyoto's opponents. Wanting to assure himself that what they were saying was not true."[59]

It is clear that Russia's ultimate decision to ratify the Protocol was not due to an ideational commitment to resolving the problem of climate change or sustainable development more broadly, nor did the government appear tempted by the potential economic benefits of the agreement itself. Instead, ratification was based on a more instrumental view of the Protocol as a means of realizing other desirable goals at the international level while simultaneously enhancing Russia's image on the international stage.

Russia behaved internationally as neoliberal institutionalists would expect, trying to maximize its gains across multiple foreign policy issues while strengthening its long-term reputation with European states as a reliable negotiating partner. At the domestic level, an institutional approach also explains the outcome best. Whereas economic, bureaucratic, and NGO voices were fairly closely balanced for and against Kyoto, the institutional framework in which the president was virtually free from public scrutiny and free of party affiliation meant that he was not constrained by those interests. He could delay, articulate inconsistent policy positions, and make a final decision based on international concerns due to his high degree of autonomy. However, this unilateral decision-making power does not extend to the stage of implementing effective policies to tackle climate change, in which many actors must participate actively.

The Politics of Kyoto Protocol Implementation

The Russian government's motivation for ratifying the Kyoto Protocol left open a number of questions about the country's implementation strategy. An interest-based approach predicts that, having ratified largely for the sake of side payments, Russia would attempt to maximize the amount of material gain it can glean from the Protocol's flexibility mechanisms. In this scenario, efforts to reduce greenhouse gas emissions would only endure as long as funds from other Annex 1 countries continue to flow into Russia. An institutions-focused approach suggests that Russia would barely comply, since its powerful executive, coupled with frequent bureaucratic reorganization, means that after a decision has been taken single-handedly by the president, there is little momentum within the bureaucracy to develop serious implementation systems. Finally, an ideas-based approach suggests that the Russian government would maximize its emissions reductions in the spirit of Kyoto to retain its identity as a cooperative partner with Europe. This could involve policies like a carbon tax, a domestic cap-and-trade system, and fines for enterprises that exceed legislated emissions quotas.

Evidence suggests that Russia is acting according to a combination of the first two approaches and not the third. In the years since ratification, climate change policy has not been at the top of the government's agenda, and while fear about climate policies constraining economic growth persists, there are signs that growing concern about industrial competitiveness and energy efficiency have increased state and private-sector interest in taking advantage of available Kyoto mechanisms. While it has been slow to develop systems for implementing Kyoto mechanisms, the Russian government has gradually created the necessary documentation and regulatory systems to participate in emissions trading and JI mechanisms. In addition, more than one hundred JI projects with Russian partners have been submitted to the UN JI Supervisory Committee since 2006, although none had received a final determination by the time this chapter was written.

Russia's overall implementation strategy was initially articulated in the February 2005 National Action Plan on Kyoto Implementation, yet that plan was extremely vague and somewhat incoherent. Pointing out the unanswered policy questions, Safonov asks, "Do we want to establish an emissions trading scheme, cap-and-trade system, or just focus on investment projects?"[60] According to M. A. Yulkin of the Environmental Investment Centre, the plan included only those government initiatives that existed prior to ratification of Kyoto, and they "cannot be taken seriously" since they do not include concrete emissions reduction targets.[61]

In December 2009 President Medvedev signed a "climate doctrine," spearheaded by the Ministry of Natural Resources. The doctrine officially acknowledges that anthropogenic climate change exists and that the effects of climate change will impose significant costs on Russia, requiring government action. But it also enumerates anticipated benefits from climate change (such as lower energy use for heating) and focuses on adaptation as a priority for Russia's national security.[62] Anna Korppoo called a draft of the document revolutionary and perhaps "comparable in political significance with that of the Stern review on the economics of climate change in Britain."[63] Critics argue that the outlined strategy has serious flaws. The document was developed without consultation of environmental or other civil society organizations.[64] It does not suggest any specific CO_2 reduction targets or deadlines. Nonetheless, it emphasizes energy-efficient technologies and renewable energy sources. In mid-November 2009, President Medvedev signed a law on energy conservation and increased energy efficiency.[65] The legislation includes mostly symbolic measures in terms of regulation, such as mandating installation of digital electricity meters and use of high-efficiency lightbulbs. Nonetheless, it also includes some promising energy conservation mandates and incentives, such as a mandate that state-funded organizations decrease their energy consumption from 2009 levels by at least 3 percent per year for 5 years, with savings from such reductions permitted to be redirected to employees' salaries; and a provision for private-sector organizations to claim rebates on taxes and loan interest paid for renovation projects that improve energy efficiency.[66]

At the most basic level, Russia needs to do very little in order to comply with the Kyoto Protocol, since its 2007 greenhouse gas emissions are estimated at more than 35 percent below 1990 levels.[67] Russia could in fact choose "compliance without implementation."[68] Requirements for compliance include completing the national emissions inventory (cadastre) and establishing a national registry in order to track emissions credit balances and transfers. Russia was slow to meet its reporting requirements to the UN Framework Convention on Climate Change (UNFCCC). It submitted only incomplete, summary inventories of its greenhouse gas emissions in its national communications reports between 1995 and 2007[69] and submitted its first full emissions inventory in early 2007—the last of all Annex 1 countries to do so.

Ideas

Russia's shallow ideational commitment to environmental protection generally and climate change prevention specifically, as revealed by the ratification debate, has affected implementation of the Protocol. While ratification appears to have been driven primarily by international pressure and side payments, implementation is a process that occurs largely outside the public spotlight and, at least in the short term, does little to affect Russia's international image. Kokorin notes that in addition to the government's "lack of urgency" in climate change policy, the perception that climate change may have some positive effects in Russia is still common.[70] Domestic concerns about investment, industrial competitiveness, and energy efficiency are more likely to influence Russia's participation in Kyoto's flexibility mechanisms than concern about climate change per se. In 2008 Vsevolod Gavrilov, deputy minister of the Ministry for Economic Development and Trade, acknowledged, "We see [Kyoto] as a means, not as an end in itself. ... It is a way to get new technology for our industries."[71]

Public opinion polls since ratification have suggested that the Russian public is becoming more aware of the problem of climate change and more eager to take action to limit it. A GlobeScan survey in 2005—after ratification—found that 59 percent of Russians considered it a "very serious" problem, up from 43 percent in 2003.[72] A 2007 BBC/Globe Scan/PIPA survey indicated that 87 percent of Russians favored taking action to address climate change, although 44 percent preferred taking "modest steps over the coming years."[73] However, in the same survey 64 percent of Russian respondents said that "they have heard little" about climate change, demonstrating the need for public education and leadership on the issue.

Given the lack of public debate about climate change policy, NGOs have realized that they still need to explain to the general public and government officials alike why the Kyoto Protocol is worthwhile. Since ratification, WWF Russia has begun a public education campaign on climate change.[74] Other supporters have suggested that NGOs form a "Kyoto Watch" program to monitor progress (or lack thereof) in implementation. Kokorin was part of a small group that convinced the Russian government to increase the transparency of the approval process for the JI projects by providing public notification of the proposals and government decisions.[75]

Institutions

Frequent bureaucratic reorganization and generally low administrative capacity have meant that despite public and private-sector interest in benefiting from Kyoto Protocol flexibility mechanisms, construction of the legal and policy framework necessary to take advantage of these mechanisms has been drawn out. Bureaucrats such as Oleg Pluzhnikov have admitted that significant time is lost when ministries are reorganized and key officials shuffled.[76] Although the Kyoto Protocol is no longer actively opposed, progress can easily stagnate when politically powerful actors do not promote implementation or bureaucratic actors are engaged in conflict over competing approaches.[77] Russian observers in both the government and the NGO community generally agree that implementation has proceeded slowly.[78] This lethargy is variously attributed to the ministries' lack of resources, laziness, or incompetence, but it also reflects the mixed signals that state officials received during the ratification debate. Officials who work inside the ministries point out that implementation is a complex process and say they are moving forward as quickly as can be expected—a credible point, given Russia's lack of detailed planning for implementation.

The 2005 National Action Plan distributed responsibilities across ministries and created an interdepartmental commission tasked with creating the legal infrastructure to implement the Protocol.[79] This commission has been headed by the Ministry for Economic Development and Trade (now the Ministry for Economic Development). RAO UES (an electricity company accounting for one-third of Russia's CO_2 emissions) and Gazprom (the world's largest gas company) are also part of the commission.[80] The plan provided only a vague sense of which ministries and agencies are responsible for various implementation tasks, with multiple ministries often assigned a single task.[81] Over time, however, the Ministry for Economic Development and Trade obtained responsibility for registering joint implementation agreements. The Ministry of Natural Resources has been in charge of the national registry. Rosgidromet is responsible for monitoring CO_2 emissions nationally. The government forestry management agency, Rosleskhoz, is responsible for monitoring forest sinks. The Ministry of Energy is responsible for decreasing emissions from the energy sector. A reorganization of the ministries in May 2008 generated uncertainty among ministerial officials about the division of responsibilities and the possible need for new legislation.[82] Nonetheless, the previously specified division of labor seems to persist, and the main consequence of frequent reorganization of ministries and personnel has been chronic delays in policy and project implementation.

Interests

In spite of environmentalists' pressure for Russia to maximally reduce greenhouse gas emissions, Russia's implementation of the Kyoto Protocol has focused more on the strategy of maximizing investment and technology transfer, although government action in this area has been less enthusiastic than anticipated. Optimism about carbon emissions trading decreased as the market effectively shrank following the US choice not to ratify. By many accounts European states are willing to purchase credits that are the result of documented, contemporary emissions reductions, but they will not purchase Russia's "hot air," or credits that are an artifact of industrial collapse.[83] Government officials from Japan, a ratifying state likely to need significant emissions credit purchases, have contracted to buy emissions credits from Hungary, the Czech Republic, and Ukraine in spite of environmentalists' criticism that they are buying "hot air."[84] In the past, Japanese officials have expressed concern about Russia's poor progress in developing an emissions accounting system.[85]

Many business and government actors, the strongest interest groups in Russia, emphasize Russia's opportunity to profit from the JI mechanism as well as from credits for improved forest management practices. Russia has the greatest potential scope for joint implementation of all participating states, although it is no longer ranked among the top three states as a host country for JI projects.[86] Both scientists and bureaucrats pointed out in interviews that the JI mechanism could be very profitable for Russia since it allows a double gain: improvement of industrial efficiency to reduce emissions and boost long-term economic growth is paid for by other state parties to the Protocol.

Several of Russia's largest firms, notably a few energy sector giants, are prepared to take advantage of JI projects. For example, during the summer of 2005, in one of the first JI agreements, United Energy System signed a memorandum of understanding with the Danish government to upgrade technology at two power plants, with an estimated 20 million euros in investment and a reduction in greenhouse gas emissions of 1.2 million metric tons to be purchased by DanishCarbon.[87] Gazprom, Rosneft, and their regional affiliates have also researched and participated in submission of greenhouse gas reduction projects to the JI Supervisory Committee, mostly aimed at reducing gas flaring at oil and gas refineries.[88] On the other hand, Gazprom has acquired a controlling stake in one of Russia's largest coal producers and is advocating the increased use of coal domestically in order to free up gas for export.[89] In its communications to the UNFCCC, the Russian government has estimated that in 2004 the energy sector accounted for more than 80 percent of all greenhouse gas emissions in Russia and so the behavior of these firms will play a significant role in how the Protocol is implemented in Russia.[90] In general, economic actors, now focused on the economic crisis and frequently dependent on good relations with state actors, do not appear to have influenced the government to speed up the domestic JI approval process.

Although the implementation of JI projects in Russia has been constrained by the government's slow construction of a legal framework, by mid-2008 all of the necessary policies were in place. In May 2007 Mikhail Fradkov, the prime minister, signed a government decree enumerating the requirements and procedures for the approval of JI projects in Russia, which made Russia eligible to approve JI projects directly at the domestic level (the so-called "Track 1" JI route).[91] This decree was replaced by another government decree in October 2009 which specified more concretely that Russia's largest bank, Sberbank, would be the executor and registrar of joint implementation and carbon credit sales transactions, while MERT would act more as a "coordinating center" for gathering expertise on projects on a competitive basis. Criteria for evaluating projects included the amount of CO_2 emissions reduction that would be achieved, how quickly, and the "economic and social effect" of the resulting reductions, as well as other formalities.[92] Encouragingly, the decree also specified very short timelines for the approval or rejection of proposed projects.

The Ministry for Economic Development began receiving applications for joint implementation projects in March 2008.[93] Gavrilov, the leading official on the Kyoto process at the ministry, warned that the government would take a strict approach toward JI projects and not aim to approve large numbers of them, commenting, "Our goal is to promote norms of ecological responsibility."[94] These statements have been variously interpreted as signaling Russia's lack of interest in developing its carbon market or as its desire to uphold high standards.

One unusual development is that for the 2008–2012 period, Russia capped its emissions trading at 300 million metric tons of carbon, each ton equaling one carbon credit (current values range from €11 to €17 on the global market), although Russian officials have discussed further lowering the limit.[95] Emission credits are divided by sector, with more than two-thirds assigned to the energy sector. Evaluations of these restrictions were mixed. Anna Korppoo and Arild Moe point to the potential for the government to withdraw its approval of JI projects at any point, noting, "The newly established regulations reflect a strong focus on controlling projects, rather than attracting them."[96] However, Kokorin argued that although progress has been slow, the Russian government has set up "a good procedure" for evaluating JI projects; in particular he praised the overall cap on emissions trading as a "tool against hot air" and the strict requirements for up-to-date technology in the JI approval process.[97]

As of January 2010, the Russian government had not approved any JI projects domestically. Frequent personnel reshuffling, the low priority given to climate change, and lingering ambivalence about the Kyoto Protocol have all been cited as reasons for the delay.[98] However, with the October 2009 decree that approves specific JI guidelines, there is every reason to believe that the first Track 1 JI projects are likely to be approved soon.

With the domestic approval process under construction, proposed JI projects in Russia so far have followed Track 2 JI procedures, in which approval is given by the UN JI Supervisory Committee. As of January 2010, 107 project design documents for JI projects in Russia had been officially submitted to the Supervisory Committee. Of those, as expected, the largest number of projects were aimed at reduction of fugitive emissions (thirty-seven) and at renewable/nonrenewable energy sources (forty-three).[99] In January 2010 Russia-based projects represented 55 percent of the total Track 2 projects proposed worldwide and 77 percent of total proposed annual emission reduction units (ERUs).[100] Nonetheless, the first Track 2 JI project that was implemented and received final verification of emissions reductions occurred not in Russia but in Ukraine, with Japan, the Netherlands, and Switzerland as partners.[101] Even with UN approval of Russia's Track 1 domestic JI process, Korppoo argues that Track 2 may remain popular because it "adds credibility to the environmental standard of the projects," partly because the JI Supervisory Committee is thought to deal with the question of additionality more effectively.[102] Track 2 also remains relevant because Track 1 projects are progressing so slowly.

The principle of additionality presents a challenge for JI project eligibility. Additionality demands that any measures taken to reduce greenhouse gas emissions are above and beyond those that would have taken place outside the incentives of Kyoto's flexibility mechanisms. Ascertaining exactly which projects generate "additional" reductions is difficult, however. For example, are projects to prevent leakage from gas pipelines "additional" if the gas conserved can be sold for a profit? The answer to this question is not straightforward, given the complexities of the gas ownership, distribution, and pricing in Russia.[103]

An alternative proposed mechanism, the Russian Green Investment Scheme (GIS), emerged as a result of the Russian government's commitment in 2000 to reinvest all of its profits from international emissions trade units (assigned amount units, or AAU) into further emission reductions.[104] Such a scheme, which would be developed in Russia rather than an official Kyoto flexibility mechanism, is designed to increase the marketability of Russia's "hot air" emissions credits by assuring skeptical Annex B governments that their expenditures are directed toward projects in Russia that generate real emissions reductions and are subject to external verification.[105] Helmut Schreiber of the World Bank argues that GIS has several advantages over a JI project-based approach because the approval process for JI projects is likely to be "very cumbersome."[106] Moreover, GIS projects, unlike JI, would not require the demonstration of additionality.[107] Even nonquantifiable emissions reduction projects, such as forest fire prevention programs—which would not qualify for JI—could fall under GIS applicability.[108] Moreover, one advantage, given Russia's late start in implementing mechanisms, is that emissions reduction credits accruing in the current Kyoto commitment period (2008–2012) could be implemented as actual emissions reductions in Russia stretching beyond 2012.[109] The development of a GIS program in Russia still requires significant planning and the resolution of a number of administrative, technical, and financing issues.[110] In January 2008 the World Bank and the Ministry for Economic Development began a joint study on Green Investment Schemes with the intention of clarifying how these projects could be implemented in Russia.

Several regional governments appear interested in using Kyoto mechanisms to attract investment.[111] For example, Arkhangelsk established an inventory system for greenhouse gas emissions from its energy sector in full compliance with requirements of the UN Intergovernmental Panel on Climate Change, and began experimenting with emissions reduction projects even prior to ratification.[112] In January 2008 Altai Krai held a conference on attracting investment from the international carbon market, emphasizing the potential for rehabilitating the forest sector.[113] In April 2008 the governor of Kirov Oblast signed a decree on implementing the Kyoto Protocol by promoting the use of gas and biodiesel.[114] The governments of Ulyanovsk and Omsk oblasts have committed to replanting forests as part of Russia's Kyoto implementation strategy.[115]

Russia is not preparing other measures that could facilitate greenhouse gas emissions reductions, such as a domestic emissions trading system or a carbon tax. An effective internal trading scheme would require a more detailed national inventory of emissions, tracking emissions not just at the national level but by firm. The NCU advocates a domestic emissions trading system, arguing that a functioning domestic market would facilitate Russian participation in the European ETS. A Ministry for Economic Development official, however, claims that this measure "is not even discussed."[116] A carbon tax is an unlikely measure due to the fact that Russia currently sells natural gas domestically at prices below that of the world market, although prices are to be liberalized by 2011, which should increase incentives for energy efficiency. Finally, investment in alternative sources of energy appears negligible, although Russian officials have expressed interest in devoting some of the country's unused farmland to the cultivation of biofuels.[117]

Conclusion

Whether the Kyoto Protocol will actually serve to limit Russia's greenhouse gas emissions depends on how the agreement is implemented, but Russian supporters of Kyoto hope that the treaty will serve as a catalyst—encouraging Russian industry to modernize and achieve greater energy efficiency. Domestic initiatives, such as President Medvedev's June 2008 decree on measures to reduce the economy's energy intensity to 40 percent of the 2007 level by 2020, and the legislation on energy efficiency, may indirectly support this goal.[118] Safonov asserts that Kyoto could resolve a number of economic, social, and environmental problems simultaneously. For example, reducing coal use to lower CO_2 emissions should also improve public health.[119] Pluzhnikov, of the Ministry for Economic Development, sees a benefit in what he terms the "Kyoto psychology," directing attention to critical economic and environmental tasks.[120] Aleksandr Ishkov, of the Ministry of Natural Resources, argues that Kyoto will help to modernize Russia's industry and energy sectors while providing an economic mechanism for solving Russia's ecological problems, including forest management.[121] Indeed, the Protocol may indirectly serve to strengthen Russia's weak environmental protection bodies.

Russia's decision to ratify the Protocol was not primarily driven by a sense of urgency about climate change prevention, either at the elite or mass level, but by its ability to achieve other desirable benefits from international partners and concern for its international image. President Putin thus acted to further Russia's material and reputational interests at the international level, taking into account multiple foreign policy objectives, as neoliberal institutionalists would predict. Russia's centralized political institutional context made it possible for the president to decide to ratify based on these foreign policy interests. However, this same decision-making context, which did not require buy-in from a wide range of actors involved in carbon emissions and which occurred in a context of frequent bureaucratic reorganization, did little to strengthen institutional capacity or expertise on climate change. This institutional context has slowed domestic implementation of the Protocol, has affected other actors' perceived interests related to the Protocol's flexibility mechanisms, and does not ensure Russia's future cooperation on climate change initiatives.

On the positive side, if Russia invests time and resources in implementing the Kyoto Protocol, it will have a greater interest in the continuation of the system. There are clear material and ideational benefits to Russia's role as a Kyoto ratifier and active implementer, not least the continued importance of Russia for the Protocol's success. Survey data suggest that, as in many countries, the public in Russia is becoming more concerned about the problem of climate change, although many citizens remain uninformed about the problem.

Russia's purely symbolic participation in the Kyoto Protocol and beyond could be detrimental in two ways, however. First, the clock is ticking on the 2008–2012 emissions reduction period, and those states that need to purchase carbon credits and invest in Russia through JI projects in order to meet their own binding targets will be in a difficult position if Russia fails to implement JI projects quickly following its late adoption of the necessary procedures. Second, if Russia does not comply in a serious fashion, it sets a worrisome precedent for the future participation of other large states attempting to develop their economies, including China, India, and Brazil.

These factors create uncertainty surrounding Russia's implementation and plans for the post-2012 Kyoto process. According to Russia's foreign minister, Sergei Lavrov, the government's current position is that Russia's participation after 2012 depends on "how we advance socially and economically, what our economic needs will be and what will be the positions of other emitters."[122] One month before the December 2009 United Nations climate change conference in Copenhagen, Prime Minister Putin announced that Russia would support a new agreement if two conditions were met: that all states representing a significant share of greenhouse gas emissions also sign, and that the role of Russia's forests as a carbon sink be taken into account.[123] While this stance may change during the course of negotiations, other observers agree that Russia is unlikely to accept a post-2012 agreement that would require real cuts in greenhouse gas emissions, especially if other states are not equally constrained. The financial crisis exacerbates Russia's desire to avoid any agreement that might disadvantage it economically.

Since ratification, Russia has taken some significant steps toward constructing a climate change policy, including compliance with the requirements of the Kyoto Protocol and the construction of a domestic apparatus, which allow for participation in Kyoto's flexibility mechanisms. Russia's new climate doctrine for the first time officially recognizes the role of human activity in contributing to climate change, and President Medvedev has now focused significant attention on energy efficiency. The government has restated its commitment to participate in international efforts to address and prevent climate change. However, the doctrine also employs the conceptual frame of national security to highlight Russia's adaptation to the effects of climate change. These developments provide further indication that, to the degree that Russia invests its attention as well as institutional and financial resources to climate change, it will pursue a policy strategy that emphasizes benefits to its own economic and geostrategic interests over the more specific goal of reducing greenhouse gas emissions.

Notes

1. Energy Information Administration 2008.

2. Kokeyev 2005. For text, see Article 3, Para. 6 of the text of the Kyoto Protocol.

3. Moe and Tangen 2000, 15.

4. Dudek et al. 2004, 132.

5. Victor et al. 2001.

6. WWF 2002.

7. Dudek et al. 2004.

8. Enserink 2004, 319.

9. Authors' interview with Aleksandr Kosarikov, deputy chair, Ecology Committee, Russian State Duma, Moscow, 5 July 2005; Kyoto Protocol to Destroy Russian Economy with Unnecessary Payments, Pravda.ru, 5 July 2005; Climate Change: Not a Global Threat, RIA Novosti, 23 June 2005.

10. Authors' interview with Natalia Olefirenko, climate project coordinator, Greenpeace Russia, Moscow, 13 July 2005; Karas 2004, 6.

11. Illarionov and Pivovarova 2004, 57; see also Institute of Economic Analysis 2004.

12. Labohm 2004.

13. Bobylev et al. 2004, 6–8.

14. Yulkin 2007, 153.

15. Golub et al. 2004, 26.

16. Lecocq and Shalizi 2004, 5–12.

17. Press Conference with Presidential Economic Adviser Andrei Illarionov, Interfax, 16 February 2005.

18. Wilson Rowe 2009.

19. Authors' interview with Aleksei Kokorin, coordinator, Climate Change Program, WWF Russia, Moscow, 29 June 2005; Greenpeace Russia, Kyoto Yes!, http://kyoto-da.org.ru/docs/kyoto.shtml (accessed 1 June 2005).

20. Authors' interview with Yuri Safonov, Moscow School of Higher Economics, Moscow, 14 July 2005.

21. Text available at http://www.environmentaldefense.org/subissue.cfm?subissue=13.

22. Fond "Obshchestvennoe Mnenie" 2005.

23. ROMIR, Facts and Figures, June 2005, http://www.rmh.ru/en/news/res_results/31.html (accessed 19 July 2006).

24. Molnin 2003. Note that this survey emphasized remote cities and urban villages, "rather than big cities where the level of information flow is higher" (Molnin 2003, 17), so the lack of public awareness shown in these statistics may be somewhat exaggerated.

25. Authors' interview with Vladimir Zakharov, director, Center for Russian Environmental Policy, Moscow, 28 June 2005.

26. Kokorin interview; Safonov interview.

27. RIA Novosti, 12 October 2004; transcript of interview with participants in the Social Forum on Climate Change, Radio Svoboda, 6 September 2003.

28. Olefirenko interview.

29. Authors' interview with Stepan Dudarev, Head, National Carbon Union, Moscow, 8 July 2005.

30. Dudarev interview.

31. Authors' interview with Oleg Pluzhnikov, Division of Environmental Economics, Russian Ministry for Economic Development and Trade, Moscow, 19 July 2005.

32. Authors' interview former senior bureaucrat from the Ministry of Energy, Moscow, 19 July 2005.

33. Karas 2004, 2–3; Olefirenko interview.

34. Karas 2004, 3.

35. Kosarikov interview.

36. Buchner and Dall'Olio 2005, 354.

37. Reuters, 4 June 2003.

38. Corwin 2004.

39. ITAR-TASS, 11 April 2002; RIA Novosti, 3 September 2002.

40. Environmental Defense Fund 2003.

41. "Counter-attack on Greenhouse Gases," *Izvestiia Science*, 3 October 2003; Putin Refuses to Say if Russia Will Ratify Kyoto Protocol, *The Independent* (London), 30 September 2003.

42. Korppoo et al. 2006, 15.

43. Mirrlees-Black et al. 2004, as cited in Korppoo et al. 2006.

44. Danilov-Danilian 2004.

45. Agence France Presse, 29 September 2003.

46. Kokorin interview.

47. Ibid.

48. Safonov interview.

49. Zakharov interview; Kosarikov interview; Dudarev interview.

50. *Russia Journal*, 5 October 2004.

51. *Radio Svoboda*, 6 September 2003.

52. Kosarikov interview.

53. *Christian Science Monitor*, 5 December 2003; BBC online, 30 September 2004; Pravda.ru, 30 September 2004, 9 February 2005; *Business Week*, 1 October 2004.

54. *Moscow Times*, 20 May 2004.

55. "Russia Traded WTO for Kyoto," *Izvestiia*, 21 May 2004.

56. Authors' interview with Alexander Golub, senior economist, Environmental Defense Fund, Washington, DC, 2 September 2005.

57. Kotov 2004, 165.

58. Wilson Rowe 2009, 607.

59. Kokorin interview.

60. Safonov interview.

61. Yulkin 2007, 152.

62. President of Russia 2009.

63. COP 15 Web site, http://en.cop15.dk/news/view+news?newsid=1373 (accessed 27 May 2009); Nature News Web site, http://www.nature.com/news/2009/090526/full/news.2009.506.html?s=news_rss (accessed 26 May 2009).

64. Bellona 2009.

65. "Federal'nyi zakon Rossiiskoi Federatsii ot 23 noiabria 2009 g. N 261-F3 'Ob energosberezhenii i o povyshenii energeticheskoi effektivnosti i o vnesenii izmenenii v otdel'nye zakonodatel'nye akty Rossiiskoi Federatsii'" [Federal Law of the Russian Federation, 23 November 2009, N 261-F3 "On Energy Savings and on Increasing Energy Efficiency and on Amendments to Various Legislative Acts of the Russian Federation"], *Rossiiskaia gazeta*, 27 November 2009.

66. Ibid.

67. UNFCCC, Summary of GHG Emissions for Russian Federation, http://unfccc.int/files/ghg_emissions_data/application/pdf/rus_ghg_profile.pdf (accessed 3 November 2009).

68. Kotov and Nikitina 2003, 9.

69. Korppoo 2004; Webster 2002.

70. Aleksei Kokorin, personal communication, 20 May 2008.

71. *Reuters*, 28 April 2008.

72. GlobeScan Incorporated 2006. Both polls used samples of 1,000 respondents nationwide.

73. BBC World Service 2007. The poll used a sample of 1,034 respondents nationwide.

74. Kokorin communication.

75. Kokorin communication.

76. Oleg Pluzhnikov, interview in RIA-Novosti, 4 August 2008.

77. Honneland and Jorgensen 2002.

78. Olefirenko interview.

79. Yamin and Depledge 2004, 148–156.

80. Authors' interview with Aleksandr Ishkov, director, State Environmental Policy Department, Ministry of Natural Resources, Moscow, 18 July 2005.

81. MERT 2005.

82. Oleg Pluzhnikov, personal communication, 30 May 2008.

83. Golub et al. 2004, 29; Lecocq and Shalizi 2004, 17–18.

84. Maeda 2009; Carr and Tomek 2009; http://www.bloomberg.com/apps/ news?pid=20601101&sid=a_9z0ESfhSL0&refer=japan; http://www.carbonoff setsdaily.com/news-channels/asia/czechs-sell-20-million-carbon-credits-to -japan-16121.htm.

85. Turner and Buckley 2006; Korppoo 2007.

86. *Point Carbon*, 15 June 2009, www.pointcarbon.com.

87. DanishCarbon press release, http://www.mst.dk/transportuk/01070100.htm (accessed 1 August 2005).

88. Gazprom 2006; JI Project Design Documents, http://ji.unfccc.int/JI_Projects/ DeterAndVerif/Verification/PDD/index.html (accessed 16 June 2009).

89. Kramer 2008; Safonov and Rechel 2007, 129.

90. Russian Federation, Progress Report, 13 February 2007, http://unfccc.int/ national_reports/annex_i_natcom/submitted_natcom/items/3625.php.

91. Resolution of the of the Russian Federation Government from 28 May 2007, No. 332; Enforcement Branch of the Compliance Committee of the Kyoto Protocol, http://unfccc.int/files/kyoto_mechanisms/compliance/enforcement_branch/ application/pdf/eligibility_list_20_june_2008.pdf (accessed 25 June 2008).

92. Government of the Russian Federation, Polozhenie o realizatsii stat'i 6 Kiotskogo protokola k Ramochnoi konventsii OON ob izmenenii klimata [Decree on Implementation of Article 6 of the Kyoto Protocol to the UN Framework Convention on Climate Change], 28 October 2009, http://www .government.ru/content/governmentactivity/rfgovernmentdecisions/archive/2009 /10/28/7498133.htm (accessed 2 November 2009).

93. Elder 2008.

94. Shuster 2008.

95. *Carbon Finance*, 30 January 2008, http://www.carbon-financeonline.com/ index.cfm?section=lead&action=view&id=10994 (accessed 1 June 2008); "Kyoto Projects Face Tough Framework," *Moscow Times*, 7 October 2009, http://www .themoscowtimes.com/article/386856.html (accessed 3 November 2009).

96. Korppoo and Moe 2007, 6.

97. Aleksei Kokorin, personal communication, 20 May 2008. See also WWF Russia, Bulletin, Spring 2007, http://www.wwf.ru/eng/.

98. "Russia JI Remains in Limbo amid Bureaucratic Shake-up," 2 June 2009, www.pointcarbon.com.

99. UNFCCC JISC, http://ji.unfccc.int/JI_Projects/DeterAndVerif/Verification/ PDD/index.html (accessed 11 November 2008). Note that the sectoral totals exceed the total number of projects as any single project may fall within multiple sectoral scopes.

100. UNFCCC JISC, http://ji.unfccc.int/JI_Projects/DeterAndVerif/Verification/ PDD/index.html; UNEP Risoe Centre 2010.

101. UNFCCC Joint Implementation, http://ji.unfccc.int/index.html (accessed 10 June 2009).

102. Korppoo 2007, 2.

103. Korppoo and Moe 2008.

104. Korppoo and Lyanguzova 2007, 104.

105. Tangen et al. 2002.

106. Authors' interview with Helmut Schreiber, Lead Environmental Economist, World Bank, Moscow office, 15 July 2005.

107. Mehling 2007, 54.

108. Korppoo and Lyanguzova 2007, 117.

109. Ibid., 105.

110. Ibid., 109–116.

111. Kotov and Nikitina 2003, 17.

112. Yulkin 2007, 158; Pravda.ru, 16 February 2005.

113. Atmosfera Informatsionnoe Agestvo, 14 January 2008, http://asfera.info/ news/one-10892.html (accessed 26 June 2008).

114. "Production of Biofuel Must Be Developed in Kirov Region —Governor," *Regnum*, 29 April 2008, http://www.regnum.ru/news/993650.html (accessed 22 June 2008).

115. *Regnum*, 27 March 2007, http://www.regnum.ru/news/803106.html (accessed 10 October 2007); http://www.regnum.ru/news/904554.html (accessed 28 May 2008); http://www.regnum.ru/news/1006839.html (accessed 26 June 2008).

116. National Carbon Union Analytical Materials, http://www.natcarbon.ru/en/ analytical/system/; Pluzhnikov communication.

117. RFE/RL, 13 March 2008; BioPact, http://biopact.com/2007/10/putin -encourages-farmers-to-produce.html.

118. Presidential decree no. 899, 4 June 2008, http://document.kremlin.ru/doc .asp?ID=046255 (accessed 20 June 2008).

119. Safonov interview.

120. Pluzhnikov interview.

121. Ishkov interview.

122. "Russia Not Saying Whether It Will Sign Treaty Replacing Kyoto Protocol After 2012," Interfax, 25 January 2008, available in Johnson's Russia List (JRL) 2008, #19. For similar comments from MERT officials, see "Russia to Support Kyoto Obligations after 2012 if Growth Not Hindered," Interfax, 7 December 2007, available in JRL 2007, no. 253.

123. Korsunskaya 2009.

References

BBC World Service. 2007. All Countries Need to Take Major Steps on Climate Change: Global Poll, 24 September. http://www.worldpublicopinion.org/pipa/articles/btenvironmentra/412.php?nid=&id=&pnt=412 (accessed 19 June 2008).

Bellona. 2009. Update: Russian Government Reviews Doctrine on Climate Change, Prompting Cheers and Jeers. http://www.bellona.org/articles/articles _2009/climate_doctrine (accessed 8 May 2009).

Bobylev, S. N., et al. 2004. *Kommentarii k stat'e Instituta ekonomicheskogo analiza "Ekonomicheskie posledstviia vozmozhnoi ratifikatsii Rossiiskoi Federatsii Kiotskogo protokola"* [Commentary to the Article of the Institute for Economic Analysis "Economic Consequences of the Russian Federation's Potential Ratification of the Kyoto Protocol"] . Moscow: Social Forum on Climate Change, Center for Russian Ecological Policy, and Environmental Defense.

Buchner, Barbara, and Silvia Dall'Olio. 2005. Russia and the Kyoto Protocol: The Long Road to Ratification. *Transition Studies Review* 12:349–382.

Carr, Mathew, and Radoslav Tomek. 2009. Japan Denies Buying "Hot Air" to Meet Kyoto Target. Bloomberg, 23 July. http://www.bloomberg.com/apps/news?pid=20601101&sid=auYplIVXDnYY (accessed 4 November 2009).

Corwin, Julie A. 2004. House of Lords or House of Valets? *RFE/RL Reports*, 16 August. http://www.rferl.org/reports/rpw/2004/08/31-160804.asp (accessed 13 February 2006).

Danilov-Danilian, Victor. 2004. What Can Russia Expect from the Kyoto Protocol? *Towards a Sustainable Russia* 27:11–13.

Dudek, D., A. Golub, and E. Strukova. 2004. Economics of the Kyoto Protocol for Russia. *Climate Policy* 4:129–142.

Elder, Miriam. 2008. Carbon Credits Get Cool Reception. *Moscow Times*, 25 March.

Energy Information Administration. US Government. 2008. Russia. http://www.eia.doe.gov/cabs/Russia/Background.html (accessed May 2008).

Enserink, Martin. 2004. Moscow Meeting Bogged Down in Acrimony. *Science* 305:319.

Environmental Defense Fund. 2003. Social Forum Urges Putin to Ratify Kyoto Protocol, 8 October. http://www.environmentaldefense.org/article.cfm?contentid=3066 (accessed 2 February 2006).

Fond "Obshchestvennoe Mnenie." 2005. Deistviia po zashchite okruzhaiushchei sredi [Activities for Environmental Protection], 7 July. http://bd.fom.ru/report/map/tb052711 (accessed 11 July 2006).

Gazprom. 2006. Environmental Report 2006. http://www.gazprom.com/documents/Ecology_Eng.pdf (accessed 25 June 2008).

GlobeScan Incorporated. 2006. 30-Country Poll Finds Worldwide Consensus that Climate Change Is a Serious Problem, April 24. http://www.globescan.com/news_archives/csr_climatechange.html (accessed 30 January 2007).

Golub, A., et al. 2004. *The Dangers of Climate Change and the Benefits for the Russian Federation of Participating in the Kyoto Protocol: A Paper Examining Questions of the Science and Economics of Climate Change.* Moscow: Environmental Defense.

Honneland, Geir, and Anne-Kristin Jorgensen. 2002. Implementing Russia's International Environmental Commitments: Federal Prerogative or Regional Concern? *Europe-Asia Studies* 54:1223–1240.

Illarionov, A., and N. Pivovarova. 2004. Ekonomicheskie posledstviia ratifikatsii Rossiisko Federatsii Kiotskogo protokola [Economic Consequences of the Russian Federation's Ratification of the Kyoto Protocol]. *Voprosy ekonomiki* 11:34–59.

Institute of Economic Analysis. 2004. Ekonomicheskie posledstviia vozmozhnoi ratifikatsii Rossiiskoi Federatsii Kiotskogo protokola [Economic Consequences of the Russian Federation's Potential Ratification of the Kyoto Protocol]. Moscow: Institute of Economic Analysis. http://www.iea.ru/text/prognoz.pdf (accessed 22 February 2006).

Karas, Jacqueline. 2004. Russia and the Kyoto Protocol: Political Challenges. Briefing note, March. London: Royal Institute of International Affairs Sustainability Programme.

Kokeyev, Mikhail. 2005. Kyoto: Saving the Polar Bears. *International Affairs* 51:118–125.

Korppoo, Anna. 2004. Russia and Compliance under Kyoto: An Institutional Approach. Chatham House Sustainable Development Programme Briefing Note SDP BN 4/01 (December). https://www.riia.org/index.php?id=175 (accessed 16 February 2006).

Korppoo, Anna. 2007. Joint Implementation in Russia and Ukraine: Review of Projects Submitted to JISC. *Climate Strategies*, October.

Korppoo, Anna, Jacqueline Karas, and Michael Grubb, eds. 2006. *Russia and the Kyoto Protocol: Opportunities and Challenges.* London: Chatham House.

Korppoo, Anna, and Irina Lyanguzova. 2007. Russian Green Investment Schemes: A Background and Practical Examples. In *Implementing the Kyoto Protocol— Chances and Challenges for Transition Countries*, 103–121. Proceedings of the Summer Academy "Energy and the Environment," Irkutsk, 21–27 August 2005.

Korppoo, Anna, and Arild Moe. 2007. Russian JI Procedures: More Problems than Solutions? Climate Strategies Briefing Paper, June 2007, http://www.climatestrategies.org/reportfiles/russian_ji_procedures.pdf.

Korppoo, Anna, and Arild Moe. 2008. Russian Gas Pipeline Projects under Track 2: Case Study of the Dominant Project Type. Climate Strategies Briefing Paper, March 2008, http://www.climatestrategies.org/reportfiles/gas_paper_final.pdf.

Korsunskaya, Darya. 2009. Putin Sees Climate Deal, but with Conditions. Reuters, 2 November. http://www.reuters.com/article/internal_ReutersNewsRoom

_BehindTheScenes_MOLT/idUSTRE5A14LQ20091102 (accessed 3 November 2009).

Kotov, Vladimir. 2004. The EU-Russia Ratification Deal: The Risks and Advantages of an Informal Agreement. *International Review for Environmental Strategies* 5 (1):157–166.

Kotov, Vladimir, and Elena Nikitina. 2003. National Framework for GHG Emission Trading in Russia. Paper presented at the OECD Global Forum on Sustainable Development: Emissions Trading and Concerted Action on Tradeable Emissions Permits (CATEP) Country Forum, Paris, 17–18 March.

Kramer, Andrew E. 2008. Gazprom Moves into Coal as a Way to Increase Gas Exports. *New York Times*, 27 February.

Labohm, Hans. 2004. Russia's Vacillations on Kyoto. *Tech Central Station*, 26 May. http://www.techcentralstation.com/052604B.html (accessed 27 January 2004).

Lecocq, Franck, and Zmarak Shalizi. 2004. World Bank Development Economics Working Group. Will the Kyoto Protocol Affect Growth in Russia? World Bank Policy Research Working Paper 3454, November.

Maeda, Risa. 2009. Japan buys CO2 rights from Ukraine. Reuters, 18 March. http://www.reuters.com/article/GCA-BusinessofGreen/idUSTRE52H4C620090318 (accessed 3 November 2009).

Mehling, Michael A. 2007. The Flexible Mechanisms of the Kyoto Protocol: An Overview. In *Implementing the Kyoto Protocol—Chances and Challenges for Transition Countries*, 49–57. Proceedings of the Summer Academy "Energy and the Environment," Irkutsk, 21–27 August 2005.

Ministry for Economic Development and Trade (MERT). Government of Russia. 2005. Kompleksnyi plan deistvii po realizatsii v Rossiiskoi Federatsii Kiotskogo protokola k ramochnoi Konventsii OON ob izmenenii klimata [Integrated Action Plan for Implementation by the Russian Federation of the Kyoto Protocol to the UN Framework Convention on Climate Change]. http://www.climatechange.ru/russia/actionplan.htm (accessed 8 February 2006).

Mirrlees-Black, J., N. Nov i, M. Grubb, A. Korppoo, and D. Newberry. 2004. *Costs and Benefits to the Russian Federation of the Kyoto Protocol*. London: Cambridge Economic Policy Associates.

Moe, Arild, and Kristian Tangen. 2000. *The Kyoto Mechanisms and Russian Climate Politics*. London: Royal Institute of International Affairs.

Molnin, A. 2003. What Do the Russians Know about Environmental Problems? *Towards a Sustainable Russia* (Center for Russian Environmental Policy, Moscow) 24:17–18.

President of Russia. 2009. Official Web Portal. Climate Doctrine of the Russian Federation (17 December). http://eng.kremlin.ru/text/docs/2009/12/223509.shtml (accessed 19 January 2010).

Safonov, Yuri, and Janine Rechel. 2007. Emissions Trading & Joint Implementation: An Economic Assessment of the Implementation Strategy from the Russian

Viewpoint. In *Implementing the Kyoto Protocol—Chances and Challenges for Transition Countries*, 123–135. Proceedings of the Summer Academy "Energy and the Environment," Irkutsk, 21–27 August 2005.

Shuster, Simon. 2008. Russia Takes "Rejection" Stance on Kyoto Projects. Reuters, 13 March. http://www.reuters.com/article/environmentNews/idUSL1384390720080313 (accessed 3 November 2009).

Tangen, Kristian, Anna Korppoo, Vladimir Berdin, Taishi Sugiyama, Christian Egenhofer, John Drexhage, Oleg Pluzhnikov, et al. 2002. *A Russian Green Investment Scheme: Securing Environmental Benefits from International Emissions Trading*. Climate Strategies.

Turner, David, and Neil Buckley. 2006. Japan Looks at Emissions Trading with Ukraine. *Financial Times* (Asia edition), 28 June. http://www.ft.com/cms/s/0/e63d427a-0641-11db-9dde-0000779e2340.html?nclick_check=1 (accessed 3 November 2009).

UNEP Risoe Centre. 2008. JI Pipeline Overview. http://cdmpipeline.org/ (accessed 11 November 2008).

Victor, David, Nebojša Nakićenović, and Nadejda Victor. 2001. The Kyoto Protocol Emission Allocations: Windfall Surpluses for Russia and Ukraine. *Climatic Change* 49:263–277.

Webster, Paul. 2002. Russia Can Save Kyoto, if It Can Do the Math. *Science* 296:2129–2130.

Wilson Rowe, Elana. 2009. Who Is to Blame? Agency, Causality, Responsibility and the Role of Experts in Russian Framings of Global Climate Change. *Europe-Asia Studies* 61:593–619.

WWF. 2002. WWF Welcomes Russian Government's Decision to Start the Process of Ratifying the Kyoto Climate Treaty. WWF press release, 11 April. http://www.climnet.org/EUenergy/ratification/russia.htm (accessed 9 February 2006).

Yamin, Farhana, and Joanna Depledge. 2004. *The International Climate Change Regime: A Guide to Rules, Institutions and Procedures*. Cambridge: Cambridge University Press.

Yulkin, M. A. 2007. Russia and the Kyoto Protocol: How to Meet the Challenges and Not to Miss the Challenges. In *Implementing the Kyoto Protocol—Chances and Challenges for Transition Countries*, 137–165. Proceedings of the Summer Academy "Energy and the Environment," Irkutsk, 21–27 August 2005.

5

Climate Leadership, Japanese Style: Embedded Symbolism and Post-2001 Kyoto Protocol Politics

Yves Tiberghien and Miranda A. Schreurs

Introduction

After the Bush administration pulled the United States out of the Kyoto Protocol in March 2001, Japan found itself the pivotal actor in the global battle over the survival of the treaty. With the United States out of Kyoto, the costs of ratification rose significantly. Japan would be expected to take painful and costly measures to reduce its greenhouse gas emissions without US industries and the public having to take similar steps. This threatened to place Japan at a competitive disadvantage with the United States and with developing countries, which were exempted from taking action under the agreement. For numerous industries, this was seen as making what was already a tough set of requirements even more unpalatable. As a result, they pressured politicians and bureaucrats to do something to ensure that they would not have to bear unacceptably high costs. This meant getting the United States to return to the agreement, abandoning the agreement, or reducing its potential impact on industry and thus on the economy as a whole.

Still, many interests within the government—especially the Ministry of Environment (MOE) and the Ministry of Foreign Affairs (MOFA)—and some industries (for example, the nuclear, insurance, and pollution control industries) had a strong interest in seeing the agreement enter into force.[1] Perhaps even more importantly, the Japanese public was largely behind the Kyoto Protocol. As one indication, the Japanese Consumer Cooperative Union, representing over 500 university, housing, medical, insurance, and retail unions and a combined membership of over 20 million urged early ratification of the agreement.[2] Many environmental nongovernmental organizations (NGOs) also called for ratification.

As a result of these competing perspectives, there was substantial political and bureaucratic debate on how to approach ratification.

Because of the global impact of Japan's decision, international diplomacy intensified. The stakes were very high for Japan's environmental and global foreign policy. Under the international spotlight, Japan was forced to take a stance. Japan did so, ratifying the Kyoto Protocol in June 2002. Six years later, as host to the G8 meeting in Toyako, Hokkaido, Prime Minister Yasuo Fukuda announced that Japan would pursue 60–80 percent cuts in emissions by 2050 under its Cool Earth Initiative.[3] In September 2009, Yukio Hatoyama, Japan's first prime minister from the Democratic Party of Japan (DPJ), announced that his government planned to pursue a 25 percent reduction goal for greenhouse gases relative to their 1990 levels by 2020.

This chapter asks two main sets of questions. First, given the power of anti-Kyoto interests and bureaucratic actors, why did the Japanese government ratify the Kyoto Protocol? In the US case, anti-Kyoto forces were able to prevent ratification. Why did the same kind of politics not play out in Japan? The balance of interest group politics, bureaucratic politics, and foreign policy priorities certainly could have led to the agreement's collapse. With an anti-Kyoto coalition including powerful elements within Keidanren (the Japan Federation of Economic Organizations), the Ministry of International Trade and Industry (MITI, renamed the Ministry of Economy, Trade, and Industry [METI] in 2001), and the ruling Liberal Democratic Party (LDP), and a prime minister (Jun'ichiro Koizumi) who was committed to strengthening US-Japan relations, it is certainly not inconceivable that Japan would have sided with the United States. After all, the proponents of the agreement were led by a weak MOE, a poorly developed EU partnership, underresourced NGOs, and an opposition party with no hope of winning the upper house elections of July 2001. And while the proponents also had supporters within the LDP, several of the strongest advocates had failed to win reelection in the previous lower house election (for example, Kazuo Aichi and Takashi Kosugi).

Japan's decision to ratify cannot be explained by the balance of interests, bureaucratic positions, electoral politics, or foreign relations alone. Another key factor was necessary to tilt the outcome in the favor of the pro-Kyoto coalition. The decision of earlier LDP leaders to pursue global environmental leadership, reinforced through discourse and bureaucratic actions, helped to build the Kyoto Protocol into a symbol of Japan's new policy identity. In other words, *embedded symbolism* constrained the ability of anti-Kyoto forces to get their concerns onto the political agenda and limited the freedom of action of political leaders in the wake of the

US withdrawal. The rallying effect of Kyoto essentially trumped the decision in favor of ratification. It allowed weaker actors to mobilize in the name of this national symbol, much as they had done at several earlier junctures when Japan's commitment to addressing global warming had come into question. Had the international agreement instead born the name of a city outside Japan, it is not at all certain that Japan's policy leaders would have chosen to side with the EU rather than the United States.

Second, why in June 2008 did Prime Minister Fukuda commit his country to emission cuts of 60–80 percent over the next forty years when the country has had so much trouble reducing its greenhouse gas emissions over the past decade? As of 2007, Japan's emissions were 6.4 percent above 1990 levels. And why did Prime Minister Hatoyama put his new government on a limb with a 25 percent greenhouse gas emission reduction goal for 2020 when his predecessor Taro Aso had pledged the country to far less? At the time Hatoyama made his announcement, the US administration under Barack Obama had yet to send any concrete signal on US intentions. Is Japan reemerging as a climate policy leader?

This chapter shows that embedded symbolism was primarily at work in the debate over ratification of the Kyoto Protocol and continues to play a role as Japan positions itself in international negotiations on a post-Kyoto successor agreement. Had this variable not been present, the balance of interest group politics and institutional politics would have pointed toward nonratification, especially given US opposition to the Kyoto Protocol. Japan's efforts to establish itself as a leader on climate change issues in the international negotiations on a post-Kyoto agreement can also be tied to the importance of Kyoto symbolism, although pending changes in US policy direction after the 2008 presidential election and growing public concern with climate change are certainly important factors as well.

It is also important to ask whether Japan's ratification of the Kyoto Protocol, its call for a 60–80 percent reduction target for 2050, and the 25 percent emission reduction goal for 2020 introduced by the DPJ really signify a break with the past, the shift toward a new economic and industrial paradigm, and Japan's embrace of an international climate leadership role. To answer this question, it is important to separate ratification and agenda setting from implementation. For Japan, the decision to ratify was basically a choice between joining the EU or siding with the United States. It was also a highly visible decision that would influence Japan's reputation and relationships with multiple audiences. Thus in many ways Japan's decision was a major one since failure to ratify would have signaled the death of the Kyoto Protocol. The 60–80 percent reduction target for 2050 proposed by Prime Minister Fukuda was a signal that Japan remained engaged but that there was a struggle between different coalitions of actors as to what kind of policies should be introduced beyond the Kyoto Protocol. Had there been a greater consensus within the LDP behind the need for dramatic and quick action, Fukuda could have made a bolder announcement, but many within the party were too closely tied to strong industrial interests, including the utilities and heavily energy-intensive industries, that were critical of Japan taking on stringent targets. The window of opportunity for change came after the election of 30 August 2009 that swept the LDP and its entrenched governance networks aside and brought to power the centrist DPJ in a coalition with two junior parties. In September 2009, new prime minister Hatoyama made a public pledge at the United Nations' annual meeting to cut Japan's emissions by 25 percent from 1990 levels by 2020, on the condition that major players such as the US and China also make important commitments. This target represents a major break with his LDP predecessor, Taro Aso, who had presented a far less ambitious target of a 15 percent reduction of 2005 greenhouse gas levels by 2020 (which equates to 8 percent below 1990 levels).

It is typically in relation to questions of implementation that the real differences in interests among actors tend to show up. While some of these battles occur within and among bureaucratic offices and are quite technical and hidden from the public eye, others go to more fundamental questions as to the nature of policies that should be introduced and where the heaviest burdens should lie. Should there be greater reliance on nuclear energy? Should a mandatory carbon emissions trading system be put in place? Should carbon taxes be introduced? As discussed below, Japan has introduced many new policy measures to meet its Kyoto Protocol target, but most have focused on voluntary measures. The outcome has been a middle-of-the-road soft implementation that positions Japan in between the EU approach (focused on mandatory emissions trading) and the Canadian approach (no effective measures). Japan has passed numerous laws and packages to encourage energy efficiency, tighten industrial standards, and spread best practices. Yet to date Japan has decided against establishing a carbon tax, introducing summer time (daylight saving time), or imposing a mandatory carbon emissions market. There is a heavy reliance on using carbon sinks, Kyoto flexibility mechanisms, and a new energy policy, although the latter partially depends on the construction of new nuclear plants.

Signaling its intentions to break with the past, the Hatoyama government plans to pursue new policies and measures to meet its ambitious reduction goals. The party is also changing how business is done, distancing itself from Keidanren and even from the bureaucracy that had worked so closely for so many decades with the LDP. The DPJ, moreover, has relatively strong links to environmental NGOs (personified by Foreign Minister Katsuya Okada's and Vice Foreign Minister Tetsuro Fukuyama's close NGO ties).

The remainder of this chapter proceeds in four steps. The first section examines how interests, institutions, and ideas affected decision making, underscoring the limitations of an analysis purely rooted in interests and institutions. The next section looks at ideas and embedded symbols. Building on the agenda-setting literature, it offers a theory of constrained policymaking in the face of an established political symbol. It also presents a political framework for the constitution of such symbols. The third section analyzes the empirical sequence leading to ratification. The final section contrasts ratification with the messier and less symbolic politics of implementation.

Interests, Institutions, and Ideas

Several plausible explanations can be given for Japan's ratification of Kyoto and the country's continued cultivation of its image as a climate change leader. These explanations are embedded in an understanding of interests, institutions, and ideas.

Interests: Japanese Industry, the Ratification of Kyoto, and Japan's Post-Kyoto Target

Japan is well known for the power of its business interests (*zaikai*). The existence of a powerful business organization, Keidanren, and the powerful MITI/METI enhanced the voice of industry in the policymaking process during the long rule of the LDP (1955–2009, with only a short period of less than one year in opposition in 1993). Industrial interests were expressed through different routes: direct public voice, policy inputs through government councils (*shingikai*), and lobbying of politicians in the conservative governing party.

Keidanren represents about four-fifths of Japanese manufacturers. In 1997, in the months leading up to the Kyoto conference, Keidanren issued a Voluntary Action Plan for the Environment, which called upon its members to voluntarily cut back their greenhouse gas and other emissions. At its start, thirty-six industries, representing 137 organizations agreed to develop plans to reduce their environmental footprint. In the area of climate change, this led to many corporations developing voluntary targets and timetables for greenhouse gas emissions reductions.[4] Keidanren pursued voluntary actions in the hope of avoiding governmental regulations.

Ever since the formation of the Kyoto Protocol, Japanese industry has shared the concerns of many US industries that developing countries were not obliged to take any measures to limit their own greenhouse gas emissions. As long as the United States was in Kyoto, Japanese industry was somewhat shielded from the competitive pressures that the agreement placed on them. But once the United States pulled out, many industries became nervous that something more than the voluntary measures they had already committed to would be required: momentum against Kyoto emerged.[5]

Industry, moreover, had been expressing concern about the cost and fairness to Japan of the Kyoto Protocol ever since its formulation. The widely held view was that Japan, with its relatively high energy efficiency levels, was being asked to carry a heavier burden than other countries.

In fact, Japan committed itself to a costly bargain by ratifying Kyoto. In 2002, Japan's CO_2 emissions were up 7.5 percent from 1990, meaning that emission cuts of 13.5 percent of 2002 levels would be necessary in a mere eight years, although the government evaluated the real gap as being closer to only 12.0 percent (+6 percent from 1990), given that temporary shutdowns in the nuclear sector had driven emissions up in the previous years.[6]

It was clear to political and business leaders that making further cuts would not be easy. Armed with this knowledge, Japanese industry issued strong words of warning regarding the implications of Kyoto ratification in the absence of participation by the United States and developing countries.[7] In 2005, when the Kyoto Protocol was coming into force, those ideas had not changed. Nobuo Yamaguchi, chairman of Japan's Chamber of Commerce and Industry, criticized the government for its "diplomatic failure" in allowing the United States to withdraw from the agreement, putting Japan at a serious disadvantage vis-à-vis Europe.[8]

Yet industry was not able to speak in a single voice. In July 2001 the head of Keidanren, Takashi Imai, made his opinion clear that Japan could not afford to stay in Kyoto if the United States stayed out.[9] But at the same time, the chairman of the Japan Federation of Employers' Association (Nippon Keidanren) expressed the position that global climate change was a problem the industrialized world needed to tackle and that therefore, the decision to ratify the bill was one that should be respected. The representative of the Japan Association of Corporate Executives (Keizai Doyukai) suggested that ratification was a positive step. The differences in these unions' positions largely reflected the industries they represented and the extent to which each depended on fossil fuels. Energy utilities and manufacturers that used large amounts of energy were concerned about what Kyoto's ratification would mean for their international competitiveness. In contrast, the nuclear industry saw in Kyoto a vehicle to justify the building of more nuclear power plants.[10] The service industry and manufacturers of consumer goods had an interest in presenting an environmentally progressive image to consumers. They were also eager to prevent boycotts of their products by environmentally conscious consumers in Japan and Europe as had already started to occur against some US companies.[11]

Because of these divisions, Keidanren did not launch an all-out fight against ratification despite its strong reservations. Instead, it focused on two points: making sure that (1) diplomats worked on developing a framework that the United States and developing countries could eventually become a part of, and (2) industry not be expected to carry the bulk of the responsibility of bringing down emissions.

Japanese industry was also not unified in its opposition to adopting post-Kyoto commitments. Thus, during the last years of the LDP's time in power, each of Japan's many, short-lived prime ministers made some form of climate commitment. In May 2007, Prime Minister Abe announced a 50 percent reduction goal for global emissions for 2050 as part of his Cool Earth 50 program. Prime Minister Fukuda upped the goal to a 60 to 80 percent reduction by 2050 in June 2007. Two years later, Prime Minister Aso introduced a medium-term goal of 15 percent below 2005 levels by 2020. None of these goals, however, came close to the European Union's 20 percent emission reduction goal for 2020 relative to 1990 levels announced in March 2007. The LDP was too closely tied to industry to follow the EU's lead. The DPJ's September 2009 pronouncement of a far more ambitious 25 percent emission reduction target below 1990 levels for 2020 represents a dramatic change and suggests that the influence of big business is at a postwar low.

Changing Political Economic Interests as a Counterpoint

Another possible explanation for Japan's decision to ratify the Kyoto Protocol lies with Japan's foreign economic and political interests. There is certainly awareness in Japan that success in the European market can be enhanced by a strong environmental positioning (both in terms of image and technology). Moreover, Japan has shown a growing willingness to show independence from US foreign policy decisions, especially in relation to various environmental treaties.[12] While the empirical record shows that Japanese policymaking is becoming increasingly independent of the United States, and Japan has sided more frequently with the EU on various foreign policy matters, with both the EU and the United States lobbying Japan, it is difficult to imagine that the EU pull would have been strong enough on its own to persuade Koizumi to choose ratification, given that so many Japanese industries were complaining that the agreement would put Japan at a disadvantage with Europe. Other factors need to be considered.

Counterbalancing Interests: The Rise of Environmental NGOs and the Role of the Media

Nongovernmental organizations concerned with such issues as environment, natural disasters, and human rights have been on the rise since the early 1990s.[13] The 1995 Hanshin earthquake, global climate change, and Japan's expanded overseas development assistance programs have ushered in a new era of (at least limited) cooperation between NGOs and government.[14] Breaking with the past confrontational relationship, at least some elements within the government—most notably the Ministry of the Environment and the Foreign Ministry—have come to accept NGOs as credible partners, information providers, and links to the public. NGOs, in turn, have developed greater expertise and ability to contribute in substantive (as opposed to simply ideological) ways to policy formulation. NGOs' growing access to policymaking through involvement in summits, ministerial councils, and Diet testimonies represents a degree of transformation in Japan's environmental policymaking. One former NGO representative, Tetsuro Fukuyama, who participated as a member of Kiko Forum '97 in the run-up to the Kyoto conference, later became a member of the House of Councilors. He maintains a strong link to environmental NGOs.

Numerous NGOs, such as Greenpeace Japan, Kiko (Climate) Forum, WWF Japan, and Friends of the Earth, A SEED JAPAN, and Citizens' Alliance for Saving the Atmosphere (CASA), repeatedly lobbied the government. In June 2001, thirteen Japanese NGOs organized the Stop Global Warming! Parade, which was attended by five hundred people in downtown Tokyo. They released a statement demanding "policymakers in the Japanese Diet and government, even without US participation, to stand firm and push ahead with the protocol."[15] Several dozen representatives of the press covered the parade.[16] The Japanese press was in general very supportive of the NGOs' activities and the Kyoto Protocol.[17] The *Nikkei Weekly* called the Kyoto Protocol's ratification a "victory" for Japan's NGOs.[18]

This changed milieu helped to counterbalance the dominance of economic interests and certainly provided a push toward ratification. The growing influence of civil society was also a factor in the DPJ's sweep to power in 2009 and their embrace of more participatory and open decision-making processes. It is doubtful, however, given their relatively small size and numbers, that NGOs on their own were strong enough to convince Koizumi of the importance of ratification. NGOs do appear to be closely tied to the DPJ and are advising the government on its climate and renewable energy policies. The weak capacities of the NGO community, however, limit the extent to which they can offer policy alternatives to the government.

Institutions: Bureaucratic Structure

The Japanese administration is both vertically entrenched and far-reaching in its regulatory reach. Japanese environmental policymaking is both top-down and divided.[19] Climate change policy is complex because it involves so many actors and interests (for example, energy, land use, transportation, construction). It is a classic case of a multifunctional shared-policy arena. MOFA is in charge of foreign relations. MOE has a strong interest in climate change but is weak relative to other ministries. METI is in charge of energy policy and most aspects of industrial policy. Its overall priority is industrial and economic competitiveness, although it also has a large interest in developing nuclear energy and new environmental technologies, and its global environmental affairs bureau often champions environmental causes. On the whole, METI opposes punitive regulations on industry and giving too much power to MOE. On balance one would anticipate the stronger METI to win battles related to climate change matters over MOFA and MOE. Yet at several junctures, including both during the Kyoto Protocol negotiations in 1997 and the ratification debate in 2001, this was not the case.

During the 1997 negotiations, three main ministries were involved in determining what Japan's negotiating position would be. The Environment Agency (the precursor of the current MOE), basing its calculations on the work of researchers at the National Institute of Environmental Studies, argued that a reduction in greenhouse gas emissions on the order of 7 to 8 percent by 2010 would be possible if an energy tax was introduced and renewable energies widely promoted. MOFA came out with a proposal for a 6.8 percent reduction by 2010. MITI had a widely divergent view, believing that emissions in 2010 were likely to be 3 percent higher than they were in 1990. MOFA and the Environment Agency eventually agreed to shift their positions down to a 5 percent reduction target. MITI countered by moving its position to a flat stabilization goal. The deputy cabinet secretary also weighed in and gave his support to the 5 percent reduction target. To have done otherwise as host to the third Conference of the Parties (COP 3) would have been problematic for Japan's foreign relations and environmental leadership goals.[20]

The same ministerial battle lines were evident at the time of ratification. In this period the Cabinet office in charge of global warming (*naikaku honbu*) was led by a METI official on loan to the Cabinet (*shukkosha*). Despite this, MOE and MOFA were successful in pushing for ratification.[21]

Counterbalancing Institution: Electoral System and Changed Party Politics

A second underlying institutional lens relates to changed party competition in the wake of the LDP's fragmentation in 1993 and the electoral reforms of 1994. The electoral reforms changed the system from one of single nontransferable votes in multimember districts to a mixed system of first-past-the-post votes in single-member districts (300 seats) and proportional representation in several large districts (initially 200 seats, changed to 180 after 2000) for the House of Representatives, which selects the prime minister. The new system, it was hoped, would lead to issue-based competition and alternation in power between two major parties.

One reason the LDP was able to stay in power for years after these reforms was its adroitness as a catchall party. To ensure reelection, Diet members must gain the support of favored interest groups as well as a large enough segment of the general public. The shock of temporarily losing power in 1993 and the arrival of coalition politics helped to reorient the LDP and created opportunities for legislative innovation. The LDP acquiesced to some of the projects presented by coalition partners, especially New Komeito, the LDP's Buddhist partner in government from 1999 to 2009. This party, which expresses a stronger concern for social and environmental issues than other parties, pressured the LDP on Kyoto at several junctures. On 12 July 2001, New Komeito formally sided with opposition parties in the Diet in urging the government to commit to ratification.[22]

These tendencies toward accommodation were further pushed after the LDP had a particularly shattering defeat in the July 1998 House of Councilors election. As a result, the party was forced to rely even more heavily on coalition partners. The ensuing sense of vulnerability made the party's leadership more open to tactical reforms.

This fluid context of changed electoral incentives and party dynamics, while not sufficient to explain the decisions of 2001–2002, formed a new political environment that was more fertile to political entrepreneurship. Indeed, despite changing incentives, the LDP remained divided between coalitions of politicians associated with particular interests. Within the LDP, the environmental coalition (*kankyo zoku*) remained a minority one; links with Keidanren and economic interests remained dominant. For the LDP's leaders, however, the calculus was different. Breaking coalitional stalemates and arbitrating in favor of Kyoto was a long-term strategic move as they pursued new urban voters and more junior politicians attempting to build up their reputation.

The long-heralded change toward an alteration of power among major political parties finally occurred with the August 2009 landslide victory of the DPJ and the concomitant collapse of the LDP. The electoral change opened the door to a far more progressive climate program than was pursued by the LDP. While the LDP made some concessions to climate change advocates, deep changes that would have impacted the party's most important industrial backers were typically avoided. The DPJ is less dependent on industry for electoral support. This is a major reason why the DPJ has announced a far-reaching greenhouse gas mitigation target.

Ideas and the Power of Embedded Symbolism

Ideas can wield a powerful influence on policy outcomes, especially when they become embedded as symbols that resonate with the general public. The Kyoto Protocol took on such significance, becoming a symbol of the pressing problem of global climate change and Japan's bid to be a larger foreign policy player and a leader in global environmental protection.

Not all policy ideas have equal symbolic potential. For an idea to rise to the status of a symbol, it must not only become part of a policy agenda but also assume a larger political significance, becoming ingrained in public and political dialog and functioning as a focal point around which expectations converge. Specific individuals, groups, or organizations work to make such associations and to transform an idea into a symbol.

Deborah Stone defines a symbol as "anything that stands for something else. Its meaning depends on how people interpret it, use it, or respond to it."[23] When an issue, such as the Kyoto Protocol, becomes a symbol of other things—like global warming, foreign policy prominence, and political leadership—it becomes imbued with larger meanings. This raises the stakes in political confrontations. Because symbols can have so much influence on policy outcomes, political actors have a strong interest in trying to shape how people understand them. Often a group of powerful actors forms around the symbol and works to attach certain definitions to it. They form a kind of "policy monopoly"[24] as they are the ones who are in a position to influence which concepts are associated with the symbol (Kyoto as a symbol of Japanese leadership in tackling a major global problem as opposed to as a symbol of costly economic cutbacks). Opponents can find it extremely difficult to change the meanings tied to the symbol.

Framing the Meaning of Kyoto

There were numerous actors who had an interest in defining the Kyoto Protocol as more than simply an international agreement. Well before the protocol was even being discussed, powerful LDP power broker and former prime minister Noboru Takeshita backed the notion of acting on climate change. For Takeshita, who had been tainted by political scandal, it was a way to reinvent his own image as a green and clean politician and to make the LDP a more modern party, in the way Margaret Thatcher, George H. W. Bush, and Mikhail Gorbachev had tried to do in their own countries.[25] Thus in 1990, after initially hesitating to act, Japan announced a voluntary target for the stabilization of CO_2 emissions at 1990 levels by 2000. And in 1992, at the United Nations Conference on Environment and Development in Rio de Janeiro, Brazil, Japan signed the UN Framework Convention on Climate Change (UNFCCC) and pledged to provide between ¥900 billion and 1 trillion over five years in environmental overseas development assistance. Takeshita was also instrumental in putting climate change on the agenda of his ally, later prime minister Ryutaro Hashimoto.[26] Hashimoto was in fact in power at the time the Protocol was negotiated. For the Environment Agency, the backing that came from Takeshita and later Hashimoto made it possible to win support for ideas MITI/METI were not behind, including the voluntary emissions reduction target in 1990 and the 6 percent reduction target negotiated at Kyoto. Hashimoto was also among a group of Diet members (twenty-four from the House of Representatives and eleven from the House of Councilors, all members of GLOBE, Japan [Global Legislators for a Balanced Environment]) who signed a letter to President Bush dated 4 April 2001 urging the United States to cooperate in addressing global warming.[27]

Other actors saw in climate change a means of pursuing different agendas. For MOFA, it was an area in which Japan could project its voice abroad as an essential component of the country's global "soft power."[28] A proactive climate change policy allowed the government to present a leadership role in an issue area of global significance, mitigate the intense economic competition of the early 1990s, and construct a new national identity centered on the concept of sustainable development.[29]

MITI/METI decided to get on the bandwagon as well, establishing an office to specifically address global warming. For Japanese industry, which had considerable experience with pollution control and energy efficiency improvements, making linkages to climate change policies was simultaneously a means to improve the image of corporate Japan, which had long been attacked for lack of attention to matters of global corporate responsibility, and to open up new business markets. For the embattled nuclear industry, climate change arguments could be used to support the building of more nuclear power plants. The important thing for METI and Japanese industry was to make sure that the international playing field remained level.

The Battle over Ratification in 2001: Interests, Entrenched Symbolism, and Political Reinforcement

Japan's immediate reaction to the Bush administration's 28 March 2001 announcement that the United States would no longer participate in Kyoto was one of surprise, dismay, and even anger.[30] On 30 March, Prime Minister Yoshiro Mori sent a letter to President Bush expressing his deep concern about the effect this would have on the international negotiations and urging the United States to work with Japan to ensure the agreement's enaction.[31] Yasuo Fukuda, the chief cabinet secretary, announced that same day, "What the Japanese government must do is to continue to call on the United States [to ratify the treaty], and keep up diplomatic efforts to ensure the Kyoto Protocol will take effect."[32]

On 9 April, Yoriko Kawaguchi, the environment minister, having just met with a group of EU delegates, made a formal statement that enunciated five points: (1) the EU and Japan share a common concern regarding the US pronouncement, (2) climate change is urgent and the developed countries have a responsibility to act first, (3) the Protocol contains tools that would enable cost-effective reduction of emissions and create economic opportunities, (4) Japan and the EU remain committed to the entry-into-force of the Kyoto Protocol by 2002, and (5) US participation is extremely important, and therefore, both Japan and the EU will urge the United States to reconsider its position.[33]

The Diet was also set in motion. One of the strongest indicators of the symbolic importance that the Kyoto Protocol had taken on was the complete support it received in both houses of the Diet. Both the House of Councilors (18 April) and the House of Representatives (19 April) unanimously passed very similarly worded resolutions calling for the United States to reenter the negotiations and for the Japanese government to "ratify the Kyoto Protocol early, and internationally, take a leadership for the entry into force of the Kyoto Protocol in the year 2002."[34] No politicians dared to speak out against Kyoto in the way their American, Australian, and Canadian counterparts did or to even abstain from voting on the resolution.

With so many indications that Japan was set on ratification, why then did so many European, American, and even Japanese observers believe that Japan might join the United States in abandoning the Protocol? Why did European leaders feel it necessary to lobby Japan so hard?[35]

On 24 May 2001, Margot Wallström, EU environment commissioner, stated that the EU would step up cooperation with Japan. She expressed concern that "it could be difficult for some of those traditionally tied very close to the United States to actually take sides against the United States."[36] The Dutch environment minister, Jan Pronk, who was slated to be the chair of the June Bonn conference (COP 6, part 2), traveled to Japan especially to meet with Kawaguchi and find out what it would take to keep Japan in Kyoto.[37]

A New Prime Minister Intent on Better US-Japan Relations
On 24 April, the LDP elected Jun'ichiro Koizumi as its president. Koizumi was popular, combative, and wanted to shake up the bureaucracy,[38] but he did not have a reputation for being a politician with much of an interest in climate change. In fact, after a group of six NGOs succeeded in winning a fifteen-minute audience with him on 30 May 2001, they came out of the meeting with the impression that Koizumi was basically leaving the matter of Kyoto to Kawaguchi.[39]

On 30 June, Koizumi met with Bush at Camp David; he left many with the impression that he was unwilling to proceed without US participation. He stated that Japan wanted to work "together with the European Union and the world in collaboration with the United States in dealing with global warming" and "that it would be more effective if Japan and the United States were to work closely with one another and that the world would benefit as a result."[40] Koizumi offered to initiate high-level Japan-US government-to-government consultations.[41] In a post-summit press conference, Koizumi stated "that Japan was willing to work until the last minute to rally support for the treaty, but that, in the end, it would not proceed without the United States."[42] The United States was emboldened by Koizumi's remarks, having read them to mean that Japan shared its negative view on Kyoto. Spencer Abraham, the US energy secretary, said on 1 July that the Protocol appeared to be dead and that the United States would continue to push alternative plans for increased research and voluntary approaches. He went on to say that he was "glad to see Japan joining us in taking that position."[43] The *New York Times* called Koizumi's statements on the Kyoto Protocol "as changeable as the weather."[44]

The Koizumi administration's ambiguous statements elicited strong reactions domestically. New Komeito urged Koizumi to ratify even if efforts to bring the United States back into the agreement failed. Japan Communist Party leader Kazuo Shii stated that Koizumi should let Washington know that it was breaking an international treaty and urge it to return to the agreement. The Social Democratic Party's Takako Doi criticized Koizumi's response as "an example of weak-kneed diplomacy." Yukio Hatoyama, leader of the Democratic Party of Japan, charged that Japan's attitude might lead to speculation that Tokyo wanted to lower the targets after being pressured by business groups.[45] Even members of Koizumi's own party, like Kenichi Mizuno, the chair of the LDP's environment committee in 2001, were pressuring Koizumi to act.[46]

Jennifer Morgan, climate change program director at the World Wildlife Fund International, summed up the situation as follows:

I think Koizumi's uncertain and ambiguous statements demonstrate what a difficult decision this is for Japan and how much rides on their decision. They are the ones who can bring this protocol into force. Their name's on it, and he's under a lot of domestic pressure to move forward. But, internationally, his key allies are split. ... The cultural situation comes in on two fronts. The first is that this is the Kyoto Protocol, ... the only international agreement with the name of a Japanese city on it. And that's something that the Japanese have pledged to fulfill. And their honor in pledging that I think plays a major role in them wanting to stick with it. But then you have a situation where making a decision to necessarily choose between two allies is very difficult—to lose face with one or the other.[47]

Koizumi may have been playing a more shrewd political game than his critics realized. He was involved in two-front diplomacy, working to appease conflicting domestic interests and foreign allies. Given the symbolic power of Kyoto, it would have been difficult for Koizumi to abandon Kyoto. With the unanimous resolutions of both houses of the Diet, Japan had signaled its intentions to ratify. Moreover, public opinion in support of Kyoto was strong. A poll conducted by the Cabinet Office (Naikakufu) in February 2002 showed that 49.8 percent of respondents wanted Japan to take the lead in ratifying Kyoto, even if the United States was not going to ratify. Another 26.4 percent supported ratification, although only on condition that the United States also ratify. Only 9.3 percent opposed ratification entirely because of the economic burden it would impose.[48] Charles Scanlon, the BBC's Tokyo correspondent at the time, noted that while for some months after the United States pulled out Japan was wavering, public opinion would not have allowed Japan to walk away from the Protocol.[49] Public opinion surveys, in fact, showed consistently strong concern about climate change. As early as 1987, an opinion poll conducted by the prime minister's office found 32 percent very worried and another 42 percent somewhat worried about climate change. Polls conducted by the prime minister's office in 1998 found 82 percent of respondents concerned about climate change and 82.4 percent in 2001.[50] Interestingly, though, the July 2001 poll found that while 67.2 percent of respondents expressed awareness of the Kyoto Protocol, 47.4 percent said they were only aware of the word and not the content of the agreement.[51] This too reinforces the importance of the Kyoto Protocol as a symbol.

As Yoshitomo Tamaki, director of the Environment and Ocean Division Policy Bureau in the Ministry of Land, Infrastructure, and Transport, summed it up: Japan ratified the Kyoto Protocol because Japan had hosted (chaired) the conference where the Kyoto Protocol was drawn up. For Japan, it was a question of face. To have withdrawn support for the Kyoto Protocol would have meant losing face. There was broad consensus in Japan on this point.[52]

Had Koizumi been as immediately supportive of Kyoto as Mori was, he would have weakened Japan's hand at the international negotiating table. This may explain Koizumi's ambiguity on the question of ratification. He showed willingness to cooperate with both the EU and the United States without letting either side know for sure where he stood. The EU needed Japan if the Kyoto Protocol was to survive. Basically, by arguing that Japan was uncomfortable with moving forward without the United States (which was in fact the case), Koizumi was creating a situation in which Japan would be able to extract many concessions from the EU that it had been unable to achieve in earlier negotiating rounds. These concessions were couched in the COP 6, part 2, and COP 7 negotiations as conditions that would be needed to keep the door open for a possible US return to the agreement. They were concessions that would also appease, to at least some extent, domestic opponents.

Winning Concessions from the EU

The sixth COP to the UNFCCC convened in Bonn in late July 2001. Going into the meeting, METI minister Takeo Hiranuma, eager to protect business interests, argued that it was necessary to make the Protocol more "flexible" and to revisit the agreement to prevent the United States from drifting away.[53] MOE officials countered that if Japan became too flexible, the Protocol's effectiveness would be greatly reduced.

Whereas the EU had long argued that there should be strict limitations on how much of a country's emissions reduction target could be achieved through use of the flexibility mechanisms or offsets in the form of carbon-sequestering sinks (forests and other carbon absorbing land uses), at Bonn the EU agreed to Japan's demands that countries be allowed to rely heavily on these instruments. The EU also agreed to drop the idea of including punitive measures for countries that failed to meet their emission reduction goals. The one major concession that Japan was unable to win was to include nuclear energy under the Clean Development Mechanism. The concessions that Japan won were seen as crucial if it were to have a chance at fulfilling its Kyoto obligations. They were also viewed as necessary if there were to be any chance of wooing the United States back into the agreement.

Japan's Formal Announcement of Its Plans to Ratify Kyoto

Having achieved most of what it had demanded in the negotiations, on 11 November 2001 Koizumi indicated in a Diet question-and-answer session that Japan would ratify Kyoto. The actual ratification process was quick. The bill was introduced in the lower house on 10 May 2002 and passed on 17 May.

The Politics of Implementation and the Reassertion of Interests and Institutions

While the power of embedded symbolism propelled the ratification process forward, it has not played an equally powerful role in relation to domestic policy implementation. Instead, interests and institutions have exerted considerable influence on the shape of policy. Japanese policies have focused on voluntary action and avoided carbon taxes or a mandatory cap-and-trade system, although in 2008 the director-general of the Global Environment Bureau of the Ministry of the Environment formed an Advisory Committee on Emissions Trading Scheme.[54] This suggests that with the LDP in power, industry was able to wield substantial influence over the kinds of implementation measures that were and were not adopted.

Types of Implementation Measures Used by Japan since 1998 and Battle Fronts

With the decision to ratify the agreement sealed, a new round of intense political debate over implementation ensued. Japan's CO_2 emissions were relatively flat from 1975 to 1990 but increased by 7.3 percent between 1990 and 1995.[55] They continued to rise over the next decade so that emissions in 2007 were 14 percent above the Kyoto Protocol target.

The LDP-led government introduced global warming legislation, amendments, and action plans in 1998, 2002, 2005, and 2006.[56] In 1998 two major steps were taken. First, the Energy Conservation Law was amended to include a wider and tougher range of energy efficiency standards. Second, the Global Warming Prevention Headquarters developed a set of Guidelines for Measures to Prevent Global Warming.[57] The guidelines spelled out plans for meeting the 6 percent reduction target through a 2.5 percent reduction for CO_2, methane, and nitrous oxide emissions; holding the increase in emissions from CFC alternatives (HFC, PFC, SF_6) to +2.0 percent; offsetting CO_2 emissions through the 0.3

percent removal by carbon sinks (through afforestation and reforestation) allowed by Kyoto, and; working to obtain approval from the international community for the idea of net removal by sinks, which would allow Japan to obtain an additional 3.7 percent reduction. Beyond this, the guidelines called for additional efforts to be made through the flexibility mechanisms.[58] These guidelines were then incorporated into the Law Concerning the Promotion of Measures to Cope with Global Warming, which outlined the responsibilities of the central government for observing greenhouse gas trends and impacts; central and local governments for introducing measures to mitigate greenhouse gas emissions; and businesses and citizens for adopting measures to limit their emissions. The Global Warming Law established broad goals and responsibilities. It did not require specific measures, although by 2001, 412 municipalities (out of the 3,000 in Japan at the time) had drawn up action plans.[59]

Once the government decided to ratify Kyoto, there was another round of fierce interministerial struggles over the establishment of sector-specific targets. In March 2002 the relevant ministries came together in the Global Warming Prevention Headquarters (headed by Koizumi) to draw up the Guideline for Measures to Prevent Global Warming. This document called on industry to (voluntarily) cut emissions by 7 percent (by 2010 from 1990 levels) and households by 2 percent. The plan requested that households trim daily showers by one minute and television time by one hour daily. It urged households to spend more time in the same room. The transportation sector came out of the negotiations in a relatively strong position, only being asked to limit emissions to a 17 percent increase from 1990 levels. Importantly, the focus of the guideline was on "technology development" and "citizen efforts" as opposed to regulations.[60] Guidelines to prioritize climate change projects as part of overseas development aid were drafted as well.[61] In May 2002 the Diet formally passed the amended Law Concerning the Promotion of Measures to Cope with Global Warming. By and large, this followed the March guidelines, although economic incentives were also introduced, such as reduced tax rates for fuel-efficient automobiles. Further measures were adopted that mandated that all government vehicles be low-emission types by 2004 and imposing energy conservation measures in new buildings.

Because the legislation avoided compulsory measures, it was criticized in forthcoming editorials and by the opposition for falling short of needed action. Heavy lobbying by industry prevented the inclusion of

economic instruments (for example, carbon taxes) that had been promoted by MOE. Instead, the plan relied on boosting nuclear power by
30 percent (with thirteen new reactors by 2012), heavy use of forest
sinks, and introduction of Kyoto flexibility mechanisms after 2008.[62]

In April 2005 the government adopted the Kyoto Protocol Target
Achievement Plan because it was clear that with the measures in place
at the time, Japan would not be able to meet its target. Still, under the
2005 Kyoto Protocol Target Achievement Plan, basic policy directions
remained unchanged from the 2002 plan. Instead, expectations for
various sectors were simply heightened somewhat.

The measures to address the persistent large lag in target achievement
consisted of a planned increase in nuclear energy, measures for the better
management of existing nuclear reactors, better conservation, and the
promotion of new sources of energy.[63] To accompany the 2005 action
plan, several legal tools were adopted: a system to recalculate, report,
and publish greenhouse gas emissions (2005); the reinforcement of energy
saving for plants, buildings, and transportation (2005); and the reinforcement of the recovery and destruction of fluorocarbons (2006). In
2006, Japan also put in place a system to acquire credits from the Kyoto
mechanisms, giving MOE a large budget to actively buy emission reduction credits on the open global market. As of February 2006, it was
reported that Japan was buying up to 20 percent of the world's CO_2
credits (through the Clean Development Mechanism). Japan allocated
¥17.6 billion (about US$170 million) for such purchases in fiscal year
2006.[64]

Another innovative component of the 2005 action plan was the launch
of the summer "Cool-Biz" campaign, heavily advertised by Koizumi and
MOE minister Yuriko Koike. The campaign requested that all working
men shed jackets and ties from June to September. Ministers and government officials were ordered to lead by example. Offices were then
requested to set the temperature of air conditioners to 28°C (82°F) and
government offices were to cut use of air conditioners in the evening. An
interesting side effect of this campaign was the stimulation of new
fashion trends and of retail sales for clothing.[65] While the plan is certainly
interesting, it was looked at by many in the environmental community
as a distraction from taking the real kinds of measures the country will
have to take to meet its goal.[66]

In June 2006 the LDP's environment committee found that the current
measures would not be sufficient. The panel urged more budget allowances and tax cuts targeting both new energy sources and forest manage-

ment. The panel singled out biomass fuels as an area that should be prioritized, including ethanol produced from sugar cane, diesel fuel from edible oil, biogas from sewage disposal sites, and wood pellets from scrap lumber.[67]

Encouragingly, the Japanese public appears prepared for tougher measures. In a 2004 opinion poll by the Yomiuri Shimbun, 45 percent of respondents supported the idea of a carbon tax.[68] An opinion poll conducted by the Naikakufu in 2006 showed that 87.1 percent of respondents showed interest in global environmental issues (up from 82.0 percent in 1998) and 60.0 percent knew about the government's Target Achievement Plan; 64.6 percent stated that current measures on industrial emissions of greenhouse gases were insufficient, 61.8 percent supported the introduction of mandatory targets by industry, and 74.1 percent claimed to participate in government-recommended measures for lowering household energy consumption. For example, 71 percent said that they were careful to turn off the electricity in rooms not in use; 67 percent claimed to select low-energy appliances when purchasing new ones; and 53.5 percent said that they were cutting back on shower time. Regarding the Cool Biz campaign, 76.6 percent of respondents knew about it, including 87 percent of employed people; 31 percent said they took measures according to the Cool Biz campaign; and 43 percent of these said that they did so expressly to fight global warming.[69]

The Asia Pacific Partnership on Clean Development, 2005
While Japan has actively worked to find ways to fulfill its obligations without paying too heavy an economic price, it also joined the United States in the Asia Pacific Partnership on Clean Development, which was formed in July 2005. This alliance brings together the United States, Australia, Canada, India, China, South Korea, and Japan. The loose partnership emphasizes technology transfers rather than fixed targets and caps.[70] METI argued that the partnership is complementary to Kyoto, does not weaken it, and is better suited to combating climate change because it puts the private sector rather than government bureaucrats on the front line.[71]

Cool Earth Strategies
In 2007, Prime Minister Shinzo Abe initiated the "Cool Earth 50" strategy, a plan for halving global emissions by 2050. The plan calls for major emitting nations to establish quantified national targets for emissions reductions based on a sector-by-sector assessment of reduction poten-

tials, commitments by developing countries, and the promotion of "innovative technologies" (such as carbon sequestration, nuclear energy, and hydrogen fuels) for CO_2 emissions reductions. These policy proposals can be contrasted with the EU calls, made at COP 13 in Bali, Indonesia, in late 2007, for industrialized states to commit to reduce their greenhouse gas emissions by 25–40 percent relative to 1990 levels by 2020.

Abe served as prime minister for a brief twelve months. His successor, Yasuo Fukuda, initiated a Cool Earth Partnership Fund: US$10 billion in grants, aid, and technical assistance to help developing countries tackle climate change. He also called for a global 30 percent energy efficiency improvement target for 2020 and committed to investing $30 billion over five years in research and development in energy and environment. In the lead-up to the G8 summit in Toyako, Hokkaido, however, he resisted European calls for the establishment of midterm post-2012 emissions reduction goal, instead pushing for an agreement among the G8 countries to work to reduce greenhouse gases by 50 percent by 2050 (notably no baseline year was given). In the lead-up to the meeting, Fukuda called for "equitable solutions" that will bring the largest emitting countries into the agreement.

A Lackluster Target

Prime Minister Taro Aso's June 2009 announcement that Japan would pursue a 2005 base year instead of the 1990 baseline used by the EU was met with considerable criticism from NGOs and within Europe. The relatively modest 2020 goal of a 15 percent reduction relative to 2005 that he offered equated to only an 8 percent reduction from 1990 levels. The goal moved Japan little beyond its –6 percent Kyoto Protocol target. The pendulum had tipped back in favor of conservative economic interests that were reluctant to upset the status quo. The interests of Keidanren prevailed, but only for a very short while.

New Times: A Return to Japanese Climate Leadership?

The historic victory of the DPJ has the potential to usher in a new period of Japanese climate leadership. The DPJ wants to bring new ideas to Japanese climate policies, weaken powerful interests that have prevented substantial policy change, and take advantage of the opportunities afforded by its large majorities in both houses of the Diet. The DPJ plans to pursue policies that were blocked by industrial interests in the past, including feed-in-tariff policies for renewable energies along the lines of what is commonly found in European countries, an emissions trading system, and possibly a global warming tax. It remains to be seen whether this ambitious agenda will succeed, especially given the DPJ's attempts to break the influence of Keidanren, bureaucratic interests, and powerful lobbying groups. There is at least the hope that in the coming years Japan may take on a more forceful climate mitigation stance and move beyond its role as middle man between the United States and the EU.

Conclusion

Whether or not Koizumi and his Cabinet ever seriously considered abandoning Kyoto is unclear. What is clear is that they recognized that the Kyoto Protocol was imbued with symbolism. What elevated Kyoto to the level of a powerful political symbol was the convergence of several factors: the initial political choices of the LDP's most prominent politicians (Noboru Takeshita and Ryutaro Hashimoto) to place their political capital on this issue and to link their party's fortunes, at least in part, to an activist environmental foreign policy; the linking of other policy goals to the Kyoto Protocol; the importance of the agreement's Japanese name;[72] the gradual crystallization of public opinion around this politically constructed symbol; and the formation of a network of NGOs which, though weak, were aided by a media that was willing to tell their side of the story.[73]

The Kyoto Protocol had been negotiated in an intense and heated conference that took place over the course of twelve days in December 1997. So important was the success of this agreement that Japan's negotiators agreed to cut greenhouse gas emissions by levels that the powerful Ministry of International Trade and Industry had said would be too costly. Nearly four years later, when the United States retreated from the agreement, Japan's leadership determined that ratification was in their best political interest. Prior to ratifying, however, they managed to reshape the agreement to make implementation somewhat less burdensome.

While Keidanren was largely opposed to ratification, for most actors, Japan was already on the path toward ratification well before the US withdrawal. While there were certainly many politicians who knew little about the agreement[74] or had doubts about it, they were certainly not vocal in their opposition in the way that some US Congressmen were.[75] Japanese politicians were well aware that environmental interests had become important to the electorate and that the media had taken a largely supportive stance. Most Diet members presumably did not have a good understanding of what the Kyoto Protocol would mean for the economy; they simply saw it as a symbol of a strong foreign policy. While it looked to the outside world like Japan might not ratify, to most Japanese observers, this was not a question. Instead, the real battle was one over the shape that the agreement would take and how strong a card Japan would be able to play in international negotiations.

It is also clear that once the agreement had been ratified and attention shifted to the important question of implementation, interest group politics became more dominant. There was limited political leadership from the LDP when it came to pushing through the kind of hard measures that will be needed to achieve Japan's target. Although Japan moved forward on Kyoto without the United States, Japan continued to engage with the United States on climate change, often taking positions that moved it closer to that country. The LDP's failure to offer a midterm 2020 target for a post-Kyoto greenhouse gas emissions reduction agreement at the G8 summit in Toyako, Hokkaido, despite Japan acting as host, suggests that governmental leaders remained reluctant to move ahead of Washington. Japan chose to keep its own options open as it waited to see the outcome of the 2008 US presidential election and bought time before introducing new regulatory measures or an emissions trading system.[76] When in June 2009 Prime Minister Aso released his modest 2020 goal, it appeared that Japan was giving up any intentions of international climate change leadership. Environmental interests failed to move Aso's government to agree to more.

A short three months later, the game suddenly drastically changed. The landslide election victory of the DPJ (in which it obtained 308 out of 480 seats in the lower house) delivered a knockout blow to 54 years of LDP dominance. Not only a new social-democratic policy direction but also new policy processes have been set in motion. The DPJ government has identified climate leadership as a priority and has publicly committed itself with impressive goals. For the first time, Japan is seriously considering instruments such as a carbon tax or an emissions trading system, even though actual implementation is not assured. At the very least, 2009 will be seen as a critical juncture; public opinion, party leadership, and NGO linkages are likely to play a stronger role in climate change policymaking under the DPJ than was the case with the LDP.

Notes

The authors would like to acknowledge the generous support of the Weyerhaeuser Company Foundation and the able research assistantship of Yoko Ikegami.

1. Hamanaka 2006.

2. "JCCU's Appeal on the Ratification of the Kyoto Protocol," Co-op for a Better Tomorrow, 16 February 2005, http://www.jccu.coop/English_here/news/new_050221_01.htm.

3. Associated Press, "Japan PM Targets Cutting Carbon Emissions by 60–80 Percent by 2050," *International Herald Tribune*, 9 June 2008.

4. Keidanren, Outline of the Keidanren Voluntary Action Plan, 17 June 1997, http://www.keidanren.or.jp/english/policy/ pol058/outline.html.

5. Sawa and Kikukawa 2004, 97–138.

6. All data from government documents established on 28 April 2005 (Ministry of Economy, Trade, and Industry, "Kyoto Giteisho Mokuhyou tassei keikaku ni motozuku torikumi" [A Plan for Fulfilling the Kyoto Protocol Target], government document, 28 April 2005).

7. Schreurs interview with Ken Takeuchi, 19 June 2006. Ken Takeuchi, who as an Asahi Shimbun journalist has observed climate change–related activities in Japan since the early 1990s, noted that after the US withdrawal, many Japanese industries and Keidanren gave him piles of information as to why Japan should not ratify.

8. "As the Kyoto Protocol Goes into Effect, Japan Faces Daunting Task to Reduce Greenhouse Gas Emissions," *Foreign Press Center Japan*, 17 February 2005.

9. "Push on with Kyoto Pact: Kawaguchi," *Japan Times*, 6 July 2001, http://search.japantimes.co.jp/cgi-bin/nn20010706a8.html.

10. Schreurs has had numerous discussions with METI officials dealing with nuclear power issues related to the Kyoto Protocol, including in June 2006.

11. Sawa and Kikukawa 2004, 107–109.

12. Kawashima (2000; 2003); Broadbent (2002). We are grateful for the insights of one anonymous reviewer on this matter.

13. Karan and Suginuma 2008; Reimann 2001; Schreurs 2004; Tiberghien 2006; Torigoe 2000; Yamamura 1999.

14. Hasegawa 2004, 44; Pekkanen 2006.

15. "Participants of the Family Parade to Stop Global Warming!," *Peace Boat news archive*, 9 June 2001, http://www.peaceboat.org/english/nwps/cn/arc/010618/index_b.html.

16. Voices from Japan, Japanese NGOs into Action, *Picture album of the parade*, http://www.neting.or.jp/eco/kanbun/before2004/NPO/keihatu/event/2001/parade/before/parade_e/parade_e.htm.

17. This was pointed out in interviews with newspaper journalists who suggested that the press supported ratification.

18. "Kyoto Protocol's Ratification Marks Victory for Japanese NGOs," *Nikkei Weekly*, 23 June 2002.

19. Fisher 2004, 70.

20. Takeuchi 1998, 159–170.

21. Tiberghien interview with METI official, February 2006.

22. "Koizumi Again Talks Reform. Rival Parties Label Proposals Vague during Debate," *Japan Times*, 12 July 2001, 1.

23. Stone 1997, 137.

24. Baumgartner and Jones 1993.

25. Schreurs 2000; Schreurs 1995.

26. Ohta 1995, 2000.

27. Global Legislators Organization for a Balanced Environment, letter to President George W. Bush, 4 April 2001.

28. Nye 2004.

29. See, for example, Broadbent 2002; Kawashima 2000; Matsumura 2000; Miyaoka 2004, 76–77; Schreurs 2002, 2005; Takeuchi 1998, 151–187; and press conference by the press secretary, Ministry of Foreign Affairs, 21 October 1997, http://www.mofa.go.jp/announce/press/1997/10/1021.html.

30. Doug Struck, "Japan Dismayed by Bush's Stance on Global Warming Accord," *Washington Post*, 28 March 2001, http://www.climnet.org/news/march2001.html#japan.

31. Ministry of Foreign Affairs, Letter from Prime Minister Yoshiro Mori to President George W. Bush Concerning Negotiations on the Framework Convention on Climate Change, 30 March 2001, http://www.mofa.go.jp/announce/announce/2001/3/0330-2.html.

32. "Japan to Keep Pressing U.S. on Global Warming," *Japan Times*, 30 March 2001, http://www.climnet.org/news/march2001.html#japan.

33. Yoriko Kawaguchi, Statement on Climate Change, 9 April 2001, Japan Center for Climate Change Actions, http://www.jccca.org/.

34. Quotation is from the House of Representatives, Japan, Resolution Concerning the Realization of International Agreement Toward the Entry into Force of the Kyoto Protocol, 19 April 2001, http://www.mofa.go.jp/policy/environment/warm/cop/ kyoto_r2.html. See also House of Councilors, Japan, Resolution Concerning the Realization of International Agreement Toward the Entry into Force of the Kyoto Protocol, 18 April 2001, http://www.mofa.go.jp/policy/environment/warm/cop/kyoto_r1.html; House of Representatives, Japan, Resolution Concerning the Realization of International Agreement Toward the Entry into Force of the Kyoto Protocol, 19 April 2001, http://www.mofa.go.jp/policy/environment/warm/cop/kyoto_r2.html.

35. Fisher 2004, 64. Fisher quotes interviews pointing to a crucial role of EU lobbying in July 2001.

36. "Kyoto Protocol Dependent on Japan and Other U.S. Allies, Wallström Says," *Japan Times*, 24 May 2001, http://www.japantimes.co.jp/cgi-bin/getarticle.pl5?nn20010524b3.htm.

37. Ibid.

38. This idea was suggested by Asahi Shimbun reporter, Ishii Toru, author's interview, 19 June 2001.

39. Kankyo NGO, Koizumi shusho ni Kyoto giteisho Hakkou ni muketa rida-shippu wo chokutetsu youbou, JCCCA (Japan Center for Climate Change Actions), vol. 31, 30 May 2001, http://www.jccca.org/cop6/cop6/cop6010530. html (accessed June 2004).

40. Ministry of Foreign Affairs, Japan-US Summit Meeting, 30 June 2001 at Camp David, the United States of America: Outline of the Talks on Climate Change, 2 July 2001.

41. "Full Text of the Koizumi-Bush Joint Statement," *Japan Times*, 3 July 2001, http://search.japantimes.co.jp/cgi-bin/nn20010703c4.html.

42. Andrew Revkin, "Burden Seems to Be on Japan to Salvage that Fast-Eroding Climate Treaty," *New York Times*, 3 July 2001, A9.

43. Bette Hileman, "Kyoto Success in Japan's Hands: Japan Waffles on Whether It Will Ratify the Protocol without the U.S.," *Chemical and Engineering News* (CENEAR), 79(28): 11.

44. Howard French, "As Changeable as the Weather," *New York Times*, 4 July 2001, A07.

45. "Koizumi Again Talks Reform," *Japan Times*, 12 July 2001, http://search .japantimes.co.jp/cgi-bin/nn20010712a1.html

46. Kenichi Mizuno, homepage, http://www.catv296.ne.jp/~mizunokenichi/ doujisinkoudokyumento.htm.

47. Jennifer Morgan, interview with Steve Curwood on Living on Earth, broad-cast, 6 July 2001, http://www.loe.org/shows/ shows.htm?programID=01-P13 –00027#feature1.

48. "50% Say Japan Should Ratify Kyoto Protocol without US," *Nikkei Net Interactive*, 2 February 2002, http://www.nni.nikkei.co.jp/.

49. "Japan Ratifies Kyoto Pact," *BBC*, 4 June 2002, http://news.bbc.co.uk/1/hi/ world/asia-pacific/2024265.stm.

50. Inoue Takashi, "Yoronchosa ni miru chikyu ondanka no henyou," *Mitsubishi Research Institute Eco Weekly*, 21 August 2006, http://www.mri.co.jp/ COLUMN/ECO/INOUET/2006/0821IT.html.

51. Naikakufu Daijin Kanbo Seifu Koho shitsu, "Chikyu ondanka boshi ni kan suru raifu sutairu ni kan suru yoron chosa," July 2001, http://www8.cao.go .jp/survey/h13/h13-ondanka/index.html.

52. Schreurs interview with Yoshitomo Tamaki, Tokyo, Japan, 16 June 2006.

53. "Kyoto giteisho no minaoshi mo—Keizaisho beikoku sanka motomeru," *Kyodo Tsushin*, 12 June 2001. See also "Kyoto giteisho shuusei mo—Hiranuma Keizai sangyousho, beikoku nuki no hakkou kangaezu," *Mainichi Shinbun*, 12 June 2001.

54. Advisory Committee on the Emissions Trading Scheme, Ministry of the Environment, Approach to Japanese Emissions Trading Scheme Interim Report

(Executive Summary), 20 May 2008, http://www.env.go.jp/en/earth/cc/ajets-ir -080520.pdf.

55. Schreurs 2002, 194.

56. Global Warming Prevention Headquarters 1998a, 1998b.

57. Global Warming Prevention Headquarters 1998a, 1998b.

58. Global Warming Prevention Headquarters 1998b.

59. Ibid. Note that the number of municipalities in Japan now is only 1,800 as a result of a process of consolidation initiated by the central government.

60. Prime Minister of Japan, Guidelines for Measures to Prevent Global Warming (Summary), 19 March 2002, http://www.kantei.go.jp/foreign/policy/ondanka/ 020319summary_e.html.

61. Hisane Masaki, Health, education targets pondered for ODA outlays, *Japan Times*, 22 March 2002, http://search.japantimes.co.jp/cgi-bin/np20020322a8 .html.

62. "Toothless Global-Warming Bill," *Japan Times*, 1 May 2002.

63. Author's interview with METI officials, Tokyo, February 2006.

64. Mayumi Negishi, "Japan's Appetite for CO_2 Credits Hits Fever Pitch," *Japan Times*, 15 February 2006, http://search.japantimes.co.jp/cgi-bin/ nn20060215f1.html.

65. "Workers Shed Coats, Ties for '06 'Cool Biz' Season," *Japan Times*, 2 June 2006, http://search.japantimes.co.jp/cgi-bin/nn20060602a8.html.

66. Discussions with members of Japan's Rainbow and Green Network.

67. "LDP Panel Urges More Action to Fight Global Warming," *Japan Times*, 2 June 2006. http://search.japantimes.co.jp/cgi-bin/nn20060602b1.html

68. "The Poll on Climate Change," *Yomiuri Shinbun*, 21 October 2004.

69. Naikakfu (Cabinet Office of Japan), "Yoron chosa: Chikyu ondanka taisaku" (Opinion Poll: Policies toward Global Warming), government document, 2006.

70. *Economist*, 30 July 2005, 39.

71. Tiberghien's interview with METI official, February 2006.

72. This point was made repeatedly in interviews and discussions Schreurs held in summer 2006 with individuals holding government, academic, and environmental positions in Japan.

73. This is a much-discussed point. See, for example, Kawashima 2000; and Shimada 2003.

74. Schreurs's interview with Mitsuko Tomon, Social Democratic Party Diet member (lower house) at the time of the Kyoto Protocol's ratification, Okinawa, Japan, July 2006.

75. James Inhofe, "The Science of Climate Change," Senate Floor Statement, 28 July 2003.

76. Kanie 2003.

References

Baumgartner, Frank R., and Bryan D. Jones. 1993. *Agendas and Instability in American Politics*. Chicago: University of Chicago Press.

Broadbent, Jeffrey. 2002. From Heat to Light? Japan's Changing Response to Global Warming. In *Sovereignty under Challenge: How Governments Respond*, ed. John Montgomery and Nathan Glazer, 109–142. Somerset, NJ: Transaction Publications.

Fisher, Dana. 2004. *National Governance and the Global Climate Change Regime*. Lanham, MD: Rowman & Littlefield.

Global Warming Prevention Headquarters (Cabinet Office, Japan). 1998a. Guidelines for Measures to Prevent Global Warming. 19 June.

Global Warming Prevention Headquarters (Cabinet Office, Japan). 1998b. Guidelines for Measures to Prevent Global Warming, Part 2: Essential Measures to Prevent Global Warming. 19 June.

Hamanaka, Hironori. 2006. *Kyoto giteisho o meguru kokusai kosho: Shi o pi suri iko no kosho keii* [The International Negotiations for the Kyoto Protocol]. Tokyo: Keio Gijuku Daigaku Shuppankai.

Hasegawa, Koichi. 2004. *Constructing Civil Society in Japan: Voices of Environmental Movements*. Melbourne, Victoria: Trans Pacific.

Kanie, Norichika. 2003. Leadership in Multilateral Negotiation and Domestic Policy: The Netherlands and the Kyoto Protocol Negotiation. *International Negotiation* 8:339–365.

Karan, P. P., and Unryu Suginuma, eds. 2008. *Local Environmental Movement: A Comparative Study of the United States and Japan*. Lexington: University of Kentucky Press.

Kawashima, Yasuko. 2000. Japan's Decision-Making about Climate Change Problems: Comparative Study of Decisions in 1990 and in 1997. *Environmental Economics and Policy Studies* 3 (1):29–57.

Kawashima, Yutaka. 2003. *Japanese Foreign Policy at the Crossroads Challenges and Options for the Twenty-First Century*. Washington, DC: Brookings Institution Press.

Matsumura, Hiroshi. 2000. *Japan and the Kyoto Protocol: Conditions for Ratification*. London: Royal Institute of International Affairs Energy and Environment Programme.

Miyaoka, Isao. 2004. Japan's Conciliation with the United States on Climate Change Negotiations. *International Relations of the Asia-Pacific* 4 (1):73–96.

Nye, Joseph S. 2004. *Soft Power: The Means to Success in World Politics*. New York: Public Affairs.

Ohta, Hiroshi. 1995. *Japan's Politics and Diplomacy of Climate Change*. New York: Columbia University.

Ohta, Hiroshi. 2000. Japanese Environmental Foreign Policy. In *Japanese Foreign Policy Today: A Reader*, ed. Takashi Inoguchi and Purnendra Jain, 96–121. New York: Palgrave.

Pekkanen, Robert. 2006. *Japan's Dual Civil Society: Members without Advocates*. Stanford: Stanford University Press.

Reimann, Kim DoHyang. 2001. Late Developers in Global Civil Society: Domestic Barriers, International Socialization and the Emergence of International NGOs in Japan. PhD diss., Harvard University.

Sawa, Akihiro, and Jingo Kikukawa. 2004. Kyoto giteisho hijun to kokusai taisaku o meguru geemu [The Game of Kyoto Ratification and Foreign Policy]. In *Chikyuu ondanka no saikenshou: Postu Kyoto giteisho no koushou ni dou nozomu ka* [A New Look at Global Warming: How to Understand the Kyoto Protocol Negotiations], ed. Akihiro Sawa and Souichirou Seki. Tokyo: Toyou Keizai Shinposha.

Schreurs, Miranda A. 1995. Policy Laggard or Policy Leader? Global Environmental Policy-Making under the Liberal Democratic Party. *Journal of Pacific Asia* 2:3–34.

Schreurs, Miranda A. 2000. Shifting Priorities of Environmental Risk Management in Japan. In *Learning to Manage Global Environmental Risks: A Comparative History of Social Responses to Climate Change, Ozone Depletion, and Acid Rain*, ed. Social Learning Group, vol. 1, 191–212. Cambridge, MA: MIT Press.

Schreurs, Miranda A. 2002. *Environmental Politics in Japan, Germany, and the United States*. Cambridge: Cambridge University Press.

Schreurs, Miranda A. 2004. Assessing Japan's Role as a Global Environmental Leader. *Politics and Society* 23 (1):88–110.

Schreurs, Miranda A. 2005. Japan in the Greenhouse: The Challenge of Addressing Rising Emissions. In *Ecological Modernization and Japan*, ed. Brendan F. D. Barrett. New York: RoutledgeCurzon.

Shimada, Kunihiko. 2003. The Legacy of the Kyoto Protocol: Its Role as the Rule Book for an International Climate Framework. *International Review of Environmental Strategies* 5 (1): editor's note.

Stone, Deborah A. 1997. *Policy Paradox: The Art of Political Decision Making*. New York: W. W. Norton.

Takeuchi, Keiji. 1998. *Chikyuu ondanka no seijigaku* [The Politics of Global Warming]. Tokyo: Asahi Sensho.

Tiberghien, Yves. 2006. The Battle for the Global Governance of Genetically-Modified Organisms: The Roles of the European Union, Japan, Korea, and China in a Comparative Context. *Les Etudes du CERI* 124.

Torigoe, Hiroyuki, ed. 2000. *Kankyou boranteia npo no shakaigaku* [Social Analysis of Environmental Volunteer NPOs]. Tokyo: Shinyousha.

Yamamura, Tsunetoshi, ed. 1999. *Kankyou ngo: Sono katsudo, rinen to kadai* [Environmental NGOs: Their Activities, Ideas, and Topics]. Tokyo: Shinzansha.

6

The Struggle of Ideas and Self-Interest in Canadian Climate Policy

Kathryn Harrison

Introduction

In ratifying the Kyoto Protocol in December 2002, Canada accepted perhaps the most ambitious commitment among all parties to the agreement. Although Canada's formal target is to reduce its emissions to 6 percent below 1990 levels by 2008 to 2012, Canadian policymakers knew that in order to comply they would need to deliver a 30 percent reduction below projected emissions by 2010.[1] The impact of such deep reductions on economic competitiveness loomed especially large after the withdrawal from the Kyoto Protocol of Canada's largest trading partner, the United States, in 2001. Since ratification, however, a succession of governments has failed to halt Canada's emissions growth, let alone to deliver the dramatic reductions necessary to achieve compliance.

The contrast between Canada's ratification of the Kyoto Protocol and its inaction with respect to compliance might suggest that ratification was a merely symbolic gesture. However, this chapter argues that Canada's decision to ratify entailed a meaningful commitment to undertake significant reductions. We are thus faced with two questions. Why did Canada ratify the Kyoto Protocol despite anticipation of significant costs? And why, given that bold commitment, has Canada made so little progress in reducing its emissions?

The politics of ratification are significantly different from those of implementation. Canadian prime minister Jean Chrétien was able to employ his considerable authority as leader of a majority party in Canada's parliamentary system to fulfill a personal commitment to ratification, despite electoral and institutional obstacles. However, the latter reasserted themselves before the ink was dry on Canada's ratification papers. As Canada turned from the relatively abstract question of ratification to the task of designing and implementing concrete policies to reduce its emissions, opposition from business and the provinces persisted even as public attention subsided. The Liberal governments of Chrétien and his successor, Paul Martin, both yielded to the business community and anxious provincial governments in proposing implementation plans that relied primarily on public spending rather than regulation. Thereafter, election in 2006 of a Conservative minority government ideologically opposed to the Kyoto Protocol further undermined implementation efforts as the new government announced that Canada would not even try to meet its target under the Kyoto Protocol.

That said, the resurgence of public attention to the environment in late 2006 prompted even the Conservative government to commit to regulatory measures to reduce Canada's emissions, while at the same time many provincial governments announced initiatives of their own. Although public pressure on climate change subsided with the onset of the global economic crisis in late 2008, the election of US President Obama and the ensuing dramatic turn in US climate policy will facilitate adoption of harmonized policies in Canada as well. Thus, despite Canada's brief divergence from its major trading partner in ratifying the Kyoto Protocol, it seems likely that the two will again converge, with Canada taking its lead from its dominant partner.

Domestic Factors in an International Context

This chapter seeks to explain two distinct outcomes: Canada's decision to ratify the Kyoto Protocol in December 2002, and Canada's failure to date to adopt effective policies to mitigate climate change. The focus of the chapter is on three broad domestic variables that influence policymakers' decisions: electoral incentives, political institutions, and policymakers' own ideals. While the chapter is primarily concerned with domestic politics, the direction and degree of international influence on both electoral incentives and policymakers' normative commitments is also considered.

Electoral Incentives

A critical motive of politicians in any democracy is that of reelection. However, while the politician faces voters only once ever few years, she or he contends with organized interest groups on a regular basis. The relative influence on those groups will depend on their size, since their members are the voters most likely to take into account the government's actions on the issue in question come election time, but more importantly on their claims to speak for the interests of the electorate at large. With respect to climate policy, Canadian politicians faced competing arguments from business organizations, who argued that emissions reductions would cripple Canada's economy, and the environmental community, which insisted that mitigation measures were not only necessary but politically popular and economically feasible.

One would expect a politician's position on this all too familiar jobs-versus-environment tradeoff to depend on both the magnitude of the costs and benefits of action and evidence of how the electorate weighs the two. In that respect, the business community's opposition was bolstered by the depth of cuts Canada needed to make to meet its Kyoto Protocol target. When Canada signed on to make a 6 percent cut below 1990 levels during the Kyoto negotiations in 1997, it knew that it would need to make a deep reduction below projected business-as-usual emissions, which were increasing as a result of both population and economic growth. However, a robust economy and booming oil sector in the ensuing years yielded emissions increases even greater than originally anticipated. As a result, as illustrated in figure 6.1, at key decision points

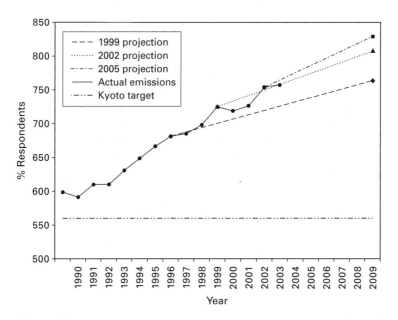

Figure 6.1
Canada's greenhouse gas emissions trajectory. *Sources:* Government of Canada 1999, 2002; Natural Resources Canada 2006.

the Kyoto Protocol target was actually moving farther away rather than closer, even as time was running out to get there.

Canada has a fossil-fuel-intensive economy, with the third highest greenhouse gas emissions per capita among major industrialized countries, after Australia and the United States. It is also a trade-dependent economy and thus vulnerable should trading partners not match its reduction commitments. Most notably, the withdrawal from the Kyoto Protocol in 2001 by the United States, which accounts for 80 percent of Canada's exports and 70 percent of imports, greatly increased Canadian business' fear that compliance costs would place their goods at a competitive disadvantage in North American markets.

In that context, it is hardly surprising that the federal government faced strong and virtually unanimous opposition to ratification and adoption of domestic emissions abatement measures from the Canadian business community. The opposition was led by a formidable alliance among peak business associations: the Canadian Council of Chief Executives, the leading voice of big business in Canada; Canadian Manufacturers and Exporters, whose members account for 90 percent of Canadian exports; the Canadian Chamber of Commerce, representing small and medium-sized businesses; and the Canadian Association of Petroleum Producers, whose members have contributed significantly to Canada's recent economic growth. While unquestionably well funded, these organizations' influence derived primarily from their employment of a majority of Canadians working in the private sector: the bottom line was jobs.

The environmental community's campaign for ratification of the Kyoto Protocol and adoption of strong domestic climate policies was led by the Sierra Club of Canada, the Pembina Institute for Appropriate Development, and the David Suzuki Foundation. While the reputation of Canadian environmental groups allowed them to "punch above their weight," their resources and access paled in comparison to those of their opponents in the business community. That said, from a politician's perspective, the relative influence of the environmental community turns on the credibility of its claim to speak for the electorate at large. We thus turn to public opinion polls.

Policymakers were well aware that public opinion was solidly in favor of the Kyoto Protocol. Indeed, throughout the ratification debate in the fall of 2002, the federal government commissioned *daily* tracking polls. Despite a high-profile campaign against ratification by business and some provinces, support for ratification declined only from 79 percent to 73

percent before rebounding to 79 percent.[2] However, complicating interpretation of the high level of support elicited by *close-ended* questions
about the Kyoto Protocol was a relatively low level of public attention
to climate change and other environmental issues, as demonstrated by
open-ended questions concerning respondents' priorities. The environment simply was not a top priority for voters before 2006. Moreover,
the fact that economic concerns were a higher priority tended to reinforce
the business community's message about the effects of ratification on
jobs and the economy. Consistent with this, David Anderson, minister
of the environment at the time of ratification, recalled that his Cabinet
colleagues "were very suspicious of the polling, even the Prime Minister.
... The numbers were just too good."[3] Similarly, the prime minister's
longtime advisor, Eddie Goldenberg, reports that the government doubted
Canadians' willingness to support the necessary implementation measures, despite their professed support for ratification.[4] It is telling that
after a high-profile and contentious debate over ratification in the fall of
2002, only half of Canadians polled in the spring of 2003 were even
aware that Canada had already ratified the Kyoto Protocol.[5] Electoral
incentives thus cannot easily account for Canada's ratification of the
Kyoto Protocol in light of the lack of salience of the issue for most voters
and the relative strength of interest group opposition. Electoral disincentives are, however, consistent with Canada's failure to date to make
progress toward meeting its Kyoto Protocol target thereafter.

Polls in 2006 indicated a dramatic resurgence of attention to the
environment in general and climate change in particular, with the percentage of Canadians citing the environment as the "most important
issue facing Canada" increasing from just 4 percent in January 2006 to
26 percent in January 2007, at which point it was the most frequently
cited issue.[6] The heightened salience of climate change among voters
transformed the electoral incentives of federal and provincial politicians
of all partisan stripes. However, as with previous "green waves,"[7] Canadians' attention to the environment was short-lived. As the price of
gasoline rose in early 2008, the environment fell from the top of voters'
minds. When a federal election was called in the fall, the environment
was in third place among public priorities after the economy and health
care.[8] However, with the onset of the global economic crisis in the midst
of the election campaign, the environment effectively disappeared from
voters' radar, not only weakening electoral pressures for action but also
strengthening the position of the business community in opposing
emissions regulations. By December 2008, only 5 percent of Canadians

identified the environment as the "most important problem" facing the country, compared to 53 percent who cited the economy.[9]

Political Institutions

This section considers two political institutions most relevant to Canadian climate policy: federalism and parliamentary government. Both demonstrate the complexity of institutional effects, which are contingent on interactions with other factors.

The effects of federalism have depended on interaction with electoral incentives. In the face of public inattention to the environment, federalism presented a significant obstacle to Canada's efforts to address climate change. Canada is a decentralized federation with a division of powers between the federal and provincial governments that exacerbates the already significant challenge of addressing climate change. With respect to the Kyoto Protocol, the federal government has a relatively weak international treaty power, in which it has acknowledged authority to negotiate and ratify treaties but not necessarily to implement them. Although the federal government arguably has significant implementation authority associated with its powers concerning taxation, trade, and criminal law, any perceived incursions into provincial jurisdiction are guaranteed to provoke opposition from provincial governments. In practice, the federal government historically has taken a relatively narrow view of its environmental authority, especially with respect to air pollution.[10]

In contrast, provincial governments own and thus have clear authority to manage "Crown lands" within their borders. With 90 percent of Canada's land still in public hands, public ownership by the provinces is significant indeed: the provinces control the natural resources most relevant to climate policy, including oil, gas, and coal on one hand, and forest sinks and sites for generation of hydroelectricity on the other. In addition, provincial governments also have clear regulatory authority over private and local matters, such as building codes and transportation planning, which are presumptive components of any greenhouse gas mitigation strategy.

The potential for federal-provincial conflict is further exacerbated by the regional nature of Canada's economy. Automobile manufacturing is almost exclusively based in Ontario, where it is the leading industry. Oil is primarily located in Alberta, and to a lesser extent Saskatchewan, Newfoundland, and Nova Scotia. Untapped hydroelectric resources are found primarily in Quebec and Manitoba, while British Columbia has the greatest opportunity to pursue carbon sequestration. Consistent with natural resource endowments, greenhouse emissions vary significantly among the provinces. As indicated in table 6.1, Alberta's and Saskatchewan's 2004 per capita emissions of 73 and 69 metric tons of CO_2eq per year, respectively, would be the highest in the world (exceeding those of Qatar) if those provinces were independent countries.[11] In contrast, Quebec, with extensive hydroelectric capacity, has per capita emissions of 12 metric tons of CO_2eq per year—half the Canadian average. Moreover, the gap between provinces is increasing as energy-intensive production from the oil sands grows in Alberta.[12] Any national effort to reduce greenhouse gas releases thus has the potential for significant regional variation in costs—and provincial governments can be counted on to step in as powerful defenders of "their" industries' interests.

Although federalism has primarily been a source of obstruction in Canadian climate policy initiatives to date, the resurgence of public attention to the environment in 2006 transformed provincial as well as federal politicians' electoral incentives, and in so doing also transformed the implications of federalism for climate policy. In particular, there was

Table 6.1
Greenhouse Gas Emissions by Province

Province/ territory	2004 Emissions per capita (MTCO2eq/yr)	Emissions growth, 1990– 2004	Share of total Canadian population	Share of total Canadian emissions growth
Newfoundland	20	4%	2%	0%
Prince Edward Island	17	10%	0%	0%
Nova Scotia	25	17%	3%	2%
New Brunswick	32	47%	2%	5%
Quebec	12	6%	24%	3%
Ontario	16	15%	39%	17%
Manitoba	17	11%	4%	1%
Saskatchewan	69	62%	3%	17%
Alberta	73	40%	10%	44%
British Columbia	16	30%	13%	10%
Yukon	13	−19%	0.1%	0%
NWT + Nunavut	22	4%	0.2%	0%
Canada	23	26%	100%	100%

Source: Author's calculation, CANSIM table 051-0001, and 2004 National Inventory Report, Annex 12 tables.

a shift from a dynamic of provincial obstruction of federal initiatives to one of innovation by provincial leaders, combined with pressure from at least some provinces for matching federal measures. That said, innovation by provincial leaders by no means guarantees action by *all* provinces. Ontario continued to resist federal regulation of its auto sector while Alberta's plans to develop its oil sands remain the critical obstacle to any effort to reduce Canada's national emissions.

As with federalism, the implications of parliamentary government are contingent on interaction with other variables. Historically, Canada's parliamentary system in combination with a first-past-the-post electoral system has tended to deliver majority governments with capacity for decisive action. However, parliamentary government has both capacity for action and inaction. Just as Cabinet can pursue its "good policy motives" in the face of electoral disincentives, so too can a parliamentary government follow its ideology in resisting electoral pressures for action. Further complicating matters is the increased likelihood of minority governments in response to a recent regionalization of Canada's party system. Since 2004, Canadians have elected three minority governments at the federal level, one Liberal and two Conservative. Comparison of the Liberal and Conservative governments reveals that it is not the government's partisan minority that is the issue so much as whether it has a *legislative* majority on specific issues. Faced with a divided opposition when it came to climate policy, the Liberal government of Paul Martin could muster support for climate measures as needed, though it was not pressured to act by Parliament. In contrast, the Conservative government of Stephen Harper has faced pressure for action on climate change from a relatively unified opposition.

Ideas

Goldstein and Keohane (1993) distinguish between ideas in the form of causal and principled beliefs. In the Canadian case both forms pointed toward ratification of the Kyoto Protocol. Although ongoing debate about the validity of climate science has the potential to undermine climate policy, a factor most evident in the US and Russian cases discussed in chapters 3 and 4, the relatively low profile of such a debate in Canada meant that the reputation and credibility of science were an important source of support for ratification and adoption of domestic mitigation policies.

We thus turn to principled beliefs or values. As demonstrated below, the values of one person in particular, former prime minister Jean

Chrétien, were decisive to Canada's ratification of the Kyoto Protocol. While Chrétien's values were by no means unique, as prime minister he was in a unique position to pursue them. That said, a prime minister with one set of values can easily be replaced by another with very different values, as Stephen Harper's subsequent repudiation of Canada's Kyoto commitment demonstrated.

Evolution of the independent variables over time within the Canadian case presents five distinct periods for comparison, each of which is considered in turn below.

Period One: The Road to Ratification

The Kyoto Commitment

Canadian climate policy is characterized by a series of ambitious but unfulfilled commitments. Despite Canada's failure even to contain emissions *growth*, successive governments have promised deep cuts, albeit with ever-receding dates for compliance.

Canada initially embraced the target proposed by the 1988 International Conference on the Changing Atmosphere of a 20 percent reduction in greenhouse gas emissions between 1988 and 2005. Two years later the federal government's Green Plan set a somewhat less ambitious goal of stabilization at the 1990 level by the year 2000. In 1992 Canada readily ratified the Framework Convention on Climate Change (FCCC), which included a similar, albeit nonbinding, goal. When the Liberal Party under Jean Chrétien won the first of three parliamentary majorities in 1993, they sought to outdo their Conservative predecessors by proposing a 20 percent cut below 1990 levels by 2005.

As the international community sought agreement on binding targets, Canada stood alongside the United States in insisting on flexibility mechanisms, including emissions trading and credit for existing carbon sinks. With the approach of the third Conference of the Parties to the FCCC (COP 3) in 1997, it was clear that Canada, like most other FCCC signatories, could not meet the target of stabilization at 1990 levels by 2000. In the lead-up to the Kyoto meeting, the federal and provincial ministers of energy and environment agreed, with the exception of Quebec (which sought a more ambitious target), that Canada's position would match the prior US commitment to reduce emissions to 1990 levels by 2010, thus extending the original deadline by a decade. However, in the opening days of the Kyoto meeting, the federal government unilaterally announced a new position, that

Canada would reduce its emissions to 3 percent below 1990 levels by 2010.

Much has been made of the fact that the prime minister personally chose a position that was more demanding than that of the United States going into the Kyoto meeting. Smith concludes that Jean Chrétien's motive was to outdo the United States for reasons of personal or national pride.[13] However, press accounts at the time suggested a very different explanation. Chrétien is reported to have received a phone call from President Clinton urging Canada to help bridge the gap and thus facilitate agreement between the US and EU positions.[14] Whatever the motive, the federal government's departure from a hard-won federal-provincial consensus drew forceful objections from provincial representatives upon their arrival in Kyoto.

The provinces were further outraged when Canada ultimately agreed to a Kyoto Protocol commitment to reduce emissions to 6 percent below 1990 levels by 2008 to 2012. Although federal officials acknowledge that the target Canada accepted was beyond any scenarios analyzed in advance of the Kyoto meeting, the explanation lies in the position of the United States. Canadian negotiators were directed by the two federal ministers leading the delegation to stay 1 percent behind the United States position. Canada's minister of the environment at the time, Christine Stewart, recalled, "We didn't do any negotiating or setting benchmarks in Kyoto without talking to the Prime Minister. He wanted regular briefings," but "I was so pleasantly surprised that our Prime Minister was willing to up the ante each time we talked to him."[15]

Canada's position represented a careful balancing of ideals and economic self-interest. On one hand, there was a desire for Canada to do its part, and to be seen to be doing its part, to address a global problem. A member of the Canadian negotiating team thus asked rhetorically, "Being good Canadians, can you imagine us letting the Americans get too far ahead of us?"[16] On the other hand, Canada was cognizant of the need to remain economically competitive with its largest trading partner. Contrary to the "one-upping the Americans" hypothesis, Canada did not beat the United States in Kyoto but rather claimed a concession because it is on the more greenhouse-gas-intensive end of that trading relationship.[17] Stewart later reflected, "As long as the US was with us, or 1 percent ahead as it turned out, Canada wasn't going to lose. This was one time where the Prime Minister could fully support the US without a lot of cost."[18] Moreover, both Canada and the United

States were reassured by their victory in security flexibility mechanisms, including international trading, the Clean Development Mechanism, and Joint Implementation, as well as credit for carbon sinks, in the Kyoto Protocol.

The National Climate Change Process

Quite fortuitously, a meeting of the provincial premiers and the prime minister was scheduled to begin in Ottawa as the Kyoto conference drew to a close. Anxious premiers emerged from the meeting mollified by three reassurances from the prime minister. First, the prime minister committed that "no region [would be] asked to bear an unreasonable burden," a phrase that would become something of a mantra for the provinces in the years to follow. Second, the first ministers agreed to undertake a thorough study of the costs and benefits of implementation before proceeding to ratification. The combination of the first two promises effectively left open the question of Canada's ratification of the Protocol just days after Canada negotiated its commitment in Kyoto.[19] Finally, the first ministers agreed that development of an implementation plan would be done in partnership with provincial and territorial governments. In response, the federal and provincial governments thus established the National Climate Change Process, co-chaired by Alberta and the federal government, a massive public consultation exercise involving some 450 experts and 225 stakeholders in sixteen "issue tables," each of which met many times over several years, an exercise one participant referred to as the "Air Canada subsidy program."[20]

The nature of the challenge Canada faced to implement the Kyoto Protocol changed dramatically in the spring of 2001 when the newly elected US president, George W. Bush, announced that the United States would not ratify the Kyoto Protocol. Since Canada's commitment in Kyoto had been predicated on the US position, many within the federal government and in provincial governments assumed that Canada would withdraw as well. However, while awaiting the plan promised by the US administration, Canada continued to press in international negotiations for interpretations of the Kyoto agreement that would make it easier for it to comply. Although the "umbrella group" led by the United States had failed to achieve the additional flexibility they sought at COP 6 in The Hague, the US withdrawal from the Protocol meant that the international community now needed *both* Japan and Russia to ratify for the treaty to enter into force. In that context, Japan and its ally Canada won important concessions, including no limits on their reliance on international mechanisms and carbon sequestration through forestry and land use changes.

Ratification

In the lead-up to the Conference on Environment and Development in Johannesburg, there was speculation that Canada would use the occasion to announce a decision to ratify the Kyoto Protocol, spurring intense lobbying activity on both sides. The business coalition argued that ratification could cost Can$40 billion and the loss of more than 450,000 jobs.[21] On the other side, pro-Kyoto members of the Liberal caucus collected signatures from 96 (of 172) Liberal members of Parliament and 23 Liberal senators, calling on the government to ratify Kyoto.[22]

Anxious Cabinet ministers were privately reassured by the prime minister's office that no announcement on the Kyoto Protocol would be made in Johannesburg. It was thus a surprise to many, not least his own Cabinet, when Chrétien announced in Johannesburg that a resolution to ratify the Kyoto Protocol would be placed before Canada's Parliament by the end of the year. Although the prime minister's speech was widely reported in the press, and more recently by Chrétien himself,[23] as an announcement that Canada would ratify the Kyoto Protocol, technically that was not what Mr. Chrétien promised. The decision to ratify international treaties in Canada rests not with Parliament but with Cabinet, which at the time of the prime minister's speech remained deeply divided on the question of ratification. However, with the receipt of the backbenchers' letter supporting ratification, and assured of support in the House from both the Bloc Québécois and New Democratic Party, the prime minister was confident that a parliamentary resolution would pass, in turn forcing his own Cabinet's hand.

The federal implementation plan released in November 2002 in support of the ratification resolution proposed measures to achieve 180 metric tons of reductions (60 metric tons short of the reductions anticipated to be needed to achieve compliance), at a cost of 30,000 fewer jobs in 2010.[24] However, what was most striking about the federal implementation plan was its lack of detail. There was a call to negotiate covenants with industrial sectors but no specifics as to which facilities would be expected to reduce their emissions and by how much. There was heavy reliance on public spending but no budgetary commitments for new projects. There were proposals for measures such as revisions to building codes that arguably could only be undertaken by provincial governments, but no commitment to do so from the provinces. Five years after Canada agreed in Kyoto to a 6 percent cut below 1990 levels and after a massive national consultation exercise, the federal government effectively released a plan to develop a plan.

Among the provinces, the prime minister's proposal to ratify the Kyoto Protocol drew support from only Quebec and Manitoba, both of which have undeveloped hydroelectric capacity. In contrast, the premier of Ontario, speaking for almost 40 percent of Canadians, stated that his province would not support Kyoto if it killed "even one job."[25] On the initiative of Alberta, Saskatchewan, and Nova Scotia, *all* provincial premiers signed a statement declaring the federal plan "inadequate" and calling on the prime minister to agree to a set of twelve principles before ratification. When Chrétien rejected the premiers' demands,[26] which would have entailed the federal government assuming all financial risk associated with implementation, discussions between the federal government and the provinces ceased, effectively terminating the National Climate Change Process.

Through the fall of 2002, members of Chrétien's caucus were remarkably candid concerning their reservations about ratification.[27] While it was virtually guaranteed that the Kyoto resolution would pass in the House with support of two of the three opposition parties, there was nonetheless potential for both embarrassment and loss of influence for the prime minister should a significant number of Liberals oppose the motion. In response, Chrétien declared the vote a matter of confidence.[28] On 10 December 2002, the House of Commons readily passed a resolution calling on Cabinet to ratify the Kyoto Protocol, with all Liberal members present voting in support. Ironically, Mr. Chrétien's authority may have been amplified by the combination of his imminent retirement and majority support within caucus for his rival, Paul Martin, since members of the Liberal caucus arguably did not want to risk an election with Chrétien still their leader.[29] The Kyoto resolution passed in the Senate on 12 December, and the following day the decision to ratify was made by Cabinet without debate, all ministers having already registered their support in the House.

Period Two: The Challenge of Compliance

When the high drama of ratification subsided, Canada was left facing the same host of challenges: a fossil-fuel-intensive economy, federal-provincial conflict, and tensions within the federal government, especially between the natural resources and environment departments. Little noticed in the aftermath of ratification was a low-key press release from Natural Resources Canada that the federal government had committed to industry that it would not have to pay abatement costs of more than Can$15 per metric ton nor make reductions greater than 15 percent below projected business-as-usual emissions for 2010.[30] The commitment, though announced only after ratification, had in fact been central to resolving divisions within Cabinet prior to ratification, with negotiations with the oil industry launched by the prime minister himself upon his return from Johannesburg[31] and thereafter conducted by his own deputy.

Although the magnitude of the concession drew little attention at the time, a price cap of Can$15 per metric ton flew in the face of economic analyses that projected a domestic marginal abatement cost in excess of Can$150 per metric ton.[32] Equally problematic was the 15 percent guarantee to "large final emitters," given that Canada anticipated that it would need a 30 percent reduction to meet its Kyoto target and industrial sources account for half of Canada's emissions. The effect of the $15/15 percent guarantee thus was to render it impossible for Canada to comply with the Kyoto Protocol other than through massive public spending on either international credits or domestic subsidies to business.

Although much work remained to put flesh on a skeletal federal plan, as the announced date of Chrétien's retirement approached the bureaucracy adopted a wait-and-see attitude in light of the ambivalence of Chrétien's anticipated successor during the ratification debate.[33] When Paul Martin succeeded Chrétien as prime minister in December 2003, he continued to equivocate given uncertainty concerning Russia's ratification and thus the Protocol's survival.[34] In the meantime, Martin called an election in the spring of 2004 which reduced the Liberals to a minority government.

A continuing stalemate between Environment Canada and Natural Resources Canada within the federal government was broken by an unlikely external actor. Seeing Canada's ratification of the Kyoto Protocol as an opportunity to demonstrate the feasibility of more aggressive action on climate change in the United States, the Rockefeller Brothers Fund sponsored a weekend retreat to discuss Canadian climate policy in early 2004, and subsequently provided a Can$60,000 grant to the Sage Foundation in Canada to fund activist Louise Comeau to advance the vision agreed to at the workshop. Comeau succeeded in gaining the ear of Prime Minister's Office (PMO) staff and thereafter worked with the

PMO to draft a new climate change plan in the fall of 2004, drawing on an economic analysis conducted outside the government with funding from the Sage Foundation.[35]

The first draft of what would eventually become "Project Green" was ready in time to send home for Christmas with the prime minister, who responded enthusiastically. Although Natural Resources Canada and Environment Canada offered characteristically opposite reactions to the draft, with "the boss" clearly on its side Environment Canada exercised growing influence over future drafts. In particular, the proposal in the 2002 plan to negotiate voluntary "covenants" with industrial sectors was rejected in favor of a regulatory cap-and-trade program. However, the quid pro quo for Cabinet's approval of a regulatory approach was reduction of the target for industrial sources from 15 percent to 12 percent. In addition, mindful of auto industry jobs in Ontario, Cabinet rejected the minister of the environment's call for tailpipe regulations in favor of a voluntary agreement with the industry. Although the resulting plan, Project Green, promised a cap-and-trade program for industrial sources,[36] this accounted for just 13 percent of the proposed reductions of 270 metric tons. In contrast, fully three-quarters of reductions were to be delivered through Can\$12 billion in public expenditures, the cornerstones of which would be the Partnership Fund to distribute money to the provinces and the Climate Fund, a massive program of subsidies to business. In addition, the Climate Fund was expected to purchase international credits and invest in the Clean Development Mechanism. However, although Canada was one of the countries that fought hardest for inclusion of international flexibility mechanisms in the Protocol, by 2005 policymakers had discovered that international trading did not play well with voters at home. One senior official explained that "no politician wanted to touch it with a ten-foot pole."[37] Another acknowledged that omission of a specific estimate for international credits was "deliberate. The government didn't want that to surface. It was the elephant in the room."[38] Although details concerning international purchases were studiously omitted from Project Green, an early PMO draft of the plan proposed over 100 metric tons of international purchases per year, constituting almost 40 percent of Canada's reductions.[39]

The federal government optimistically estimated that Project Green would deliver compliance with the Kyoto Protocol at a cost of Can\$12 billion (although that figure did not account for ongoing investments to maintain those reductions). However, an independent analysis by Mark Jaccard and colleagues projected that at that level of expenditure Project

Green would fall about 100 metric tons per year short of the 270 metric tons per year reduction needed relative to business as usual and would merely slow rather than reverse emissions growth.[40]

Period Three: Retreat from the Kyoto Target

Canada's effort to fulfill its commitment under the Kyoto Protocol, while faltering under the Liberals, ground to a halt with the January 2006 election of a Conservative minority government. The party and its leader, Stephen Harper, both have strong roots in oil-rich Alberta. In 2002, as then leader of the Canadian Alliance Party, Harper decried the Kyoto Protocol as a "socialist scheme to suck money out of wealth-producing nations" predicated on "tentative and contradictory scientific evidence."[41] When the Alliance merged the following year with the more centrist Progressive Conservative Party, the new Conservative Party moderated its positions in an effort to appeal to voters across the country. The Conservatives' 2006 election platform thus did not even mention the word Kyoto, although it referred to the Liberals' propensity to "sign ambiguous treaties and send money to foreign governments for hot air credits," promising that a Conservative government would develop a "'made-in-Canada' plan" to deliver "clean air, clean water, clean land and clean energy."[42]

Within weeks of assuming office, the new minister of the environment announced that it was "impossible for Canada to reach its Kyoto target,"[43] without pulling "every truck and car off the street, shut[ting] down every train and ground[ing] every plane" in Canada,[44] a claim that assumed no reductions in other sectors and no reliance on the Kyoto Protocol's international mechanisms. Consistent with the latter, the Harper government committed that it would not "send Canadian tax-payers' dollars overseas."[45] However, cognizant of the continued popularity of the treaty, the minister walked a fine line, insisting that Canada "respected" the Kyoto Protocol but simply "need[ed] new targets."[46]

The new government quickly canceled many of its predecessors' climate programs, including the voluntary One Tonne Challenge, energy conservation subsidies for homeowners, and regulations for industrial sources that were under development. The least noted but perhaps most significant change was that the Harper government simply declined to establish the Climate and Partnership Funds, which together accounted for 80 percent of Canada's projected emissions reductions under Project Green.

While quick to cancel its Liberal predecessors' spending programs, the Conservative government was not shy about announcing politically astute expenditures of its own. The government's first budget committed Can$2.2 billion for public transit, which focus groups had identified as a "winner" with voters,[47] and Can$220 million per year for a tax credit for transit pass holders promised during the election campaign. Since the vast majority of those tax credits will go to those already using public transit, the cost to taxpayers per metric ton of CO_2 emissions reduction was projected to be a whopping Can$2,000, a far cry from business' cap of Can$15 per metric ton.[48] The government also announced its intention to develop a regulation to require 5 percent ethanol in gasoline across the country by 2010, a rare case of a regulatory measure welcomed by both the agriculture and petroleum sectors, further sweetened by Can$345 million in government subsidies to the ethanol industry.[49]

The much-anticipated "Made-in-Canada" plan was unveiled in October 2006. The government repeatedly emphasized its commitment to "action" and "mandatory requirements" in contrast to its Liberal predecessors' "inaction" and ineffective voluntary programs. However, consistent with polls taken prior to the 2006 election, which indicated that air quality rather than climate change was voters' top environmental priority,[50] particularly in suburban ridings that were a key electoral target for the Conservative party,[51] the government sought to shift the focus from greenhouse gases to conventional air pollutants. With respect to climate, the government announced its intention to *begin consultations* on new regulations for automobiles and large final emitters to take effect in 2011, with targets to be determined. While critical of emissions increases under the Liberals' watch, the Conservatives promised only to end emissions *growth* by 2025.

Period Four: Made in Canada, Again

The "Made in Canada" plan was uniformly panned by the opposition parties, environmentalists, and the media, while positive comments from the oil and gas industry did little to lend the initiative credibility.[52] Although the government's strategy was consistent with preelection polls, the politics of global warming had changed dramatically in the intervening year as the environment surged to the top of the public's agenda. The electorate's renewed attention to environmental issues prompted competition among all parties to demonstrate their green credentials. The opposition parties' legislative majority on the issue enabled them to pass the Kyoto Protocol Implementation Act, which mandated that within sixty days of its passage, "the Minister shall prepare a Climate Change Plan that includes a description of the measures to be taken to ensure that Canada meets its obligations" under the Kyoto Protocol. The act's inclusion of nondiscretionary language backed by a deadline is unusual among Westminster parliamentary systems, reflecting the unprecedented case in Canadian parliamentary history of the opposition passing a bill without support of the government of the day.

Although the government submitted a plan to Parliament by the deadline, it defied the act in acknowledging that its plan would not ensure compliance with the Kyoto Protocol.[53] Environmental groups quickly launched a lawsuit in federal court. However, although the Liberal leader of the opposition had previously declared that government defiance of the act would be tantamount to a "coup d'etat,"[54] none of the opposition party leaders was willing to provoke an election over the issue.

The Conservative government responded to the resurgence of public attention to the environment with a host of climate policy announcements of its own. In January 2007 the prime minister replaced his embattled minister of the environment with a more experienced colleague. The government then held a series of press conferences across the country to announce over Can$5 billion in environmental spending, much of it restoring programs of the previous Liberal government, repackaged under the banner of "ecoACTION." At the same time, the government repaired relations with the provinces by committing Can$1.5 billion to the Clean Air and Climate Change Trust, similar to the Partnership Fund it had canceled the previous year.

The Conservatives thus followed the Liberals' lead, swallowing an ideological poison pill of environment-related spending. However, there were significant differences between the Liberal and Conservative spending strategies. Having rejected both the Kyoto Protocol target and the Protocol's international mechanisms, the Conservative government has favored investments in technology that are unlikely to yield near-term reductions, in contrast to the Liberals strategy of funding domestic offsets and purchasing international carbon credits. While the Liberals' Project Green undoubtedly overstated its effectiveness in projecting 270 metric tons of reductions per year below business as usual, an equally optimistic Conservative plan projects reductions of just 70 metric tons per year, expected to leave Canada at least 34 percent above its Kyoto Protocol target during the commitment period.

The Harper government also released a new regulatory plan, "Turning the Corner," in the spring of 2007, purporting to end Canada's emissions growth by 2012 (rather than 2025, as proposed in the government's first plan) and thereafter to achieve a 20 percent reduction below 2006 emissions (about 2 percent below 1990) by 2020. However, the reduction projection rests on an unrealistic assumption that firms will either reduce their own emissions or purchase comparable overseas credits, rather than taking advantage of what for most will be a less expensive option of investing just Can$15 per metric ton in a new Climate Change Technology Fund, which would not be expected to yield emissions reductions in the near term.[55] An independent analysis by Jaccard and Rivers projects that even with the proposed regulatory measures, Canada's emissions will continue to grow, reaching 30 percent above 1990 levels by 2020.[56]

The surge in public attention to climate change also had an effect at the provincial level. Three provinces—British Columbia, Manitoba, and Quebec—committed to matching California's motor vehicle tailpipe standards, while others, with the notable exception of Ontario, encouraged the federal government to match that standard nationally. British Columbia led the provinces, with a legislative commitment to reduce its emissions to 33 percent below 2007 levels (10 percent below 1990) by 2020, backed by a North America's first revenue-neutral carbon tax. In addition, British Columbia, Ontario, Manitoba, and Quebec have committed to participating with US states in the Western Climate Initiative's cap-and-trade program. While actions by provincial leaders are promising both in and of themselves and because they offer reassurance to other provinces that would be reluctant to regulate unilaterally, they do not guarantee action by *all* provinces. Of greatest concern, the climate plan unveiled by the province of Alberta, which accounts for roughly one-third of Canada's emissions, has committed only to a 14 percent reduction relative to 2005 emissions—18 percent *above* 1990 levels!—by 2050.

Period Five: Made in the USA

In 2008 and 2009, the politics of climate change in Canada saw two significant developments, each pushing climate policy in a different direction: a decline in public attention to the environment hastened by the onset of a global recession, and the election of US President Barack Obama, which heralded a 180-degree turn in the climate policies of Canada's neighbor and closest trading partner.

As previously noted, public attention to the environment began to decline in early 2008 but remained strong as summer approached. In response, the Liberal Party, led by former minister of the environment Stéphane Dion, made a bold decision to offer a revenue-neutral carbon tax as the centerpiece of its platform. In June 2008 the party released its "Green Shift" proposal, calling for a tax on fossil fuels, beginning at Can$10 per metric ton of CO_2 and increasing to Can$40 over four years, and a host of tax cuts to ensure revenue-neutrality for the government.

The Liberals were rewarded with a resounding electoral defeat in October 2008. While the depth of public support for a carbon tax was questionable even with the environment at the top of the polls, the Green Shift was undermined by two additional factors. First, it was discredited by partisan attacks from both the left and right. From the left, the New Democratic Party, arguing that a carbon tax would unfairly burden "working families," proposed a cap and trade that would "make big polluters pay," conveniently neglecting the costs that would be passed on to consumers. From the right, Prime Minister Harper dismissed the credibility of the proposed matching tax cuts and described the Liberals' carbon tax as an "insane" measure that would "wreck the economy" and "screw Canadians."[57] For good measure, the Conservatives countered the Liberals' carbon tax with a promise to *cut* taxes on diesel fuel. Second, the onset of a global recession in the midst of the election campaign not only undermined what public support may have existed for painful measures to address climate change but also shifted voters' attention to the economy, an issue on which the Conservatives enjoyed a solid lead over the Liberals.[58]

The Liberal Party lost a quarter of its seats in the election and jettisoned its leader two months later. Although the new leader, Michael Ignatieff, had distinguished himself from Dion in the contest for the party's leadership in 2006 by proposing a carbon tax, with hindsight of the 2008 election, Ignatieff repudiated the Green Shift. A leading political commentator has since described carbon taxes as the new "third rail of Canadian politics. Touch it and die."[59]

The Conservatives picked up seats at the Liberals' expense but remained in a minority position. However, the new government not only faced weaker electoral pressure to reduce greenhouse gas emissions but also clear signals that the economy was Canadians' priority. In contrast to previous governments' rejection of the need for tradeoffs between environment and economy, the new minister of the environment, Jim Prentice, called for "balance between measurable environmental progress and steady economic growth." Lest there be any doubt as to the government's priorities, the minister promised, "We will not—and let me be clear on this—aggravate an already weakening economy in the name of environmental progress."[60]

While the shift in voters' priorities signaled retrenchment of Canada's already feeble climate policies, the concurrent election of Barack Obama provided a boost for efforts to address climate change on both sides of the Canada-US border. As discussed in chapter 3, Obama immediately signaled an about-face from the previous administration in calling on the Environmental Protection Agency to reconsider its rejection of California's tailpipe standards and to revisit the question of regulation of greenhouse gas emissions under the Clean Air Act. Moreover, Obama called on Congress to pass a strong and broad-ranging cap-and-trade program based on hard caps and full auctioning of permits.

The prospect of more aggressive efforts to address greenhouse gas emissions in the United States presents both an opportunity and a challenge for Canada. Action by the United States will ease opposition to regulation from the business community in Canada, since the implications for competitiveness of regulatory costs are greatly reduced if Canada's major trading partner undertakes comparable measures. At the same time, however, two measures under consideration in the United States represent a potential threat to Canadian industries. The first is the euphemistically labeled "border adjustments" found in the most prominent bills before Congress, which anticipate financial penalties for import of goods from countries that do not match US standards. While the political incentives for Canada to harmonize with US standards for comparable sectors mitigate that threat to some degree, the prospect of tariffs on Canadian exports to the United States will ensure that Canadian policymakers are ever mindful of the need to keep up with their neighbors.

More significant is the threat posed by well-to-wheels "low-carbon fuel standards" of the sort already adopted by California and proposed by other US states and congressional Democrats. Low-carbon fuel standards will discourage US refiners' reliance on oil produced from Canada's tar sands, since the energy-intensive processes to separate oil from soil result in significantly higher greenhouse gas emissions than conventional production. The tar sands already account for half of Canada's oil exports to the United States, a figure that is expected to grow—along with associated greenhouse gas emissions—in years to come. At the urging of the Canadian oil industry and oil-producing provinces, the

Canadian government has stepped up its lobbying efforts in Washington. At the same time, however, Canadian environmentalists have launched their own campaign calling for an end to the US import of "dirty oil" from Canada. The campaign included a public letter to President Obama and full page ads in US newspapers in advance of the president's first visit to Canada.

After two "made-in-Canada" plans, it has become increasingly clear that the next round of Canadian climate policy will be made in the United States. The day after the US election Harper proposed a joint effort to develop a North American cap-and-trade system akin to the European Emissions Trading Scheme. However, preoccupied with the formidable challenge of passing their own legislation, US officials have for the most part rebuffed Canada's overtures. Similarly, on the occasion of President Obama's first visit to Canada, he and the prime minister agreed only to launch a "clean energy dialogue." The first product of that initiative, an agreement by each country to commit Can$3.5 billion for development of technology for carbon capture and storage, refers only to the technology's application to coal-fired power plants, a priority for the United States, not tar sands facilities, which are a priority for Canada (but a less viable candidate for carbon capture).[61] Canada committed to match US fuel economy standards the day after they were announced by President Obama.[62] Finally, in June 2009, the Canadian minister of the environment acknowledged that the draft cap-and-trade plan intended to take effect in 2010, which the government had committed to publish by the end of 2008, was indefinitely on hold pending details of the forthcoming US regulatory regime.[63] Ironically, although the United States' renewed commitment on climate change will push Canada toward stronger action, in the short term it is providing cover for a government reluctant to impose regulatory burdens on business during an economic recession.

Conclusion

The Canadian case presents two very different outcomes to be explained: a bold decision to ratify the Kyoto Protocol in 2002 despite significant costs (period one), and Canada's apparent inability in practice to take meaningful actions to reduce its emissions (periods two, three, and four), though with the promise of change in period five. Table 6.2 summarizes how the dependent variables and policy outcomes have evolved over time.

Table 6.2
Evolution over Time of Independent and Dependent Variables

	Period 1 1988–2002	Period 2 2002–2006	Period 3 2006	Period 4 2007–2009	Period 5 2009–
Public pressure	Inattentive	Inattentive	Inattentive	Highly attentive	Inattentive
Business opposition	Strong opposition	Very strong opposition	Very strong opposition	Weaker opposition	Weaker opposition
Policymaker's ideology	Strong commitment by Jean Chrétien	Paul Martin ambivalent	Antipathy from Stephen Harper	Antipathy from Stephen Harper	Antipathy from Stephen Harper
Federalism	Strong provincial opposition but no veto over ratification	Provincial opposition with potential veto over implementation	Weakening opposition as provincial leaders begin to emerge	Provincial innovation and calls for national standards but opposition from some provinces	Provincial innovation, calls for harmonization with US, but still opposition from some provinces
Parliamentary government	Majority government	Minority government with legislative majority	Minority government with legislative minority	Minority government with legislative minority	Minority government with legislative minority
Outcome	Ratification; "Climate Change Plan for Canada"	"Project Green": commitment to Kyoto target via public spending	"Green Plan 2": rejection of Kyoto target, cancellation of programs	"Turning the Corner": rejection of Kyoto target, but tightening of domestic measures	"US-Canada Clean Energy Dialogue," commitment to harmonization with US cap and trade program

Ratification

Neither the institution of federalism nor electoral incentives were favorable to Canada's ratification of the Kyoto Protocol. However, Jean Chrétien's normative commitment to the Kyoto Protocol carried the day, facilitated by the prime minister's considerable capacity as leader of a majority within a parliamentary system.

Why was Chrétien so strongly committed to ratification? When asked what motivated the prime minister, to a one Cabinet colleagues and officials in regular contact with the prime minister (five ministers and six senior officials) offered remarkably close variations on the words of former minister of the environment David Anderson: "First and foremost, he genuinely believed it was the right thing to do." Interview subjects also emphasized Chrétien's commitment to multilateralism, which, a PMO official offered, "was always a strong article of faith for him."[64] That said, it is easier for a politician to follow his moral compass at the end of his career, when electoral and intergovernmental considerations presumably weigh less heavily.

The generous deal negotiated with the business community in the lead-up to ratification prompts the question, Did Canada ratify with no intention of ever complying? A central agency official explained, "The level of literacy [within Cabinet] on these issues was extremely low."[65] Moreover, there had been discussion within Cabinet of the limited consequences that would befall Canada should it fail to meet its target.[66] Weighing against these factors, however, was a very real debate that occurred among the subset of Cabinet members who were highly engaged on the issue. It is unlikely they would have bothered over a mere ruse. Moreover, the very public debate surrounding ratification necessitated putting a concrete plan on the table that would serve as a benchmark for evaluating the government's subsequent actions. While it is plausible that in voting to ratify the Kyoto Protocol many Cabinet members doubted that Canada would *fully* comply, the evidence suggests that they were self-consciously taking on a very real and challenging commitment.

The Implementation Gap

Good intentions clearly have not been enough, however. Not only will Canada fail to comply with the Kyoto Protocol, but its emissions have been moving farther from, rather than closer to, its target. The vast majority of measures proposed in the four implementation plans announced since the Kyoto Protocol was negotiated have never been implemented. Why, after making such a bold commitment to ratification, has Canada failed so abysmally to control its emissions?

Implementation differs from ratification in several respects. Such limited public attention as was prompted by the symbolism of ratification of an international treaty quickly evaporated as the government moved on to the technical questions associated with implementation. In contrast, the strength of business and provincial opposition increased as the imposition of costs moved closer to reality. Moreover, the institutional challenge presented by federalism is arguably greater at the implementation stage. While provincial governments do not have formal capacity to block ratification, the breadth of their jurisdiction over natural resources and public infrastructure necessitates provincial cooperation with respect to implementation.

In addition to the change in the task at hand, from ratification to implementation, two other factors changed between period one and period two. First, the new prime minister's ambivalence about the Kyoto Protocol resulted in two to three years' delay. Second, there was a newfound recognition that public spending offered a vehicle for the government to assert its continued commitment to a popular international agreement without alienating either business or provincial opponents. In effect, the government bought off both business and provincial opposition with inattentive taxpayers' money.

In theory, that strategy was equally available to the Conservative government that assumed office in period three. However, significant changes in Canadian climate policy introduced by the Harper government in 2006, including repudiation of Canada's Kyoto Protocol target and cancellation of proposed regulations and expenditures, suggests that ideology carried the day. Although the legislative majority that supported stronger action on climate change theoretically offered a constraint on the government, the government's defiance of the Kyoto Protocol Implementation Act underscores that the one mechanism the opposition parties have to call the executive to account, a vote of nonconfidence, is a blunt and thus ineffective tool.[67]

Conditions changed again in period four with a dramatic surge in public attention to climate change. In response, the business community relaxed its opposition, presumably in order to influence the shape of inevitable tax or regulatory programs.[68] And as provincial governments responded to the demands of their own electorates, the implications of federalism for the federal government were also transformed. While resistance from key provinces remains a critical obstacle, unilateral actions by other provinces have increased pressure from the business community for federal measures to "level the playing field." The about-face of the Harper government in embracing environment-related spending and tightening its regulatory proposals suggests that credible public demand for action can trump party ideology.

While Canada still has no regulation of greenhouse gas emissions, the changes in US climate policy that have followed President Obama's inauguration suggest that change is on the horizon in Canada as well. Given the close integration of the two economies, actions to reduce greenhouse gas emissions in the United States will reduce the economic effects of, and thus political opposition to, adoption of comparable measures in Canada. And if the opportunity to respond to voters' expectations at a low cost is not enough, the threat of trade retaliation will undoubtedly ensure that Canada closely follows the US lead.

International Influences
The analysis thus far has focused on domestic factors, but the question remains: To what extent were domestic politics influenced by international factors? That is, how did international influences shape electoral incentives and norms in Canada's domestic political debate?

With respect to electoral politics, the international context to date has been, on balance, an obstacle to ratification and especially implementation. While Canadian environmentalists were certainly well networked with their counterparts in other countries, support from allies outside the country was not a significant factor in the ratification debate. While *political globalization* thus was a minor supportive factor at best, *economic globalization* has posed a significant challenge. The business community's opposition to the Kyoto Protocol was strengthened by Canada's heavy reliance on international trade, particularly after the withdrawal of Canada's main trading partner from the Kyoto Protocol. And while business interests did not prevail on the ratification question, they have done so thus far with respect to implementation, effectively rendering Canada's ratification a moot point.

That said, if the United States adopts measures to reduce its emissions, as seems increasingly likely, this obstacle will be largely neutralized. Indeed, the combination of pressures from domestic producers for a "level playing field" with respect to product standards (though not necessarily for emissions standards) and the threat of US trade sanctions will likely create upward pressure on Canadian climate policy.

It is difficult to assess the effects of international ideas on Canadian climate policy, not least because it is difficult to distinguish between international and domestic norms with respect to environmental protection. That said, two leaders' views with respect to international institutions did have some influence, though in opposite directions. Jean Chrétien's colleagues cited the prime minister's commitment to multilateralism as an important factor underlying his decision to ratify, while skepticism of international institutions was cited by a central agency official as a reason for the Harper government's rejection of international trading and thus repudiation of Canada's commitment under the Kyoto Protocol.

Steven Bernstein has argued that a package of causal and principled ideas he labels "liberal environmentalism" facilitated Canada's commitment to the Kyoto Protocol by "mak[ing] it more difficult to argue that the treaty is anti-competitive or growth."[69] That ideal is hard to reconcile with the heated debate about the implications of the Kyoto Protocol for economic competitiveness that has taken place in Canada, in which the win-win rhetoric of sustainable development confronted the reality of winners *and losers*. In that sense, Canada's ratification of the Kyoto Protocol represents an even stronger test of the power of principled beliefs than suggested by Bernstein. By the same token, however, Canada's failure to follow through on that commitment reveals the fragility of politicians' values in the absence of institutional and especially electoral support.

In conclusion, electoral incentives have offered both the strongest obstacle to and the greatest opportunity for policy change. While Prime Minister Chrétien was able to follow his principles to ratify the Kyoto Protocol, both he and his successors were wary of adopting the difficult measures necessary to achieve compliance in the absence of compelling evidence of public willingness to pay. However, the residue of renewed public concern for the environment combined with a reduction in business opposition as a result of actions undertaken in the United States are poised to overcome remaining institutional obstacles and the governing party's ideological antipathy. A decade after the Kyoto Protocol was negotiated, during which Canada's emissions steadily increased, one can only hope that the window of opportunity will open wide enough.

Notes

Research for this chapter was supported by the Fulbright Foundation and by a grant from the Weyerhaeuser Company Foundation to the University of British

Columbia. I am grateful to Tyler Bryant and Katherine Boothe for superb research assistance, to Steven Bernstein, Doug MacDonald, Heather Smith, and Lisa McIntosh Sundstrom for insightful comments on an earlier version of this chapter, and to the thirty-one individuals who generously gave their time for interviews (seven current or former Cabinet ministers, eighteen federal and provincial public servants, three environmentalists, and one industry spokesperson). Any errors of fact or of interpretation are mine alone.

1. Government of Canada 2002.

2. EKOS Research Associates 2002.

3. Author's interview with David Anderson, March 2006.

4. Les Whittington, "Liberals Knew Kyoto a Long Shot; but Chrétien Aide Says Signing Accord a Vital Step Forward," *Toronto Star*, 23 February 2007, A6.

5. EKOS Research Associates 2003.

6. Strategic Counsel 2007.

7. Harrison 1996.

8. Brian Laghi, "Harper Tories on the Brink of Majority, Poll Finds," *Globe and Mail*, 2 September 2008, A1.

9. Environics press release, 4 June 2009.

10. Harrison 1996.

11. "CO_2 equivalent" (CO_2eq) combines emissions of all six greenhouse gases covered by the Kyoto Protocol by translating them into equivalent emissions of CO_2 based on each gas's global warming potential.

12. Natural Resources Canada 2006.

13. Smith 1998, 28.

14. Giles Gherson, "Chrétien Returns from Europe Transformed into a Born-Again Enviro-PM," *Vancouver Sun*, 31 October 1997, A9; Rosemary Speirs, "The PM and His Greenhouse Policy," *Charlottetown Guardian*, 7 November 1997, A6.

15. Author's interview with Christine Stewart, March 2006.

16. Author's interview, February 2006.

17. Canada's justification for the 1 percent concession was that the United States was expected to reduce its emissions by increasing imports of Canadian natural gas, the production of which would increase Canada's emissions.

18. Author's interview with Christine Stewart, 2006.

19. Norm Ovenden, "Klein Works on Kyoto Veto," *Vancouver Sun*, 13 December 1997, A4; Joan Bryden and Norma Greenaway, "PM Promises to Consult with Provinces on Gas Emissions," *Vancouver Sun*, 12 December 1997, A10.

20. Rabe 2005.

21. Canadian Manufacturers and Exporters 2002; Alan Toulin, "Ottawa May Go It Alone on Kyoto: Speculation Rife that PM Will Commit at Earth Summit:

Cabinet Gets Ratification Plan Next Month, Could Be Approved without Provincial OK," *National Post*, 29 August 2002, A1.

22. Susan Riley, "Liberal Caucus Draws Green Line," *Ottawa Citizen*, 26 August 2002, A12.

23. Chrétien 2007, 388.

24. Government of Canada 2002.

25. Steven Frank, "Where There's Smoke ...," *Time*, 21 October 2002, 160 (17):47.

26. The full statement can be viewed at http://www.scics.gc.ca/cinfo02/830767004_e.html. With respect to the principles rejected by the prime minister, see Joe Paraskevas, Peter O'Neil, April Lindgren, and Joan Bryden, "Provinces Fail to Budge PM on Kyoto: Chrétien Says Deal Must Be Passed in Interest of 'Future Generations,'" *Ottawa Citizen*, 27 November 2002, A6.

27. Les Whittington, "Ottawa Eyes $5 Billion Kyoto Incentive Plan," *Toronto Star*, 21 September 2002, A22; Andrew Coyne, "The Line on Kyoto: Ratify and Renege," *National Post*, 18 November 2002, A15; Joe Paraskevas, "McLellan Sidesteps Kyoto Queries: Minister Will Have to Choose between Alberta, Caucus in House Vote," *Ottawa Citizen*, 29 November 2002, A12.

28. The prime minister justified the unusual decision to declare a nonbinding resolution a matter of confidence on the disingenuous grounds that the government had committed to ratification in the September 2002 throne speech. However, the throne speech only committed to a *vote* on ratification.

29. Chrétien 2007.

30. Dhaliwal 2002; Jean Chrétien, letter to John Dielwert, Chairman, Canadian Association of Petroleum Producers, n.d.

31. Chrétien 2007, 388.

32. Bataille et al. 2002.

33. Coyne, "The Line on Kyoto: Ratify and Renege," A15.

34. Steven Chase, Mark Mackinnon, and Patrick Brethour, "Martin Goes Cool on Kyoto," *Globe and Mail*, 3 December 2003, online edition.

35. Sage, IISD, and Jaccard and Associates 2005.

36. Government of Canada 2005.

37. Author's interview, February 2006.

38. Author's interview, February 2006.

39. Consistent with this, analysis of a similar plan estimated 120 MT/year of international purchases (Sage Centre, International Institute for Sustainable Development, and M. K. Jaccard and Associates 2005).

40. Jaccard et al., 2006.

41. Stephen Harper, Canadian Alliance fundraising letter, 2002, cited at http://www.cbc.ca/canada/story/2007/01/30/harper-kyoto.html.

42. Conservative Party of Canada 2006.

43. Jeff Sallot, "Kyoto Plan No Good, Minister Argues," *Globe and Mail*, 8 April 2006, A5.

44. Environment Canada 2006.

45. Ibid.

46. Ambrose 2006.

47. Bill Curry, "Transit Trumps Climate Change, Ottawa Told," *Globe and Mail*, 1 September 2006, A5.

48. "Transit Tax Credit Proposal Expensive Way to Cut CO_2," *Edmonton Journal*, 7 April 2006, B12.

49. Environment Canada, 2007.

50. Sears 2006.

51. Simpson, Jaccard, and Rivers 2007, 97.

52. Front-page headlines in Canada's two national newspaper were "Critics Blast Ottawa's 'Shameful' Green Plan," and "Emission Rules Begin in 2010: Tories' Clean Air Plan Too Slow, Too Vague."

53. Environment Canada 2007.

54. Alexander Panetta, "Bid to Kill Kyoto Bill Fails," *Globe and Mail*, 14 February 2007.

55. National Round Table on the Environment and the Economy 2007.

56. Jaccard and Rivers 2007.

57. Jeffrey Simpson, "Distortion, Incoherence in the Carbon Tax's Wake," *Globe and Mail*, 26 September 2008, A19.

58. Brian Laghi, "Harper Tories on the Brink of Majority, Poll Finds," *Globe and Mail*, 2 September 2008, A1.

59. Jeffrey Simpson, "Time for a Little Mea Culpa," *Globe and Mail*, 3 January 2009, A15.

60. Notes for an address by the Honorable Jim Prentice, minister of the environment, to the Bennet Jones Lake Louise World Cup Business Forum, 28 November 2008. Emphasis in original.

61. Juliet O'Neill, "Canada, US Join in $7B Plan for Carbon; 'Clean Energy,'" *National Post*, 4 March 2009, A5.

62. Brian Laghi, "Canada to Match U.S. Car Fuel Rules," *Globe and Mail*, 20 May 2009, A10.

63. Gloria Galloway, "Emissions Rules Delayed to Match U.S. Timetable," *Globe and Mail*, 29 May 2009, A12.

64. Author's interview, March 2006.

65. Author's interviews, February 2006.

66. Whittington, "Liberals Knew Kyoto a Long Shot," A6.

67. Bergman, Müller, Strøm, and Blomgren, 2003, 157.

68. Canadian Council of Chief Executives 2007.

69. Bernstein 2002.

References

Ambrose, Rona. 2006. Testimony before the Standing Committee on Environment and Sustainable Development, 5 October.

Bataille, Christopher, et al. 2002. *Construction and Analysis of Sectoral, Regional and National Cost Curves in Canada. Part IV: Final Analysis Report.* M. K. Jaccard and Associates.

Bergman, Torbjörn, Wolfgang C. Müller, Kaare Strøm, and Magnus Blomgren. 2003. Democratic Delegation and Accountability: Cross-National Patterns. In *Delegation and Accountability in Parliamentary Democracies*, ed. Kaare Strøm, Wolfgang C. Müller, and Torbjörn Bergman. Oxford: Oxford University Press.

Bernstein, Steven. 2002. International Institutions and the Framing of Domestic Policies: The Kyoto Protocol and Canada's Response to Climate Change. *Policy Sciences* 35:203–236.

Canadian Council of Chief Executives. 2007. *Clean Growth: Building a Canadian Environmental Superpower.* October.

Canadian Manufacturers and Exporters. 2002. *Pain without Gain: Canada and the Kyoto Protocol.* Ottawa: Canadian Manufacturers and Exporters.

Chrétien, Jean. 2007. *My Years as Prime Minister.* Toronto: Knopf Canada.

Conservative Party of Canada. 2006. *Stand Up for Canada.* Ottawa: Conservative Party of Canada.

Dhaliwal, Herb. 2002. Letter to Mr. John Dielwert, Chairman, Canadian Association of Petroleum Producers. 18 December.

EKOS Research Associates Inc. 2002. Climate Change and Kyoto. October–December.

EKOS Research Associates Inc. 2003. *Canadian Attitudes toward Climatic Change. Spring 2003 Tracking Study, Final Report.* March.

Environment Canada. 2006. Ambrose Wants Realistic, Results-Oriented Approach to Climate Change. News release. 11 May.

Environment Canada. 2007. *A Climate Change Plan for the Purposes of the Kyoto Protocol Implementation Act—2007.* Ottawa: Environment Canada.

Goldstein, Judith, and Robert Keohane, eds. 1993. *Ideas and Foreign Policy: Beliefs, Institutions, and Political Change.* Ithaca: Cornell University Press.

Government of Canada. 1999. *Canada's Emission Outlook: An Update.* National Climate Change Process Analysis and Modelling Group. Ottawa: Government of Canada.

Government of Canada. 2002. *Climate Change Plan for Canada.* Ottawa: Government of Canada.

Government of Canada. 2005. *Project Green. Moving Forward on Climate Change: A Plan for Honouring Our Kyoto Commitment.* Ottawa: Government of Canada.

Harrison, Kathryn. 1996. *Passing the Buck: Federalism and Canadian Environmental Policy.* Vancouver: UBC Press.

Jaccard, Mark, et al. 2006. *Burning Our Money to Warm the Planet: Canada's Ineffective Efforts to Reduce Greenhouse Gas Emissions.* Toronto: CD Howe Institute.

Jaccard, Mark, and Nic Rivers. 2007. Estimating the Effect of the Canadian Government's 2006–7 Greenhouse Gas Policies. CD Howe Institute e-brief, 12 June.

National Round Table on the Environment and the Economy. 2007. *Response of the National Round Table on the Environment and the Economy to Its Obligations under the Kyoto Protocol Implementation Act.* Ottawa: NRTEE.

Natural Resources Canada. 2006. *Canada's Energy Outlook: The Reference Case 2006.* Ottawa: Natural Resources Canada.

Rabe, Barry. 2005. Moral Super-Power or Policy Laggard? Translating Kyoto Protocol Ratification into Federal and Provincial Climate Change Policy in Canada. Paper presented at the Annual Meeting of the Canadian Political Science Association, June.

Sage Centre, International Institute for Sustainable Development, and M. K. Jaccard and Associates. 2005. *Let's Do It! A Plan for Implementing Kyoto and Beyond.* Winnipeg: International Institute for Sustainable Development.

Sears, Robin V. 2006. The Politics of Climate Change: From One Government to the Next. *Policy Options* (October): 6–11.

Simpson, Jeffrey, Mark Jaccard, and Nic Rivers. 2007. *Hot Air: Meeting Canada's Climate Change Challenge.* Toronto: McClelland and Stewart.

Smith, Heather. 1998. The Provinces and Canadian Climate Change Policy. *Policy Options* (May): 28–30.

Strategic Counsel. 2007. A Report to the Globe and Mail and CTV. State of Canadian Public Opinion: The Greening of Canada. 26 January.

7

Climate Clever? Kyoto and Australia's Decade of Recalcitrance

Kate Crowley

It is not in Australia's interests to ratify the Kyoto Protocol. The reason it is not in Australia's interests to ratify the Kyoto Protocol is that, because the arrangements currently exclude—and are likely under present settings to continue to exclude—both developing countries and the United States. For us to ratify the protocol would cost us jobs and damage our industry. That is why the Australian Government will continue to oppose ratification.[1]
Prime Minister, John Howard, 2002

Introduction

Until 2007 only two developed nations had refused to ratify the Kyoto Protocol, the United States and Australia, and while their positions on the international stage seemed remarkably similar, at the domestic level they diverged significantly. The key difference, it is argued here, was that while Australia refused to ratify, it was nevertheless committed to meeting its Kyoto target of an 8 percent increase of greenhouse gas emissions by 2008–2012. This could only have made sense to the Coalition government if pursuing this target did not damage jobs, industry, and the economy, and throws into question the effectiveness of its domestic plans for reducing emissions. This chapter argues that Australia's pursuit of its Kyoto target was symbolic, "climate clever"[2] rhetoric designed to play to a concerned domestic audience, and that achieving the target has only been possible because of land use changes rather than any real effort such as restructuring the energy industry. Given the lack of action to reduce emissions, this also throws into question the Coalition government's claims that its +8 percent target represented a 17 percent cut in projected business-as-usual emissions on 1990 levels to 2012, with emissions otherwise growing 25 percent without the Kyoto target. If this were true, there would be evidence of massive policy efforts to reign in energy emissions, where in fact there has been none.

There is a critical need, therefore, to link Australia's international position on the Kyoto Protocol with its domestic policy agenda. Academic analysis of Australia's position has tended to focus either on its recalcitrance at the international level or on its policy efforts at the domestic level, rather than on the more complex task of linking these levels.[3] This chapter aims to make these links by considering international behavior, domestic policy, and the paradox that the Coalition government had not ratified the Kyoto Protocol but was pursuing its Kyoto target. The chapter employs both international relations and comparative politics approaches in exploring this global-domestic dynamic. It focuses on the politics and policies of the Coalition government, led by John Howard, prime minister in the decade from 1997 to 2007, from Australia's signing of the Kyoto Protocol and the launching of greenhouse policy initiatives until the election of the Labor government. It examines Australia's domestic circumstances and its argument for its +8 percent Kyoto target before examining its electoral, normative, and institutional context and then both the pathway to nonratification and domestic policy efforts.

Australia's climate change policy changed dramatically in late 2007 with the ratification of Kyoto by the newly elected Labor government, just in time for post-Kyoto talks in Bali and for its climate change minister to co-chair post-Kyoto roadmap negotiations. The normative tone of Australia's rhetoric changed abruptly too, from self-interest to global citizenry, albeit with the caution of a new government, which is now being criticized for not embracing 25–40 percent global emission cuts on 1990 levels by 2020. Even so, from opposition Labor forged a new direction on climate change. Following the release of the Stern report, it held a national summit on climate solutions and commissioned analysis of the efficacy of future emissions cuts from Australian National University economist Ross Garnaut, delivered in 2008. Labor also campaigned in 2007 on an aggressive, innovative climate change platform, which forced significant concessions from the Coalition government. Both the Labor opposition and the Coalition government committed to domestic cap-and-trade emissions trading, but Labor committed to 60 percent emissions reductions from 1990 levels by 2050 and promised AU$3 billion in climate change funding over four years, tripling the government's commitment. Labor's announcement of a 20 percent mandatory renewable energy renewable target by 2020 drew a 15 percent target from the government, which had previously proposed to abandon its 2 percent scheme, and Labor rejected entirely the government's faith in nuclear energy.

Australia's Kyoto Concessions

Australia is a carbon-intensive economy, entirely unprepared as yet for drastic cuts to its emissions, with coal still its largest export and dominant power source, and its export industry generally highly reliant on generating greenhouse gas emissions. Given its energy source, transport costs, and population profile,[4] it is easily the top net greenhouse gas emitter of the industrialized nations at 25.4 metric tons per year of CO_2 equivalent ($MtCO_2eq$) per capita (in 2007)—about 30 percent higher than the United States.[5] In global terms, it contributes about 3.9 percent of the emissions of industrialized countries, or 1.4 percent of global emissions with only 0.32 percent of the global population.[6] Australia did negotiate an 8 percent increase in emissions above 1990 levels by 2008–2012 at Kyoto in 1997, which it argued would be a significant cut in business-as-usual emissions.[7] It also negotiated the so-called "Australia clause," stipulated in Article 3.7 of the Protocol, which allows any country with net land clearing in 1990 to include the equivalent emissions in its baseline. Australia was the only Annex 1 developed country to benefit from this, with easy credit then yielded toward its +8 percent target from the net land clearing it had been experiencing in 1990.[8] The credit came as the boom in land clearing in 1990 plummeted shortly thereafter and has continued to fall (see table 7.2). Without this credit, Australia's emissions would stand at 25 percent over 1990 levels, with no obvious efforts then having been made by the Coalition government to meet the +8 percent target beyond halting land clearing.[9] Indeed, energy emissions have accelerated along business-as-usual trend lines under the Coalition government over its decade in office.

Any depiction of Australia internationally as an excessively self-interested state in terms of its position on the Kyoto Protocol needs to assess the accuracy of its claim to special-case status among the Annex 1 developed nations. Australia's special-case argument rests on its heavy reliance on fossil fuels for energy, the transport issues associated with its size as the sixth largest country in the world, its above-OECD-average population growth, its still changing land use patterns, and its export-based economy.[10] Australia is also a "new world" economy—new in the sense that its economy is only two hundred years old, and "new world" in the sense of its Asia-Pacific location and strong trading ties with East Asian nations. These include ties with developing nations that are exempt from the first Kyoto commitment period, so that Australia's trade competitiveness would suffer if the costs of production increased while those of its East Asian trading partners did not.[11] Australia's reliance on coal for power is a massive 85 percent, double the OECD average,[12] and best paralleled by China's reliance at 67.7 percent. These two countries have shared a self-interested defense of their cheap coal-based energy despite international criticism and, in Australia's case at least, a greenhouse policy context that has been highly protective of the fossil fuel industry.[13]

Aside from its reliance on coal, much of Australia's special-case argument also applies to Canada, which did not argue for increased emissions but finds it equally difficult to cut emissions levels.[14] Australia rested its case on the principle of differentiation, which the Coalition government appropriated and reinterpreted as the need for Australia's special treatment. In Kyoto Protocol discourse, *differentiation* refers to the need for the differing treatment for developing countries or for differentiation among countries within the context of a European target.[15] Australia's pursuit of increased emissions and land use concessions, and its spoiling behavior in international fora during the Coalition government's term in office, was self-interested in terms of protecting both the national economy and Australia's fossil-fuel-based interests. But it also raises questions about the legitimacy of domestic policy during the Coalition decade, which has been criticized as too closely aligned with the interests of the fossil fuel industry. By not ratifying the Kyoto Protocol, the government was able to pursue its economic, growth, and trade agendas unhindered and to offset its emissions reduction inaction with land use concessions. Australia's self-interest was greatly criticized at Kyoto in 1997. Indeed, Hamilton argues that it was only tolerated in the interests of achieving an agreed Protocol.[16]

Australia and the United States have both seen Kyoto as a threat. Australia did effectively negate that threat in the first commitment period, with its land-clearing concessions, but it would have had to face significant cuts in energy-related emissions in the second commitment period and so refused to ratify. Yet if policy attempts were really in train to actually cut emissions below business-as-usual levels as promised, and if they were proving effective, then abatement costs should have been less of a deterrence post-2012. Again, as critics have claimed, the cost of not acting on global warming is not something that the Coalition government considered; nor did the government consider the benefits of acting early, in terms of lessening the cost in the longer term, or the cost of being excluded from global carbon trading and other Kyoto mechanisms.[17] Neither was energy efficiency promoted, where abatement could have been achieved quickly and cheaply. Investment in alternate energy was likewise ignored. Hamilton argued, for example, that Australia's consumption of fuel is wasteful, that it has never been addressed, and that efficiency efforts would offer quick wins relatively easily.[18] In failing to cut emissions thus far, Australia is not well placed post-2012. While the details of the second commitment period are yet to be negotiated, emissions cuts will be critical. Australia loses its land-clearing concession post-Kyoto unless it is renegotiated, will need to now deeply cut energy emissions, and may also be expecting, as a late ratifier, to suffer a penalty of having to reduce emissions by an extra 30 percent.[19]

Electoral Interests, Normative Divides, and Institutional Context

On the international stage, Australia has therefore gained huge Kyoto concessions, with its target of an increase in emissions and generous Kyoto accounting concessions to 2012, but there was great uncertainty about the post-Kyoto period and hence the failure to ratify. This international Kyoto recalcitrance can be explained by an ideological prioritization of domestic jobs, concern for growth of industry and the economy, and by the closeness of business-government relations under a conservative government. However, it is necessary to go beyond these factors to understand the Coalition government's rhetoric and agenda on domestic climate change policy over the last decade and its pursuit of its Kyoto target: the electoral, normative, and institutional policy contexts must be taken into account. Before leaving international consideration aside, however, it is worth dispensing with the simplistic explanation that Australia was mimicking US behavior on climate change policy and in rejecting ratification. As one of the last two developed nations left to ratify, Australia had come under strong and sustained normative pressures to ratify from other nations, from transnational nongovernmental organizations, and from expert, epistemic communities.

Given the conservatism of the Coalition government, its close relations with the United States, and its support for the invasion of Iraq as a member of the US president's "coalition of the willing," the mimicry argument does make sense. However, the argument fails to consider

Australia's domestic circumstances, namely, that the Coalition government was pragmatically motivated to seek practical outcomes for Australia's own benefit in terms of its export economy and reliance on coal for energy and production. There are good reasons, then, for suggesting that its interests fortuitously aligned with the United States on nonratification rather than having been dictated by them,[20] although it is true that Australia has long been a ready follower of the United States for reasons of culture, history, identity, and values.[21] So while Australia's relations with the United States have been influential and may have played some role in Australia's nonratification, policy pragmatism and ideological conservatism were more significant. By contrast with the Coalition government, the Rudd Labor government has already begun to pressure the United States to follow its own return to multilateralism by rejoining international post-Kyoto talks as a ratifying member after the 2008 presidential election. Arguing that Australia was simply mimicking the United States also entirely misses Australia's trade-exposed position in the Asia-Pacific region: as a carbon-intensive economy, it would be disadvantaged by agreeing to emissions reductions in its energy industry that are not made by its lesser-developed trading competitors in the region.

Electoral Interests
Australia's position on Kyoto thus far is not entirely straightforward to the outside observer. However, it becomes even more of a paradox considering the strength of domestic opinion over the last decade in favor of the Kyoto process and ratification. In 1997, when the Protocol was being developed, 80 percent of Australians believed that Australia should sign it, and in 2001, when it was being resisted by both the United States and Australia, 80 percent of Australians still favored ratification, without the United States if necessary. Public opinion has supported not only the Kyoto Protocol but also the need for strong government action over the last decade, with Australians believing their government was not doing enough about climate change. In 1997, 90 percent of Australians believed this; in 2003, 78 percent; and in 2006, 86 percent. What is interesting to note is that the environment itself was not a highly *ranked* issue of concern over most of this time, with 3 and 5 percent of respondents identifying it as the "most important problem" facing Australia for most of the 1990s, and only rising to 6 percent before the 2001 federal election.[22] The failure of the Labor opposition to prioritize environmental issues before the elevation of Kevin Rudd as prime minister is also appar-

ent in polling over the last decade, with the public fairly evenly divided as to whether Labor or the Coalition government should be in charge of the environment. Beginning around 2005, though, Australians began to rank environment higher on their list of concerns, so that by the 2007 election campaign, Australians were ranking environment as their top issue of concern.[23]

In July 2006, cross-national polling showed that Australians were the most concerned of the nations polled that "the way the world produces and uses energy is causing environmental problems including climate change." Multination polling the next year similarly found that Australians were the most in favor of measures to combat climate change (92 percent), even if the cost was significant (69 percent), and that 95 percent of Australians believed climate change would pose a threat to national interests over the next decade. So in the lead-up to the federal election, Australians were more worried about climate change than any other global issue, and more worried about it than any other nation in the world.[24] By 2007, the domestic polls were not looking good in general for the Coalition government, but on environment and climate they were particularly devastating. Seventy-four percent of respondents were not satisfied with the government on climate change; 74 percent favored a carbon tax, which the government had always rejected; and 77 percent did not trust the government at all on environmental issues.[25] The Coalition government had weathered bad opinion polls and polls indicating high levels of support for Kyoto for over a decade. But it was remarkable that Howard shifted rhetoric only slightly in 2007 from climate change skepticism, which had long been his mantra, to climate change "realism." This he defined as not embracing every gloomy prediction but responding in a measured way—and in a way that doesn't hurt the Australian economy.[26]

The high levels of public support for climate action do explain the Coalition government's emphasis on meeting its Kyoto target, without stressing how this was done, and the need to play rhetorically to its domestic audience. That the public remained so concerned for so long would suggest that it was not convinced by the government's efforts or that these efforts were not seen to be as significant as failure to ratify the Kyoto Protocol. Equally, in the public's eyes, the government's climate change skepticism, prioritization of maximizing economic growth, and rejection of Kyoto played strongly to fossil-fuel-based interests. The government was criticized in particular for its close relations with the Australian Industry Greenhouse Network, comprising industries such as coal, electricity, aluminum, petroleum, minerals, and cement.[27] It was also criticized for blurring government-industry boundaries in the drafting and managing of policy, the funding of research into the cost of abatement, and the inclusion of industry on international government delegations.[28] Environmental organizations and alternative energy groups, by contrast, were treated as outsiders without favor or influence over government policy. Pro-Kyoto groups promoting alternative energy and sustainable business were equally excluded.[29] Environmental groups were consequently very active in civil society and responsible in part for the high levels of public concern, but the Labor opposition did not champion public opinion because of its own internal divisions over climate change. The Coalition government's effective exploitation of such divisions in the opposition's ranks was a hallmark of its decade in power[30] and deflected climate change pressure away from government.

Ideas

Despite public opinion, the dominant characteristic of the Coalition's climate change policy was an unwavering, ideological prioritization of domestic jobs, industry, and the economy, and a closeness of business-government relations, which held captive the climate policy agenda. For over a decade the Coalition was dogmatic, consistent, and pragmatic in its rhetoric, its nonratification, its protection of fossil-fuel-based industries, and its failure to address energy emissions. In terms of political philosophy and ideology, the Coalition was unambiguously pro-business and unified in its support of the prime minister's position of climate skepticism—right up until the 2007 federal election. Only then, with the Rudd opposition gaining ground and the public responding to its support for the Kyoto Protocol and bona fide emissions cuts, did the Coalition environment minister Malcolm Turnball, a potential leadership contender, signal any sympathy with the public's concern. The Coalition government was masterful in its use of pragmatic language about the need to defend jobs, industry, and the economy to completely overwhelm any counterarguments from Kyoto supporters. It appropriated ambiguous language to serve its ends: *differentiation*, for example, meant making special allowances for Australia, and *no regrets* meant policymaking at no cost rather than taking early action. Most crucially for Australia's reputation, the government also reinterpreted leadership on climate change to mean a unilateral asserting of national over global interests, blocking negotiations contrary to Australia's interests, and treating developing nations as equal competitors.

In terms of Australian political parties, the Coalition comprises parties of the right, whereas the Labor Party, with its origins in working-class perspectives, is generally more liberal and oriented toward social justice. The Labor Party is not, however, naturally a leftist party with regard to environmental issues—and certainly with regard to climate change. It has always had strong ties to trade unions, and historically it has proved itself as prepared as the Coalition parties to sacrifice natural resources for the sake of the economy. But both Coalition and Labor federal governments have been responsible for ensuring the establishment of world heritage areas in Australia, and both types of governments have introduced innovative environmental policies and legislation. Even so, there is greater room under a Labor government for *ethical* debates, for example over the obligations of global citizens, or the moral aspects of nonratification, or the environmental injustices of the behavior of developed nations.[31] When the Kyoto Protocol came into force for ratifying parties in 2005, the Coalition government combined its economic rationalism with its skepticism to attack Kyoto's global utility as an effective emissions abatement mechanism. It argued that Kyoto was dead without the participation of the world's largest emitters, the United States and developing nations,[32] and it advocated a regional, trade-based, self-regulatory alternative.[33] The Kyoto Protocol's global, moral, and regulatory style never suited the Coalition government's philosophy, which was defined by regionalism, self-interest, the free market, and a clear rejection of multilateral, global efforts like Kyoto.[34]

Institutions

The conservative political philosophy of the Coalition government, aligned as it was with business and industry interests, powerfully countered public opinion and was not effectively challenged by the Labor opposition for over a decade, until the 2007 election campaign. The incumbency of the Coalition government and the policy and political dominance of its conservative leader, John Howard, were further significant factors in explaining Australia's failure to ratify Kyoto. The Coalition government won office in 1996, 1998, 2001, and 2004, before eventually losing in a landslide to the Rudd Labor opposition in 2007, by which time commentators were noting that it had grown increasingly distant from the aspirations of mainstream Australia.[35] The Australian public was concerned for this entire time about the threat of climate change, as we have seen, although climate change did not become a prominent issue among voters until around 2005. Having supported

Labor in government for thirteen years from 1983, however, the public were not going to readily abandon the Coalition, which had at the 1996 federal election adopted a more brazen, innovative, and thoughtful environmental policy platform than had the Labor government. Indeed, Labor prime minister Paul Keating had completely alienated conservationists.[36] The Howard government grew ever more politically powerful then and gradually more radically conservative; it was able to exploit its control of Parliament, including both houses from 2004, when it unexpectedly won control of the Senate. In part, as a consequence of the government's enhanced power, the states and minor parties in the Senate barely influenced climate change policy.

The question remains as to what institutional capacity there was to counter the Coalition government's climate policy recalcitrance and neglect. First, with Australia's parliamentary system, the prime minister was entirely supported by his own Cabinet, and the opposition lacked the numbers in the House of Representatives to influence policy.[37] The minor parties elected to the Senate—the Democrats and the Greens—both attempted to influence climate policy before 2004. The Australian Democrats were able to use their balance of power in the Senate to negotiate abatement programs, renewable power, and alternative-fuel programs in exchange for supporting the Coalition government's tax on goods and services.[38] The Australian Greens introduced the Convention on Climate Change (Implementation) Bill 1999, and the Kyoto Protocol Ratification Bill 2002, which were defeated by the Coalition government in the House of Representatives.[39] Federalism is more promising, with the federal government having no direct environmental powers under the Australian Constitution, and residual powers belonging to the states, which may or may not chose to act to reduce emissions. But the federal government has a number of indirect methods of attempting to control state environmental policy, funding being the most obvious, and it can create legislation and can appeal to the High Court if challenged by the states on constitutional grounds. Federalism has also enabled the states to move past the Coalition government's recalcitrance by, for example, creating carbon rights, internal mandatory emissions trading schemes,[40] legislation to control land clearing, and emissions abatement requirements for developers.[41]

Australia's Kyoto Recalcitrance

All the elements of the Coalition government's climate policy are evident in its refusal to ratify the Kyoto Protocol, its conservatism, prioritization of maximum economic growth, unilateralism, climate skepticism, its protection of its fossil fuel industries, and its cheap, coal-based energy-trading advantage. Things were very different in the late 1980s under the Hawke Labor government, which aspired to international leadership on global warming without at that stage having to deal with the reality of Australia's carbon-intensive domestic circumstances. With the election of the Rudd government, thus far there has been a shift away from the Coalition's self-interested obstructionism and a reassertion of the principles of multilateralism on climate change and of Australia as an engaged environmental broker. It is interesting to note, however, that Labor prime minister Keating, who succeeded Hawke, was more of a climate change realist than Hawke and less of an environmental policy enthusiast. When Hawke lost the leadership to Keating in 1991, the environment consequently fell as an issue of government concern, with Keating's dismantling of key environmental institutions and processes.[42] This was critical for greenhouse policy, with Hawke's aspirations being replaced by Keating's apathy and his emphasis on voluntarism, both paving the way for the ensuing Coalition government policy.[43] These leader-laggard-leader stages are described below, with an emphasis upon the Coalition's decade, Australia's recalcitrance on the Kyoto Protocol, and its self-interested international posturing.

From Geneva to Kyoto

Australia had been an early accepter in the late 1980s of the principle of developed nations acting first on greenhouse gas emissions reduction despite the associated costs. Its early commitments were ambitious but untested, prior to domestic efforts, and tied even then to economic and trade-based caveats.[44] Policy shifted, under Keating, at the first Conference of the Parties (COP 1) to the United Nations Framework Convention on Climate Change UNFCCC in Berlin in 1995, with Australia fighting targets, emphasizing costs, calling for differentiation, and no longer accepting developed-nation responsibility. Australia's leader-to-laggard shift was entrenched at the 1996 COP 2 in Geneva by the newly elected Coalition government. Australia made a serious effort, with an attitude noted as positively hostile, to derail the Kyoto process, questioning Intergovernmental Panel on Climate Change IPCC science, opposing legally binding targets, and advocating differentiation—but only for itself.[45] It went armed with economic analysis to prove its case as atypically vulnerable to emissions reduction as a carbon-intensive nation. This analysis was later found by the Commonwealth Ombudsman to have been improperly funded by the fossil fuel industry and undertaken by a research body whose membership included energy industry leaders but actively excluded environmentalists.[46] The analysis stated that reductions proposed would cause GDP to decline 2 percent, with each Australian citizen AU$9,000 worse off over ten years and the loss of tens of thousands of jobs, causing enormous damage to the economy. The per capita economic cost would be twenty-two times higher for Australia than for the European Union, six times higher than for the United States, and would see Australian wages reduced by 20 percent by 2020.[47]

While the COP 2 in Geneva established the need for a legally binding treaty, it left open the possibility of different targets for individual countries. Australia again argued at the 1997 COP 3 in Kyoto against binding targets and against the need for countries to either cut back or reverse the prevailing upward trends in greenhouse gas emissions.[48] It no longer accepted the basic "Kyoto rationale" of a three-step process, that is, (1) stop emissions growth, (2) cut emissions, and only then (3) forge a global regime by involving developing nations.[49] Instead, Australia emphasized its special-case argument, again drawing international and domestic criticism.[50] Ian Lowe gives a compelling firsthand account of Australia's behavior, which Hamilton observes was embarrassing for other Australians, with even the United States criticizing Australia's spoiling efforts.[51] Other governments were scandalized by its irresponsible stance, Lowe suggests, bringing talks to the brink of collapse, until a closed-door, late-night session agreed at 3 a.m. to Australia's differentiated target and at 4 a.m. to include allowances for changes in land use.[52] So Australia did achieve its +8 percent target and critical "Australia clause," but its all-night ruse only succeeded in the end due to the parties' goal of achieving unanimous agreement.

Australia Fails to Ratify
Australia's role as a spoiler in the Kyoto process continued into 2000 at COP 6 at The Hague, Netherlands, when talks between the parties collapsed without agreement on how to implement the Kyoto Protocol, in part because Australia and the United States wanted to broaden the definition of *carbon sink*.[53] Australia argued for the definition of acceptable CO_2-absorbing forests to be extended to include vegetation such as saltbush, planted to alleviate salinity, and nonnative exotics, a position opposed by environmentalists. Indeed, it was reported that pot plants ended up dotting The Hague during the talks with signs denoting them as Australian "sinks."[54] COP 6 resumed in Bonn in 2001, where the parties agreed at last on the extensive use of flexibility mechanisms.

Australia's environment minister declared that his country's concessions would ensure that it need do nothing new—like actually cutting emissions;[55] land use concessions alone would suffice in meeting its +8 percent target. The difference between this target and Australia's projected business-as-usual emissions (even including the land use mechanism) was not mentioned, with the minister either underplaying the efforts that would be required to reduce emissions below business-as-usual levels or setting business-as-usual at inflated and irrelevant levels.

By the conclusion of COP 7 in Marrakesh, after the withdrawal of the United States, Australia had achieved the outcomes it had been seeking on the definition of carbon sinks (that is, existing forests, reafforestation, and improvements in managing forestry, cropland, and grazing land). These outcomes included no restrictions of credits from afforestation and reforestation, the inclusion of revegetation as a sink activity, and no penalties for new fast-growing, short-rotation forest plantations. It was decided, however, that no sink credits could be carried beyond 2012.[56] Despite achieving its concessions, Australia announced in 2002, after the reelection of the Coalition government, that it would not ratify the Kyoto Protocol but would instead pursue its own course based on a dual doctrine of differentiation, or special treatment, for Australia and "no regrets," or no-cost, policies. The Kyoto Protocol came into force on 16 June 2005 after Russia ratified. The Howard government continued to track its +8 percent Kyoto target in an attempt to demonstrate that nonparties can take effective action, and remained a UNFCCC party with accounting and reporting obligations. It also promoted the Asian Pacific Partnership on Clean Development and Energy (AP6)—a trade-based regional regime without emissions reduction targets—which is the type of regional model that Australia was hoping would model potential post-Kyoto arrangements.[57]

The Asian Pacific Partnership
Australia intensified its criticism of Kyoto after it came into force as a way of deflecting concern that it was now a nonparty, with the environment minister dismissing Kyoto as a "political stunt, not a serious way of addressing the issue."[58] Australia's rejection of environmental multilateralism was much criticized from all quarters, as was Australia's self-interested pursuit of the AP6 arrangement with the United States, Japan, China, India, and Korea. With these nations accounting for 50 percent of global emissions, and Kyoto covering only 25 percent in the first commitment period, Australia advocated the AP6 as superior and potentially

more effective.[59] The AP6 provided an attractive alternative for Australia, being a pragmatic arrangement that promotes specific trade benefits rather than carrying costs for each of its partners. It also embodies the region's material and security interests, resource endowments, and development needs and promotes market liberalism over regulatory approaches to climate. This "mini-lateral" effort, Aynsley Kellow argues, was precipitated by the Kyoto Protocol imposing costs, not benefits, on participating nations, while failing to meet its own targets and failing to offer a way beyond 2012. It is not possible to explore the effectiveness of the Kyoto Protocol here, but it is worth reflecting that Australia's resistance to it has been motivated, Kellow argues, by Kyoto's Eurocentrism, which is unsuited to the Asian Pacific.[60]

It will take some time for Australia to salvage its reputation on climate change, given the recalcitrance of the Coalition government and its consistent self-interest, although Rudd made a very positive start at post-Kyoto talks in Bali. The AP6 was thought by the Coalition to provide a useful forum for regional dialog, but it is not defined by a philosophy of abatement or any sense of moral responsibility for developed nations to act first. It also stumbled when the US Congress refused to approve funding for it, with Republican Senator John McCain dismissing it as a public relations ploy.[61] Australia's pursuit of the AP6 did show that it was looking for a climate change solution suited to its economic interests, free of adverse trade and employment effects, and promoting its energy industry. The Coalition government was convinced that the Kyoto Protocol would fail without the United States, and without early involvement by the developing nations, but its tactics may have encouraged those nations to also adopt self-interested, concession-seeking behavior in post-Kyoto negotiations. On the international stage, Australia has had a clear record of self-interested recalcitrance over the Howard decade with its refusal to ratify the Kyoto Protocol and its refusal to cut its energy emissions. It has negotiated a Kyoto target and concessions that allow it to conduct business as usual, which set the scene for the Coalition government's neglect of climate change policy, its most significant initiative having been to offset burgeoning energy emissions with reductions in land clearing.

Policy Efforts and Effectiveness

The Coalition government maintained that its policy efforts over the Howard decade were innovative and effective in terms of tracking

Australia's Kyoto target, while not threatening jobs, industry, or the economy—no-regrets, no-cost policymaking in action. However, to its critics, Coalition policy isolated Australia among developed nations; was poorly funded per capita on a comparative basis; failed to promote energy efficiency, alternate energy, or energy industry restructuring; and emphasized voluntary over market-based or regulatory instruments. The Coalition government ignored advice by a Senate review committee to go beyond no-regrets, no-cost measures.[62] The Coalition government's key programs were the 1997 Safeguarding the Future Package, the 1998 National Greenhouse Strategy, the 1999 Measures for a Better Environment Package, and the 2004 Securing Australia's Energy Future measures (table 7.1).[63] In the 1997 Package, the Coalition maintained and extended the Keating Labor government's emphasis on voluntary action, research, and information dissemination in its climate change policy. It boosted spending from AU$180 million in 1997 to over $2.5 billion during the 1997–2007 decade. In comparative terms, however, this was a meager effort at the lower end of spending by developed countries—at $4 per capita, similar to Canada but well below US and Japanese levels.[64] Coalition government spending efforts were later criticized by the independent Australian National Audit Agency as inadequate, ineffective, and inefficiently managed and unlikely to deliver significant greenhouse gas emissions reductions.[65]

The 1998 National Greenhouse Strategy saw the establishment of the Australian Greenhouse Office, which the Coalition government claimed as a world first despite the New South Wales state government and the Republic of China having already established their own such offices. Otherwise, this National Greenhouse Strategy emphasized intergovernmental cooperation and relations on greenhouse gases reduction efforts and planning as a way of reducing duplication by governments in their abatement efforts. The 1999 Measures for a Better Environment Package reflects the influence of the Australian Democrats discussed above, while the 2004 Securing Australia's Energy Future white paper has been criticized as "brazen in its aggressive affirmation of continuing fossil fuel interest."[66] Several recurring themes have emerged in the general criticism of the government's approach, including concern over the lack of measures tackling burgeoning energy emissions, the government's focus on protection of the coal industry, its failure to support alternative energy, and its "touching belief" in clean coal.[67] Concerns have also been voiced regarding slow and inadequate policy implementation, haphazard planning, lack of integration of climate objectives into other policies, and

Table 7.1
Australian Policies and Programs 1996–2006[1]

Safeguarding the Future: Australia's Response to Climate Change (1997)
This program establishes the Australian Greenhouse Office,[2] the extension of
the Labor government's voluntary Greenhouse Challenge program for
industry, the MRET, the renewable energy equity fund and commercialization
program, energy efficiency measures in building and appliance codes, motor
vehicle fuel efficiencies, plans to triple Australia's forest plantations by 2020,
and support for local government uptake of the Cities for Climate Protection
program.

The National Greenhouse Strategy (1998)
This strategy updates and replaces Labor's Strategy and is consistent with the
principles of cooperative government, namely, cooperative decision making,
reduced intergovernmental conflict, and more certainty in decision making.
Besides reducing duplication in abatement efforts, it aims to ensure that
policies, programs, and actions are coordinated. Implementation focuses on
(1) improving public awareness and understanding of greenhouse issues, (2)
limiting greenhouse gas emissions, and (3) developing adaptation responses.

Measures for a Better Environment (1999)
This funding package reflects the Australian Democrats' renewable energy
and energy efficiency priorities by providing for cost-effective, large-scale
greenhouse gas abatement, particularly in substantial emissions reduction or
substantial sink enhancement; renewable energy capacity for remote, especially
indigenous, communities; funding for photovoltaic systems, with subsidies for
solar hot water, and to promote commercialization of renewable energy,
alternative fuel usage, and household energy reduction.

Securing Australia's Energy Future (2004)
Additional measures announced since 1999 take the federal spending to AU\$2
billion, including measures in the 2004 Energy White Paper (Kemp and
Downer 2004) and measures announced in the 2004–2005 federal budget,
some of which appear to overlap with previous programs and may involve
extensions. Included is AU\$334.4 million for reducing Australia's greenhouse
gas emissions, AU\$500 million for low-emission technologies, AU\$100 million
for renewable technologies, and AU\$75 million for demonstration Solar Cities.

---

1. *Sources:* Australian Greenhouse Office 2004; Campbell 2006; Commonwealth
of Australia 2004; Kemp and Downer 2004; Lyster 2004.
2. Included in the Howard government's early fiscal efforts was the establishment in 1998 of the world's first national greenhouse office as the key agency
on greenhouse matters, dedicated to cutting greenhouse gas emissions, with
responsibilities including whole of government policy coordination and program
delivery.

slow progress in gaining agreement on state measures.[68] Voluntarism was criticized as light-handed, weak, and ineffective, with an inability to provoke more than 10 percent of publicly listed companies into action and paralleled by such steep energy emissions rises as to question its impact at all.[69]

Table 7.1 also reflects the failure of the Coalition government to introduce a domestic cap-and-trade emissions trading scheme (which it rejected because its competitors did not have such a scheme) and to introduce carbon taxes (which it ruled out as punitive). The key federal regulatory measure has been the Mandatory Renewable Energy Program, introduced in 1998, which encourages renewable energy generation, emissions abatement, and the sustainability of renewable energy sources. This was aimed at electricity wholesalers and large users to increase the relative share of all electricity generated from renewables by an additional 2 percent, or 9,500 gigawatt-hours, per annum by 2010, with the 2 percent target maintained until 2020.[70] Other regulatory measures listed in table 7.1 refer to a broad range of appliance and efficiency standards, building codes, labeling schemes, fuel quality regulations, and licensing agreements—mostly introduced in cooperation with the states. Pressure to adopt domestic emissions trading had come from two of the government's own environment ministers, in 2000 and in 2003, as well as from the states, and most recently from the International Energy Agency. In November 2006, the prime minister established a government-business task force on emissions trading, which did support the establishment of a domestic cap-and-trade scheme.[71] This was announced as a possibility by the Coalition moving into the 2007 election year, to broad public support, although without any elaboration on how the scheme was expected to operate or what it was expected to achieve.

With such criticism of Australian abatement policy and the failure of the Coalition government to adopt effective policy instruments as well as its emphasis on voluntarism and ineffective spending, it would be surprising if greenhouse gas emissions had actually been reduced. The most critical, symbolic gesture by the government was its commitment to its +8 percent Kyoto target. The latest tracking of the target is shown in table 7.2, which is aggregated from recent data sets and indicatively reflects the significance of land use accounting in Australia's 1990 baseline.[72] It shows that Australia is on track to achieve its target without having to make absolute cuts in energy emissions, with energy increases being offset by significant land-clearing decreases since 1990. Reporting to the UNFCCC documents some progress on emissions change, the most

Table 7.2

Greenhouse Gas Emissions and Projections (MtCo2eq), 1990, 2003, 2010[1]

Sector	1990	2003	2010 abatement	2010 business as usual	2010 with measures	Percent of 1990
Energy	287	374	46	476	430	150
Stationary	196	268	35	341	306	156
Transport	62	80	2	89	86	140
Fugitive from fuel	30	26	8	46	38	127
Industrial processes	25	32	8	46	38	150
Agriculture	91	97	1	96	96	105
Waste	19	11	12	28	16	81
Subtotal	422	514	67	646	580	137
Land use, land use change, and forestry	129[2]	6	21	44	24	35
Forest lands	0	0	n/e	−21	−21	0
Land use change	129	6	21	65	45	n/e
Total net emissions	552	521	88	690	603	109

n/e: not estimated

1. These data rely on the Australian Greenhouse Office (Australian Greenhouse Office 2005a, 2006; Australian Bureau of Statistics 2006). Columns may not add due to rounding.

2. The LULUCF baseline is hugely significant to meeting the Kyoto target and has previously been reported at 85.9Mt, not 129Mt. Improved accounting methods may account for the difference in figures, as the Australian Greenhouse Office claims; however, the revised baseline makes it easier for Australia to meet its Kyoto target.

recent data for which is shown in table 7.2 in the 2003 column. Another report and progress update are expected shortly.[73] On the basis of the 2003 information, it can be seen that emissions due to land use, land use change, and forestry have dropped from 129 $MtCO_2eq$ in 1990 to 6 $MtCO_2eq$ in 2003. In the energy sector, which includes transportion, there has been an increase in the same period from 287 to 374 $MtCO_2eq$, while there has been little significant change in the other sectors. Recent tracking of the Kyoto target shows that Australia's policy measures will result in 88 $MtCO_2eq$ of abatement from business as usual by 2010. However, energy and industrial emissions will increase 150 percent and be entirely offset by plunging land use change, which might have happened regardless of action taken by the Coalition government.

It is clear then that the Coalition government's policy climate was conducive to burgeoning greenhouse gas emissions. Australia's most recent report to the UNFCCC breaks down mitigation into cross-sectoral and sectoral reporting. Abatement in the energy sector is of considerable significance, with analysis showing that the projected cuts in this sector from business as usual will be achieved by abatement of 47 $MtCO_2eq$ (that is, 37.6 $MtCO_2eq$ in stationary energy, 2.2 $MtCO_2eq$ in transport, and 7.2 $MtCO_2eq$ in fugitive emissions). However, the federal and state governments will contribute equally to abatement in stationary energy, with greenhouse gas abatement in New South Wales alone matching the entire federal government effort. Indeed, there is very little projected abatement from intergovernmental programs addressing stationary energy, with only 3.3 $MtCO_2eq$ projected to be achieved by means of increases in energy efficiency and local action programs. The other interesting feature of the reporting is program type, with state programs (comprising 20 $MtCO_2eq$ of the projected 47 $MtCO_2eq$ abatement in the energy sector) being entirely regulatory. Of the federal government programs, those that are voluntary account for approximately 20 $MtCO_2eq$ and include the Greenhouse Challenge programs for industry as well as minor green power and energy efficiency programs. The Mandatory Renewable Energy Program was the key federal government regulatory program for the Coalition but boasted a projected abatement of only 6.6 $MtCO_2eq$.[74]

The legitimacy of the Coalition government's abatement efforts was further undermined by the shifting methods used to determine baseline information and business-as-usual projections to 2010 between reporting periods, both in reporting to the UNFCCC and by the Australian Greenhouse Office. There are bona fide adjustments to accounting methods between reporting periods; however, this makes it difficult to compare reduction efforts and to determine their legitimacy over time. In terms of context, the Coalition government's resting of its abatement policy on the no-regrets principle has led to its narrow emphasis on voluntary programs. Colin Hunt argues that this has been inefficient and burdensome to the taxpayer and should be replaced by an economy-wide tax or permit-trading scheme that would price emissions.[75] Indeed, it is surprising that a government committed to market liberalism did not do this but instead sheltered the coal industry and energy production from market forces and restructuring for so many years. In terms of other policy contexts, the states are responsible for emissions reductions in transport, land use, planning, and energy use and supply; Australia as a nonparty to the Protocol had no access to Kyoto market mechanisms and international carbon trading.

Conclusion

This chapter has considered Australia's position on climate change in the international context against the legitimacy of its domestic efforts and has examined the paradox of the Coalition government refusing to ratify the Kyoto Protocol while embracing and pursuing its Kyoto targets. From the perspective of a conservative, self-interested, unilateralist national government, the Coalition's recalcitrance on ratification and its defense of jobs, industry, and economy do make sense. Its rhetoric about achieving its Kyoto target also makes sense for three reasons. First, this target represents an increase in emissions; second, the target can be reached by reducing land-clearing rates; and third, Australia's concerned public would not abide complete inaction on climate change. The fact that the Coalition remained in power for so long does not mean, however, that this rhetoric about meeting Australia's Kyoto target was convincing. Indeed, most Australians remained concerned about the adequacy of the Coalition government's efforts for over a decade. John Howard was remarkably effective in ensuring the Coalition's longevity, while the Labor opposition was ineffective, weak, divided, and subject to ongoing internal tensions over its own leadership and so unable to project any coherent message on climate change. Moreover, although the public was concerned about climate change, environmental issues were not an issue of high priority among Australians until the last few years before the Labor government was elected in 2007. In these circumstances, the Coalition government could afford to pursue climate change policy that was ideologically driven and shaped by its very close relations with fossil-fuel-based industries, with environmental organizations and the minor political parties only very ineffective counterinfluences.

The Coalition government's failure to reduce the country's greenhouse gas emissions was therefore ideologically driven, with electoral or institutional influences having little effect on climate policy other than to inspire government rhetoric. The Coalition ignored not only public opinion (which was often distracted by other issues) but also international pressures to ratify, legislation proposed by the Australian Greens, the warnings of Australian scientists and economists, and the criticism of both the Australian National Audit Office and a Senate review committee. It negotiated with the Australian Democrats only because they held the balance of power in the Australian Senate, and with the states on emissions reduction initiatives only because they have constitutional power over the environment (the federal government has the money). Recalcitrance at the international level and neglect of emissions reduction at home is a poor legacy for the Coalition to bequeath to the Rudd Labor government, because Australia now has a decade of inaction to catch up on in one of the world's most carbon-intensive economies. The Coalition's legacy includes its offsetting of Australia's burgeoning energy emissions against land-clearing reductions as well as a policy context defined by voluntary measures, inadequate spending and investment in research, and a lack of effective regulation and market-based mechanisms. The Rudd government's ratification of Kyoto reflects its embrace of climate change as a real concern and its confidence that it can negotiate the policy and political difficulties that will be associated with real emissions cuts. Australia has begun debating the realities of these difficulties, as they are now beginning to emerge, in an open and transparent fashion, for the very first time.

Australia is the highest greenhouse gas emitter per capita in the world, albeit only a marginal contributor to global emissions, and its Coalition government clearly placed national economic self-interest before abatement. It has been argued here that economic interest only partially explains nonratification politics and the government's much criticized policy efforts. The interests of the fossil fuel industry have dominated and were closely aligned with the prime minister's climate change skepticism and his government's economic rationalism. That the Coalition government withstood strong normative pressure, at home and abroad, to ratify Kyoto, restructure the energy industry, and significantly reduce emissions is testimony to how secure it was over its decade in power. Indeed, this chapter has found only modest institutional influences on climate change politics and policy in that time, through the actions of minor parties in the Senate and reviews by agencies, independent bodies, and committees. If the government was faking its climate change efforts by relying on land clearance reductions to cover burgeoning energy emissions and was ineffectively targeting and funding its policies, these inadequate measures did not affect the Coalition's electoral success until 2007. Indeed, the Coalition government behaved as classically self-interested, signing onto the Kyoto Protocol in 1997 and committing to the principal of global emissions reductions—but only on the condition that its own emissions were able to increase. Its "climate clever" legacy of inaction may have been politically and economically clever, in the Coalition government's own pragmatic self-interested terms, but it will make effective abatement all the more difficult after 2012.

Notes

1. Howard 2002, 3163.

2. The Coalition called its approach to climate change "climate clever" during the 2007 federal election campaign.

3. For example, see, on the former, Hamilton 2001; Lowe 2004; and Macdonald 2005a. On the latter, see Australian National Audit Office 2004; Lyster 2004; and Pollard 2003.

4. Australia's population growth has been 15 percent over 1990 to 2002 (1.2 percent in 2005).

5. For 2007 figures, see Australia Government Department of Climate Change, National Greenhouse Gas Inventory http://www.climatechange.gov.au/inventory/2007/index.html.

6. Australian Greenhouse Office 2005a.

7. See table 7.2. When Kyoto targets were being negotiated in 1997, Australia was projecting that its greenhouse gas emissions would rise by 25 percent, given business as usual from 1990 levels to 2010. It argued that its Kyoto target of increased emissions would then in fact represent a steep 17 percent cut in projected future emissions. See Baumgartner and Midttun (1987) on the need to treat business-as-usual projections with great caution.

8. Pittock 2005, 187; Australian Conservation Foundation 2001. Australia is the only developed nation still clearing land; indeed only Brazil, Indonesia, Sudan, Zambia, and Mexico clear more land each year than Australia does. Land clearing causes both waste gases and changes in surface reflectivity that contribute to global warming, and its cessation is essential to maintaining biological carbon storage.

9. See table 7.2, where the fall is anticipated to be from 129 $MtCO_2eq$ in 1990 to 24 $MtCO_2eq$ to 2010. The Australia Institute has questioned the accuracy of this figure in Cooking the Greenhouse Books, *On-Line Opinion*, 2 March 2007. http://www.onlineopinion.com.au.

10. Australian Greenhouse Office 2005a, 1–2.

11. Roarty 2002,7.

12. Macdonald 2005a, 226.

13. Heggelund and Andresen 2006.

14. Harrison, chapter 6, this volume.

15. Schreurs and Tiberghien, chapter 5, this collection.

16. Hamilton and Reynolds 1998, 12; Hamilton 2007, 77.

17. See for example Hunt 2004; Pittock 2005.

18. Hamilton 2007, 47; Pittock 2005, 260.

19. Hunt 2004, 162.

20. Lightfoot 2006, 459; Elliott 2001, 268.

21. Macdonald 2005b.

22. Australian National University/Social Research Centre 2008.

23. Ibid. See also *Sydney Morning Herald*, 26 November 1997, p. 1; "Greenhouse Gas," The Australian's Newspoll Research, 2001; Hamilton 2007, 69, 209; "Climate Change the No. 1 Concern for Australians," News Limited media release, 17 January 2007.

24. See the BBC World Service, 19 Nation Poll on Energy and the World Public Opinion Poll 2007, both at www.worldpublicopinion.org.

25. "Climate Change the No. 1 Concern for Australians," 17 January 2007.

26. See the 7.30 Report ABC TV program transcript at www.abc.net.au/7.30/content/2007/s1842640.htm.

27. In particular, the Australian Industry Greenhouse Network, comprising industries such as coal, electricity, aluminum, petroleum, minerals, and cement, is argued to have had undue influence over government policy.

28. Hamilton 2001, 2006; Lowe 2004; Papadakis 2002; Lyster 2004, 565; Commonwealth Ombudsman 1998; Janine Cohen, *The Greenhouse Mafia*, transcript of a Four Corners investigative journalism program broadcast on 13 February 2006 by the Australian Broadcasting Corporation, http://www.abc.net.au.

29. Hamilton 2006, 14; 2007, 130. Environmental groups include the Australian Conservation Foundation, Greenpeace, and the World Wildlife Fund for Nature. Pro-Kyoto business groups include Environment Business Australia, the Renewable and Sustainable Energy Roundtable, the Australian Business Council for Sustainable Energy, the Australian Wind Energy Association, and the Australian Business Roundtable on Climate Change.

30. Manne 2004.

31. See Kellow 1998; Hamilton 2001; and Macdonald 2005a.

32. Hamilton 2007, 170. It is true that this language was identical to, and thus mimicry of, the United States'.

33. The AP6 solution that is discussed below.

34. J. Holmes, "What Price Will You Pay To Avert Climate Change?," Australian Broadcasting Commission, 2006.

35. Brett 2007.

36. See Papadakis 1996.

37. See Parkin and Summers 2002, 7–14.

38. Commonwealth of Australia 2004, 58.

39. The House of Representatives and the Senate enjoy equal law-making powers, with approval of both required to pass legislation.

40. The states also support a national scheme.

41. Three states have regulated to promote renewable energy, Queensland requiring 13 percent of power sold or used to be gas, Victoria requiring 10 percent of power sold or used to be renewable by 2010, and South Australia requiring 20 percent of power sold or used to be renewable by 2014.

42. Economou 1999, 71.

43. Hamilton 1999, 38–42.

44. Hamilton 2001, 32; Macdonald 2005a, 221; Taplin 1995, 17. Following the 1988 Toronto Conference on Climate Change, the 1989 Hague Summit, and the 1990 World Climate Conference in Geneva, Australia committed to stabilizing greenhouse gas emissions at 1988 levels by 2000 and reducing emissions by 20 percent by 2005.

45. Macdonald 2005a, 225.

46. Commonwealth Ombudsman 1998, 131. Australian economists also signed a statement that this analysis overstated Australia's case (Hamilton 2001, 56).

47. Australian Bureau of Agricultural and Resource Economics 1997; Lyster 2004, 564.

48. Papadakis 2002, 265.

49. Lowe 2004, 262.

50. Papadakis 2002, 265.

51. Hamilton 2001; Macdonald 2005a, 226.

52. Lowe 2004, 259–260.

53. The United States withdrew from negotiations in March 2001, following the election of George W. Bush.

54. *The Australian*, 22 November 2000; Macdonald 2005a, 228. Article 3.3 of the Protocol does define a forest tree as exceeding two meters, but land-use clearing and change is much less well defined, although allometric equations have been defined for estimating vegetation biomass (Australian Greenhouse Office 2005b).

55. Macdonald 2005a, 228.

56. Roarty 2002, 5.

57. Hamilton 2007, 223.

58. Macdonald 2005a, 228.

59. The regime will only reduce global emissions 1 percent, not the 60 percent that is needed by 2050 (Australian Greenhouse Office 2004).

60. Kellow 2006, 287. On the viability of Kyoto, see Depledge 2006.

61. Hamilton 2007, 190.

62. Commonwealth of Australia 2000; Lyster 2004, 574.

63. Australian Greenhouse Office 2004, 12; Kemp and Downer 2004.

64. Pollard 2003.

65. Australian National Audit Office 2004. Four years after seven programs were announced, the Australian National Audit Office found that 71.1 percent of the original budget estimates had been committed but that only 23.4 percent had actually been spent.

66. Christoff 2005, 29.

67. Lowe 2004, 262.

68. Commonwealth of Australia 2000.

69. Taplin 2004, 498; Commonwealth of Australia 2000; KPMG 2006; *The Australian*, 28 July 2005.

70. This program, legislated by the Renewable Energy (Electricity) Act 2000, has been criticized as too lenient. The new Labor government has promised to extend the scheme to 20 percent renewable power by 2020.

71. *The Age*, 19 February 2007.

72. This is an indicative table because data sets vary between reporting periods as accounting processes change. It is difficult to reconcile the data sets and the changes between them.

73. Note that the difference between the original business-as-usual projection and the current projections lies in part in the assumed future impact of existing government policies.

74. Australian Greenhouse Office 2005a, chapter 4.

75. Hunt 2004, 156; Campbell 2006.

References

Australian Bureau of Agricultural and Resource Economics. 1997. Emission Targets Costly for Australia and Japan. Media release. 28 April. www .abareeconomics.com/research/climatechange.

Australian Bureau of Statistics. 2006. *Measures of Australia's Progress. ABS Catalogue No. 1370.0.* Canberra: Commonwealth of Australia.

Australian Conservation Foundation. 2001. Australian Land Clearing, a Global Perspective: Latest Facts and Figures.

Australian Greenhouse Office. 2004. Tracking the Kyoto Target 2004: Australia's Greenhouse Emission Trends 1990 to 2008–12 and 2020. Canberra: Australian Greenhouse Office, Department of Environment and Heritage. http://www .greenhouse.gov.au.

Australian Greenhouse Office. 2005a. *Australia's Fourth National Communication on Climate Change: A Report under the United Nations Framework Convention on Climate Change.* Canberra: Australian Greenhouse Office, Department of Environment and Heritage. http://www.greenhouse.gov.au.

Australian Greenhouse Office. 2005b. Strategic Plan for the National Carbon Accounting System for Land Based Sources and Sinks 1999–2001. Canberra:

Australian Greenhouse Office, Department of Environment and Heritage. http://www.greenhouse.gov.au.

Australian Greenhouse Office. 2006. Tracking the Kyoto Target 2006: Australia's Greenhouse Emission Trends 1990 to 2008–12 and 2020. Canberra: Australian Greenhouse Office. http://www.greenhouse.gov.au.

Australian National Audit Office. 2004. The Administration of Major Programs: Australian Greenhouse Office. Audit Report No. 34 2003–04 Performance Audit, Canberra: Commonwealth of Australia.

Australian National University/Social Research Centre. 2008. Public Opinion towards Governance: Results from the Inaugural ANU Poll, April. http://www.anu.edu.au/anupoll/content/publications/report/governance_april_2008/ (accessed 30 September 2008).

Baumgartner, T., and A. Midttun. 1987. *The Politics of Energy Forecasting.* Oxford: Clarendon Press.

Brett, Judith. 2007. Exit Right: The Unravelling of John Howard. *Quarterly Essay* 28:1–96.

Campbell, Ian. 2006. Greenhouse Accounts Show Australia Is Still on Target for 108 Percent. Media release by the Minister for the Environment and Heritage, Senator the Hon. Ian Campbell, 23 May 2006.

Christoff, Peter. 2005. Policy Autism or Double Edged Dismissiveness? Australia's Climate Policy under the Howard Government. *Global Change, Peace and Security* 17 (1):29–44.

Commonwealth of Australia. 2000. The Heat Is On: Australia's Greenhouse Future. Proceedings of an Inquiry by the Senate Environment, Communications, Information Technology and Arts Committee.

Commonwealth of Australia. 2004. Kyoto Protocol Ratification Bill 2003 [No. 2]. Proceedings of an Inquiry by the Senate Environment, Communications, Information Technology and Arts Committee, 25 March.

Commonwealth Ombudsman. 1998. Report of the Investigation into ABARE's External Funding of Climate Change Modelling. www.ombudsman.gov.au/publications_information/Special_Reports/abare.pdf.

Depledge, Joanna. 2006. The Opposite of Learning: Ossification and the Climate Change Regime. *Global Environmental Politics* 6 (1):1–22.

Economou, Nick. 1999. Backward into the Future: National Policy-Making, Devolution and the Rise and Fall of the Environment. In *Australian Environmental Policy: Studies in Decline and Devolution,* ed. Ken Walker and Kate Crowley, 65–80. Sydney: University of New South Wales Press.

Elliott, Lorraine. 2001. Friends, Allies or Collaborators: Environmental Policy in the US-Australian Relationship. *Australian Journal of International Affairs* 55:261–273.

Hamilton, Clive. 1999. Justice, the Market and Climate Change. In *Global Ethics and Environment,* ed. N. Low, 90–105. London: Routledge.

Hamilton, Clive. 2001. *Running from the Storm: The Development of Climate Change Policy in Australia.* Sydney: University of New South Wales Press.

Hamilton, Clive. 2006. The Political Economy of Climate Change. Miltorpe Lecture, Macquarie University, Sydney, 8 June.

Hamilton, Clive. 2007. *Scorcher: The Dirty Politics of Climate Change.* Melbourne: Black Ink Agenda Press.

Hamilton, Clive, and Anna Reynolds. 1998. Land-Use Change in Australia and the Kyoto Protocol. Presentation at the Fourth Conference of the Parties of the Framework Convention on Climate Change. Bunos Aires, 12 November.

Heggelund, Gørild, and Steinar Andresen. 2006. China's Climate Change Policy: No Commitments but Still Some Implementation? Paper presented at the workshop Global Commons and National Interests: Domestic Climate Change Policies in an International Context, Peter Wall Institute, 9–10 June, University of British Columbia.

Howard, John. 2002. Hansard. *Commonwealth Parliamentary Debates 5* (June): 3163.

Hunt, Colin. 2004. Australia's Greenhouse Policy. *Australasian Journal of Environmental Management* 11 (June):156–163.

Kellow, Aynsley. 1998. Australia in the Greenhouse: Science, Norms and Interests in the Kyoto Protocol. Paper presented to the Annual Conference of the Australasian Political Science Association, Christchurch, New Zealand.

Kellow, Aynsley. 2006. A New Process for Negotiating Multilateral Environmental Agreements? The Asia-Pacific Climate Partnership beyond Kyoto. *Australian Journal of International Affairs* 60:287–303.

Kemp, the Hon Dr. David, and the Hon. Alexander Downer. 2004. Climate Change—A Long Term Plan. Press release issued by the Minister for the Environment and the Minister for Foreign Affairs and Trade, 15 June.

KPMG. 2006. *Carbon Disclosure Project Report 2006: Australia and New Zealand.* Sydney: Investor Group on Climate Change Australia/New Zealand.

Lightfoot, Simon. 2006. A Good International Citizen? Australia at the World Summit on Sustainable Development. *Australian Journal of International Affairs* 60:457–471.

Lowe, Ian. 2004. In Manne 2004, 245–266.

Lyster, Rosemary. 2004. Common but Differentiated? Australia's Response to Global Climate Change. *Georgetown International Environmental Law Review* 16:561–591.

Macdonald, Matt. 2005a. Fair Weather Friend? Ethics and Australia's Approach to Climate Change. *Australian Journal of Politics and History* 51:216–234.

Macdonald, Matt. 2005b. Perspectives on Australian Foreign Policy, 2004. *Australian Journal of International Affairs* 59:153–168.

Manne, Robert, ed. 2004. *The Howard Years.* Melbourne: Black Ink Agenda Press.

Papadakis, Elim. 1996. Environmental Policy. In *Government, Politics, Power and Policy in Australia*. 5th ed., ed. Andrew Parkin, John Summers, and Dennis Woodward, 452–467. Frenchs Forest, NSW: Longman Cheshire.

Papadakis, Elim. 2002. Global Environmental Diplomacy: Australia's stance on global warming. *Australian Journal of International Affairs* 56:265–277.

Parkin, Andrew, and John Summers. 2002. The Constitutional Framework. In *Government, Politics, Power and Policy in Australia*. 7th ed., ed. John Summers, Dennis Woodward, and Andrew Parkin, 1–21. Sydney: Pearson Longman.

Pittock, Barry. 2005. *Climate Change: Turning Up the Heat*. Melbourne: CSIRO Publishing.

Pollard, Paul. 2003. *Missing the Target: An Analysis of Australian Government Greenhouse Spending*. Discussion Paper Number 51. Canberra: Australia Institute.

Roarty, Mike. 2002. The Kyoto Protocol: Issues and Developments Through to COP7. Parliament of Australia: Department of Parliamentary Library.

Taplin, Roslyn. 1995. International Cooperation on Climate Change and Australia's Role. *Australian Geographer* 26 (1):16–22.

Taplin, Roslyn. 2004. Australian Experience with Greenhouse NEPIs. In *Governance for Industrial Transformation: Proceedings of the 2003 Berlin Conference on the Human Dimensions of Global Environmental Change*, ed. Klaus Jacob, Manfred Binder, and Anna Wiezorek, 491–501. Berlin: Environmental Policy Research Centre.

8

Chinese Climate Policy: Domestic Priorities, Foreign Policy, and Emerging Implementation

Gørild Heggelund, Steinar Andresen, and Inga Fritzen Buan

Introduction

China is a key country in the international climate regime for two reasons. First, it is important in the global climate change process because it is the world's largest emitter of greenhouse gases; moreover, China's emissions are increasing steadily. Second, its status and influence in the G-77 give it prominence in climate negotiations. As the world's largest developing country, with an influential voice in the United Nations, China has the potential to lead the developing world in the future climate regime. It has been an active participant in climate negotiations and ratified the Kyoto Protocol in 2002, but as a developing country it has refused to take on any commitments.

Although its political and economic clout have increased considerably over the past two decades, China stands out compared to the other states covered in this volume. Politically, China is still a one-party communist state. This has important implications for how to understand its climate policy and its role within the international climate regime. As there are no free elections, the role of the public is marginal. Also, there is no competition or disagreement between political parties, as we see in most democratic states. Due to the centralized nature of the regime, the role of non-state actors—whether green nongovernmental organizations (NGOs) or scientists outside the government bureaucracy—is less significant than in democratic countries. The absence or weak nature of these actors is expected to weaken the climate policies of China. "Softer" factors like knowledge and ideas will thus probably be less influential here than in the West. To the extent that pressure is exerted on China to lead a more aggressive climate policy, we expect this to come primarily from abroad. However, so far, such pressure has had little or no effect. Thus the making of climate policy in China will be more of a closed game among relevant ministries and other agencies. This does not mean that the process will be characterized by consensus. We expect that the aphorism "where you stand depends upon where you sit" also applies in the making of Chinese policy.[1]

The most important interests explaining the broad lines of Chinese climate policy are linked to the country's economic policy, particularly its energy policy. These interests are represented first and foremost by the National Development and Reform Commission (NDRC), the key player in the making of China's climate policies. The NDRC is a powerful macroeconomic agency that sees climate policy through the prism of economy and energy. This is also the case for other key actors, such as the Ministry of Foreign Affairs (MFA). However, there are actors with a more proactive position, primarily the Ministry of Environmental Protection (MEP), and non-state actors, such as scientists. Thus we regard the relevant institutions as actors, and their positions depend on their institutional roles.

China has no "hard" commitments to deliver on and thus there were no economic costs associated with its ratification of the Kyoto Protocol. However, this lack of commitments does not mean that China has not introduced measures that may lead to emissions reductions, in particular through its energy policies. China is also actively involved in the Clean Development Mechanism (CDM).

In the second section we present the three main determinants, or interests, that are decisive for China's climate change policy: economy, energy, and perceived vulnerability. Our main assumption is that the primacy of economic growth leads China to downplay the global climate issue. As a point of departure, the nature of the energy mix in combination with the strongly increased energy consumption also pull in this direction. However, increased preoccupation with energy efficiency as a means to achieve energy security may have a positive effect on greenhouse gas emissions. This may also be the case for a growing sense of vulnerability to the effects of climate change. In the third section we turn to the main *institutions* involved in China's climate change policy. We will discuss their role and influence and study them as actors in the making of climate policy. We explore whether "hard" economic interests of energy and economy are the only decisive factors in these institutions or whether non-state actors, mostly scientists, also influence the process. Thus we begin by examining China's climate policy through these broad lenses. In the third section we turn to explaining how these interests are manifested in the work of the relevant institutions in Chinese climate policies. As will be demonstrated, China's domestic climate policy has been a part of its energy policy since the beginning and has therefore been weak. China sees global climate goals primarily as an *international* issue, yet developments in the last few years may indicate changes in this attitude. We present China's stance in the international negotiations in the fourth section, where we seek to explain why external pressure to take on commitments has had little significance. In the fifth section we discuss the country's preferred way of participating in Kyoto Protocol activities—the CDM. In conclusion, we sum up the status of China's climate policy and briefly discuss possible ways forward.

Main Interests in Chinese Climate Policy: Economy, Energy, and Vulnerability

Economic Interests

China's main official priorities are economic development, poverty alleviation, and social stability. Neither environment in general nor climate policy in particular has a similarly high priority. Since the late 1970s and the initiation of Deng Xiaoping's new economic policy, industrialization for exports has been the way to achieve these prioritized goals. The results of this policy have become evident in rapid economic growth and higher living standards for several hundred millions of people. China remains a developing country, but due to rapid economic development, its gross domestic product (GDP) per capita (PPP) reached US$6,000 in 2008.[2] Still, in 2006 the World Bank estimated that more than 135 million Chinese people had consumption levels below US$1 per day.[3]

The strong economic growth has come at a price, however. With a population of nearly 1.3 billion people, diminishing natural resources, serious environmental pollution, and rapid economic growth, China exhibits all the signs of a typical developmental dilemma. Even though negative environmental effects associated with economic growth are recognized by the authorities, economic growth remains *the* most urgent priority. Officially this is needed to bridge the growing gap between rich and poor, illustrated by the leadership's decision to focus on the rural poor.[4] However, we expect that the urge to become a leading world power is also an important motivation behind the strong economic growth. These overriding economic priorities are extremely important for China's stance on the issue of climate change. In short, either taking on commitments under the Kyoto Protocol or implementing an active domestic climate policy is regarded as threatening to the economic development of the country.

Energy

Energy is a common denominator in the climate change discussion in China. It is not only the basis for economic development but also an important cause of domestic pollution and global emissions. Economic growth in China remains enabled by fossil-fuel-based energy, and expanded energy consumption has been critical to the country's development. Energy policy is therefore one of the key priorities in China's development process. China's large emissions are mainly caused by its heavy reliance on fossil fuels. Figures published by the Netherlands Environmental Assessment Agency put China on top of the list of global greenhouse gas emitters in 2007 (aggregated, not per capita).[5] Its esti-

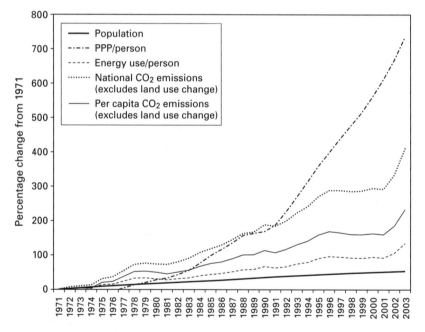

Figure 8.1
Economic development, population growth, energy use, and emissions of CO_2, China, 1971–2003. Purchasing Power Parities (PPPs) are the rates of currency conversion that equalize the purchasing power of different currencies by eliminating the differences in price levels between countries. See OECD Statistics Directorate n.d. *Source:* World Resources Institute, CAIT. http://cait.wri.org/cait .php?page=graphsingle.

mates had risen to 24 percent of global emissions in 2008, compared to 21 percent by the United States.[6] However, Chinese experts have argued that calculating per capita emissions give a more accurate picture of its contribution to the problem.[7] They also emphasize that a large part of China's huge emissions are a result of production for exports of goods that are in high demand in the West. By 2030 China's emissions are expected to represent more than one-quarter of the increase in world emissions.[8]

China has managed to reduce the rise in greenhouse gas emissions through its aggressive population control.[9] Figure 8.2 provides different scenarios for future carbon dioxide emissions.

Energy policy is closely linked to climate policy. In fact, China's energy policy has been the main driving force in its domestic climate policy. Cheap energy has made rapid economic growth, reduced poverty,

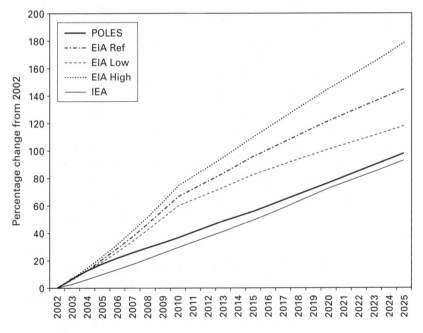

Figure 8.2
CO_2 Emissions projections, China, 2002–2025. The projections come from different models: POLES (model developed at Institut d'Économie et de Politique de l'Energie, Grenoble, France); EIA (Energy Information Administration, USA); IEA (International Energy Agency). See Greenhouse Gas Sources & Methods, November 2005, World Resources Institute. http://cait.wri.org/downloads/cait _ghgs.pdf. *Source:* World Resources Institute, CAIT. http://cait.wri.org/cait .php?page=graphproj.

and raised standards of living possible. It should be noted, however, that while China's energy consumption doubled from 1980 to 2000, its GDP *quadrupled*.[10] In 2001 China announced plans to quadruple its GDP by 2020 while again "only" doubling its energy consumption. This delinking of economic growth and energy use from 1980 to 2000 was positive from an emissions perspective. It is difficult to say whether the ambitious plans for 2020 can be implemented, however, as energy consumption once more is growing faster than GDP.[11] China experiences increasing demand for energy as the economy develops and the standard of living rises; these developments will lead to higher emissions.

China has 114 billion metric tons of proven coal reserves, making this its most important energy source.[12] In 2005 it consumed 2.2 billion metric tons, an increase of more than 90 percent since 1990.[13] Despite strongly increasing production, there have been power shortages, and the government's response has been to build new power plants.[14] China is also attempting to shift toward cleaner fuels, however. Coal burning amounted to 69.4 percent of total energy consumption in 2006 (figure 8.3) but is expected to constitute 53 percent in 2030, a considerable reduction—if the goal is met. Oil has also become an important energy source and a source of pollution. China is pursuing a rather aggressive policy toward other developing countries, not least in Africa, to secure its increasing demand for energy. Increased energy consumption and energy shortages are obvious reasons for this renewed political focus on energy. The fast-growing transportation sector—the fastest growing sector in China—will add greatly to the challenge. In 2007 there were 31 million motor vehicles on Chinese roads, and that number is projected to reach 150 million by 2030.[15] Road transportation is expected to be the primary cause of growth in petroleum consumption and a major source of emissions.

China's continued reliance on coal results in considerable domestic air pollution and greenhouse gas emissions. Curbing local air pollution is a priority of the Chinese leadership. Consequently, as a result of the increasing importance of energy issues, China has introduced important energy policy changes. Its attempts to reorient its energy mix may be significant for future greenhouse gas emissions. Energy conservation and renewable energy now top the political agenda. The key policy document for energy conservation, the *China Medium and Long-Term Energy Conservation Plan* (2004),[16] highlights this. Another initiative is the government work report presented by Premier Wen Jiabao at the National People's Congress (NPC) in March 2006, which emphasizes energy effi-

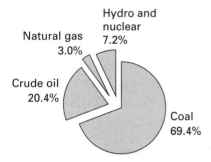

Figure 8.3
China's energy mix. Nuclear power was not specified in the China Statistical Yearbook but is often merged with hydropower. According to the NDRC, hydropower and nuclear power amount to 7.6 percent of total primary energy production in 2002. See National Development and Reform Commission 2005. *Sources:* National Bureau of Statistics of China 2007; National Development and Reform Commission 2007.

ciency as a key measure of economic growth and proposes a 4 percent reduction in energy intensity for 2006.[17] From 2006 the energy consumption per unit of output for all regions and major industries will be made public on an annual basis. Wen stressed again in the 2007 work report to the NPC the necessity to meet the energy saving and pollution control targets between 2006 and 2010, despite previous years' failure to reach the goals set.[18] The premier announced that the State Council would report annually to the NPC, starting this year, on the progress made in saving energy and reducing the discharge of major pollutants. Moreover, the eleventh Five-Year Social and Economic Development Plan (2006–2010)[19] lists energy conservation and increased energy efficiency as major objectives, the goal being to reduce the ratio of total energy use to GDP by 20 percent in 2010 compared to 2005. The 2008 government work report to the NPC emphasized that "this year is crucial for meeting the obligatory targets for energy conservation and emissions reduction set forth in the Eleventh Five-Year Plan."[20] The Renewable Energy Law, which went into effect in January 2006, states, among other policy goals, that 15 percent of all energy is to come from renewable sources by 2020. This law and related implementation regulations have given momentum to China's renewable-energy sector.[21] The energy mix chart below (figure 8.3) nevertheless illustrates the difficulty in reducing coal consumption, which indeed grew by nearly 2 percent, from 67.7 in 2004 to 69.4 in 2006, while hydro and nuclear remained the same.[22] Importantly, a new Energy Law is currently under review by the NPC Standing Committee, and is likely to be passed in 2010.[23] China's focus on the energy dilemma is also reflected in the above-mentioned National Climate Change Program, where the main objectives are energy-related.

In sum, the dominant national interests behind China's fossil-fuels-driven economic growth are the main explanation for the weak domestic climate policy. However, given its ambitious plans for energy efficiency and conservation, China may be able to reduce its greenhouse gas emissions—compared to a business-as-usual scenario—even though its *motivation* will be primarily economic. Another factor that may contribute to a more proactive climate policy is perceived vulnerability following from climate change.

Indications of Increased Vulnerability
Chinese scientists have played a major role in attracting attention to the country's vulnerability. So far, policymakers have not been equally concerned, arguing that climate change has been characterized by scientific uncertainty. However, as the effects of and potential economic losses due to climate change are causing increasing concern, this sentiment is changing. This is illustrated in the 2006 *National Assessment Report on Climate Change*, commissioned by the National Climate Change Coordination Committee (NC4; see section three) and compiled by a number of scientists.[24] The authorities have begun to pay greater attention to vulnerability and realize that China will have to prepare for more extreme weather. As was stressed in the *Assessment Report*, extreme climate events such as floods in the middle and lower reaches of the Yangtze River and in southeast China now occur more frequently. Severe droughts are frequent in the north and northeast. The *Assessment Report* concludes that the trend toward a warmer climate is consistent with the global warming trend of the past century and that the warming trend after the mid-1980s is significant. Increased precipitation in some regions in China has occurred, while other regions have experienced a decrease. The report also concludes that warming trends in China in the past twenty years especially can be attributed to increased greenhouse gases in the atmosphere related to human activities. Moreover, it states that the increase in temperature will be considerable in the next twenty to one hundred years. Increasing temperature levels could negatively affect agricultural production—a sector already under pressure due to environmental degradation and pollution. Food production could be reduced by as much as 37 percent by the second half of the twenty-first century, thus seriously impacting food security.

In sum, China is highly vulnerable to climate change. The vulnerability issue may become more important if the climate becomes more extreme, as is now envisioned in the Fourth Assessment Report (AR4) published by the Intergovernmental Panel on Climate Change (IPCC) on 2 February 2007.[25] Awareness of vulnerability and adaptation is fairly new in China. However, the growing emphasis on the need for adaptation activities indicates that climate change is increasingly perceived as a potential threat to national interests by Chinese decision makers. For China, as is the case for most developing countries, relatively limited administrative capacity and particularly vulnerable rural areas make adaptation challenging.[26] Should many people be negatively affected as a result of natural disasters linked to climate change, this might contribute to a more aggressive domestic climate policy. The last IPCC report may be an important step in that direction. In its poverty reduction efforts, China will probably have to consider the linkage between climate change and the vulnerability of the poor.

Two main Chinese interests (economy and energy) have so far pointed to a very cautious and reluctant stance. Increased preoccupation with vulnerability—as well as more emphasis on energy efficiency—pulls in the other direction. We now turn to the question of how these general background variables, or interests, are reflected in China's decision making.

Domestic Policymaking: The "Hard Coalition" Has the Upper Hand

The Role of Key Institutions
In this section we outline the most important institutions in Chinese climate policymaking. Until 1998 responsibility for climate change coordination was with the China Meteorological Administration (CMA), which was mostly preoccupied with the scientific aspects of the matter. In 1998 the State Development Planning Commission, renamed the National Development and Reform Commission in March 2003, was charged with coordinating Chinese climate change efforts, following the governmental reorganization. The responsibility being delegated to the NDRC, the most influential governmental agency in the fields of economy, energy, and climate change, signified that climate change was no longer perceived solely in scientific terms but increasingly in political and economic terms. Domestic climate policy was thereby seen largely through the prism of energy and economy. Moreover, the NDRC chairs the NC4, a high-level interministerial committee that coordinates climate change

work among ministries and other agencies in China (see figure 8.4 below). The Climate Change Office, established within the NDRC in 1998, functions as its secretariat.

The NDRC's Energy Bureau has had primary responsibility for China's energy industry since 2003. It was given responsibility for energy supply, while energy consumption and efficiency belong to the Department of Environment and Resources Conservation. China does not have a separate energy ministry, but such an establishment is being discussed as a means to achieve more efficient implementation of energy policy.[27] To reflect the increasing importance of energy issues, an Office of the National Energy Leading Group was established in 2005 at the ministerial level, headed by the NDRC chairman. This office was in charge of overall energy strategy. It served the National Energy Leading Group, a high-level task force that met annually and was led by Wen Jiabao. Moreover, a new NDRC vice-chairman post, responsible for energy and environment, was established and was held by a former minister of the State Environmental Protection Administration (SEPA). These developments illustrate both that energy has been elevated to the highest political level and that there is a specific focus on climate. It is also noteworthy that a Leading Small Group on climate change and energy

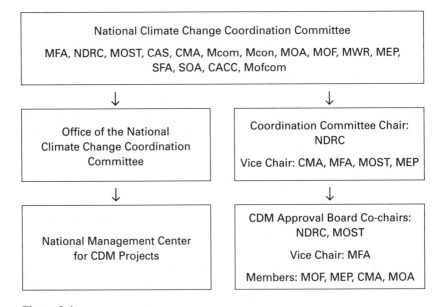

Figure 8.4
Organization of China's CDM apparatus.

saving has been established and is headed by Wen,[28] indicating that the issue of climate change is now a priority at the highest leadership level. Whether these new institutions will effect real change remains to be seen, but in the first meeting of the group, in July 2007, Wen stressed the urgency of climate change action and energy-related measures.[29] Similar sentiments were stressed again at the Leading Small Group's meeting in June 2009.[30]

One of the most influential ministries represented in the NC4 is the Ministry of Foreign Affairs (MFA), which plays a key role in the international political process on climate change. It has been less involved in the scientific and technical aspects. The MFA is a "hardliner" in stressing the significance of economic considerations, Chinese sovereignty, and the responsibility of developed countries taking the lead on the issue and providing necessary assistance and technology transfers. In general, the MFA has been in line with the position of the NDRC in climate policy-making, emphasizing the primacy of China's development needs. Climate change is seen as being a foreign policy issue and is therefore influenced by other issue areas under the purview of that ministry, discussed in the next section. This also spills over to the domestic arena and reinforces the rather passive Chinese role.

However, other actors are pulling in a more proactive direction. One of them is the Ministry of Science and Technology (MOST), another key ministry in the NC4. MOST established a research program on climate change in the 1990s and its officials have traditionally been sympathetic to environmental concerns.[31] MOST is the ministry with the broadest technical expertise about the CDM in China's bureaucracy and has been vital for China's CDM development. MOST is represented in the delegation at the UNFCCC Conferences of the Parties (COPs), and one of its officials is a representative on the CDM Executive Board.

The Ministry of Environmental Protection (MEP), previously SEPA, which was given full ministerial status in the government reshuffle in 2008, is also proactively addressing climate issues. It has participated in climate change work since the 1980s[32] but has become more vocal in the past few years and is a member of the NC4. It is also on the CDM Approval Board and established a CDM team in 2004. Given its role and mandate, MEP favors more proactive Chinese domestic climate policies and has also used climate change to promote alternative energy sources.[33] With the growing focus on the effects of climate change, MEP's role becomes more important. Together with MOST, it was responsible for overseeing the chapter on the effects of climate change in the above-mentioned *National Assessment Report*.

The Role of Non-state Actors

The role and influence of independent non-state actors in China can be expected to be moderate. However, to an increasing extent their voices are being heard, particularly those of the scientific community. Chinese scientists have been involved in climate change work since the early 1990s. Together with the Chinese Academy of Sciences (CAS), the China Meteorological Administration is one of the lead agencies in the scientific discussion on climate change.

High-level Chinese scientists have openly expressed concern about China's rising emissions.[34] A recent publication that illustrates this is *Climate and Environment Changes in China*, edited, among others, by Qin Dahe, former director of the CMA. It portrays climate change impacts in China, directly linking climate change to human activity. Chinese researchers are also heavily involved in international coopera- tion projects on climate change.[35] The CMA represents China in the IPCC, and Qin Dahe is the co-chair of the IPCC Working Group I. Twenty-eight Chinese experts were selected for the write-up of the IPCC's AR4.[36] Scientists are also included in the Chinese delegations of the Conferences of the Parties.[37]

Economists have also become increasingly involved in climate change work and conference delegations. Most of them underline the need for China to develop before taking on commitments. Others argue that taking the increasing international pressure into account, China should take on some binding reductions if technology transfer is guaranteed and if there is an increased focus on reducing carbon intensity.[38] Input is thus frequently provided by think tanks at research institutes, academies, and agencies.[39] It is difficult to establish how much real independence these actors have, however. Some of these think tanks are set up as indepen- dent bodies; others are subordinate to commissions or ministries. Con- sidering the nature of Chinese climate policy so far, it seems that their influence has been modest. However, their mere inclusion in the process would have been unthinkable only a few years ago.[40]

The more open and inclusive approach is also reflected by increased media attention to climate change. The majority of coverage concerns scientific aspects of climate change and the need to increase energy effi- ciency and reduce energy consumption. Less attention is paid to the political aspects of the global climate change. China's official climate change Web site (www.ccchina.gov.cn) posts many articles that discuss international and domestic climate change. However, the launch of the IPCC's AR4 was given only low-key coverage in the Chinese media.[41] A press conference on 6 February 2007, organized by the State Council led by Qin Dahe, was the first occasion on which an official publicly commented on the IPCC reports in the Chinese media.

NGOs are emerging actors in energy and climate change policy through involvement in the Journalist Forum on Energy (of which the purpose is to increase knowledge among TV and newspaper journalists) and the "26 Degrees" campaign, which urged companies, embassies, and other institutions to set air conditioners to 26 degrees Celsius to save electricity and protect the environment.[42]

In sum, several actors are engaged in formulating China's climate policy within various state institutions. The most important ones are NDRC and the MFA. The NDRC sets the agenda and is *the* decisive actor on domestic issues. As the NDRC has responsibility for both economic policy and energy policy, this defines and sets the limits for climate policy. As climate change is being defined primarily as a sensitive foreign policy issue, the MFA exercises great influence both internationally and domestically. So far, these actors represent the core Chinese national interests on the issue and have been the "winning coalition" in the making of Chinese climate policy. It is therefore no surprise that these two supervised the third part of the First National Climate Change Assessment, the socioeconomic assessment of climate change mitigation.

MOST, MEP, and the scientific community want to pursue a more proactive policy both domestically and internationally. However, as the issue is perceived primarily in terms of economy, energy, and foreign policy, they have so far had limited influence. Nevertheless, the more open and inclusive process of recent years, allowing for more critical voices, indicates that changes may be under way. There are very recent signs that the Chinese leadership is concerned about the effects of climate change on China, in particular in relation to the country's economic growth. Behind the scenes, presentations to the Politburo by Chinese climate experts signal the first time that regular Politburo study sessions are being devoted to climate change.[43] However, even if the Chinese authorities show increasing *willingness* to deal with energy efficiency and climate change, their *ability* to do so is uncertain, as China's implementation record is often characterized by problems of coordination, both vertically and horizontally.[44]

China on the International Scene

China has been an active participant in international climate negotiations since the beginning, usually acting in concert with the G-77. It ratified the Kyoto Protocol in August 2002. This was announced at the World Summit on Sustainable Development (also called the Earth Summit) in Johannesburg, probably to get the maximum positive attention.[45] As no costs of any kind followed from the ratification, this has likely not been the source of much internal controversy, even if the matter will have been the subject of high-level discussions. Chinese negotiators have repeatedly emphasized that developing country follow-through on the UNFCCC is contingent on the developed countries providing new and additional funding and transfer of technology. Their main argument has been that China is still a developing country.[46] Even though the level of development in its coastal regions is high, this is not representative of the rest of the country. They argue that increased emissions must be allowed in order for China to continue to develop its economy and industry. The argument of low per capita emissions—one-eighth of the US rate and about half of the world average—has been convincingly used in negotiations.[47] Chinese negotiators have contrasted the "survival emissions" of developing countries with the "luxury emissions" of developed countries, saying that the developed countries should change their own patterns of production and consumption rather than force developing countries to remove food from people's tables.[48] Thus moral arguments about equity loom large in the Chinese position on the international scene. In contrast to the role of moral claims in the industrialized countries discussed in other chapters of this volume, in China moral arguments are perceived as legitimate reasons to continue to increase emissions and *not* to take on binding commitments.

These arguments are reinforced by stressing the historical responsibility for global warming: Beijing's position is that since the United States and EU countries industrialized long before China, it is their responsibility to lead. During the negotiations, China also stressed that it has carried out a number of measures, substantially cutting emissions compared with a business-as-usual scenario.[49] Energy efficiency and conservation measures, energy pricing, increased use of renewable energy, and population control have been implemented for other reasons, but the Chinese argue that they nevertheless have led to emissions reductions—and that that is what matters. The arguments used by China (and other G-77 countries) are supported by conclusions in the IPCC's AR4 that emphasize the need to address climate change as an integral part of sustainable development policies.[50] At COP 12 (2006) in Nairobi, China's presentation of its national policies included estimates of the emissions reductions these policies are projected to achieve.[51] China's opposition to taking on commitments has also been made easier by US climate policy. The US withdrawal from the Kyoto Protocol was branded "irresponsible behavior" by the Chinese MFA.[52] The withdrawal is criticized in terms of equity. As long as the United States is not willing to take on commitments and its energy use continues to increase, they ask why China should take on commitments.[53] Although China officially condemns the US position, it no doubt makes it easier to defend its own positions. In this sense the US position is an advantage to China as the United States takes most of the international heat. Chinese observers have stated that if the United States takes on commitments, this will increase the pressure on China to do the same.[54] In turn, while the United States in the 1990s pressed for major developing countries to take on commitments, this no longer made sense for the Bush administration after 2001.[55] Thus at COP 8 (2002) in New Delhi, the United States shifted strategy and supported the G-77 in its rejection of discussing post-2012 commitments.

China is a leading actor in the G-77 and is held in high regard because it is a shrewd and well-prepared negotiator. There are no indications of its intending to leave the G-77 in the near future.[56] It may also be argued that China depends as much on the G-77 as the latter does on China. The membership underlines that China is still a developing country, thus justifying its steep increases in greenhouse gas emissions, since the right for developing countries to develop is an integral part of the Kyoto Protocol. This also tends to bolster the Chinese opposition to taking on commitments, which China emphasized again at the Group of Eight summit in Japan in July 2008.[57] It is important to note, however, that all countries, including China and the United States, at COP 13 (2007) in Bali for the first time were willing to engage in official negotiations on a new climate treaty, which the UNFCCC countries aim to finalize at COP 15 in Copenhagen in 2009. Also, it was not China but India that drove the hardest bargain among the G-77 countries at COP 13. One reason may be that India's per capita CO_2 emissions (1.8 metric tons) are below the Chinese level (5.1 metric tons).[58]

Although the UN is seen as the most important climate change arena for China, the country has become increasingly active in other international and regional structures, reflecting China's need for and will to solve the challenges associated with domestic energy and climate change.

One such process is the Major Economies Initiative, initiated by the United States and composed of eighteen of the world's largest economies (and greenhouse gas emitters). Another attractive channel of cooperation for China is the Asia-Pacific Partnership on Clean Development and Climate, established in July 2005. Here the United States is a member together with China, which is an interesting sign of a new "alliance" between the United States and key developing states. Other members are Australia, Canada, India, Japan, and South Korea. The group aims to reduce greenhouse gas intensity through technology and voluntary partnerships, without impeding economic growth.[59]

China scholars generally agree that China used to be skeptical of international regimes—wary that they would infringe on Chinese sovereignty.[60] However, this may gradually be changing, as China is also interested in establishing and preserving an image as a responsible power.[61] According to Chinese officials, the role of the UN in global environmental governance is deemed increasingly important by China.[62] China aspires to be seen as a nation abiding by rules and regulations of international environmental regimes. China's submission of its initial National Communications to the UNFCCC in November 2004 must be understood in that context.[63] The pressure to take on commitments, or at least have a more aggressive domestic climate policy, is intensifying with China's increased economic weight and this is increasingly acknowledged by Chinese officials and reported in the media.[64] Incomes are rising and the estimated value of income, in terms of purchasing power parity, is four times higher than the official Chinese figures.[65]

China's National Climate Change Program can also be viewed as to some extent responding to the growing international attention to China's increasing emissions. When the Kyoto Protocol was negotiated in 1997, China indicated that it would not even consider taking on emission reduction commitments until it had achieved a "medium level of development," indicating a level of per capita annual income of US$5,000.[66] This argument appears to have diminished in relevance and is seldom heard now. Indeed, China has stated that it will remain a developing country for some time to come; the *National Assessment Report on Climate Change* states that GDP will reach US$11,290 per capita in 2050.[67] Although China has become more willing to enter into dialog at the climate negotiations in the past few years, its opposition to binding commitments has not changed.[68]

It is hard to predict where China will go on the international scene. However, the current US administration and a more active Congress have already shown that the United States has turned toward a more proactive climate policy than the Bush administration.[69] This will in turn increase the pressure on China, having recently overtaken the United States as the world's largest greenhouse gas emitter in absolute terms.[70] The "moral" pressure for China to take on some kind of commitments may therefore become stronger and more legitimate. While definitely significant this pressure can easily be countered by pointing to very low per capita emissions in China compared to the wealthy nations. The effects of the pressure are also weakened by the closed nature of the Chinese political system and the fact that the "hardliners"—the NDRC and MFA—are in firm control of the process. Also, the domestic factors are, as in the United States, by far the most important drivers in the making of China's climate policy. Much will depend on the negotiation process leading up to COP 15 (2009). The Annex 1 countries will have to demonstrate more clearly than before that they are willing to take the lead both in terms of emissions reductions and assistance to the G-77. This is a precondition for getting major developing economies like China and India on board. Even if this happens, however, it is unlikely that China will take on economy-wide commitments. However, some kind of "softer" political commitments, often referred to as "nationally appropriate mitigation actions," may be possible.[71]

The Clean Development Mechanism: Emerging Chinese Implementation

The one way in which China is willing to implement direct climate policies is through the CDM, which together with joint implementation and emissions trading represent the Kyoto Protocol's "flexible mechanisms." Through the CDM, Annex 1 developed countries can invest in emissions reduction projects in non-Annex 1 developing countries. The UN in turn grants them Certified Emission Reductions (CERs) to help with their reduction commitments at home, one CER representing one metric ton of reduced CO_2 equivalent.[72] The second objective of the CDM is to assist developing countries in achieving sustainable development. The so-called "additionality" requirement is central to the CDM. For a project to be approved and CERs issued, the developers must establish that the planned emission reductions would not have occurred without the additional incentive provided by the credits. Since the CDM does not reduce emissions—any decrease in the host countries being offset by an increase in countries buying CERs—such "false credits" from nonadditional projects would increase overall emissions.[73]

China was initially skeptical of the flexible mechanisms, seeing them as instruments whereby the developed countries could escape responsibility. There was also concern that they may cause a diversion of official development assistance from developed countries. However, China's position has changed since the COP 7 (2001), the so-called Marrakech Accords.[74] It now actively supports the CDM because it provides opportunities that coincide with China's main interests for climate policy: economic development and energy. The ministries and commissions responsible for economic and energy interests are also the most powerful on climate policy. They see the CDM as beneficial and have made it a policy priority. The common view among key state actors is that CDM projects can benefit China. The country's priority areas for the CDM also reflect its political interests, as demonstrated below.

China has developed a national apparatus for identifying, approving, and implementing CDM projects (see figure 8.4). In 2004 it announced that the NDRC would take on the role of Designated National Authority (DNA) of the CDM. Next, the State Council in 2005 published the *Measures for Operation and Management of Clean Development Mechanism Projects in China.*[75] It repeats Beijing's stance of making no commitments and once again articulates the fear of reduced development assistance. Two issues raised in the document have drawn particular attention from international CDM investors. The first concerns ownership. Article 11 of the *Measures for Operation and Management* requires that the CDM project developers must be enterprises that are wholly or majority Chinese-owned. As CERs are considered national property, the revenues from their sales are to go partly to the Chinese state through a CDM levy, which makes the projects more costly to investors. The second issue is a 2 percent tax on projects in the priority areas. Heavier taxes are to be levied on HFC-23 and PFC projects (65 percent) and N_2O projects (30 percent). These are not priority areas and are regarded as less conducive to sustainable development despite their high global warming potential and therefore high value in terms of CERs. The fees collected from these projects will go into a fund managed by the MFA and jointly administered by the NDRC and other relevant ministries for "supporting activities on climate change."[76] Further details remain unclear. The Asian Development Bank and the World Bank are assisting the operation of this fund by providing assistance on capacity building and on the development of a CDM fee collection mechanism.[77]

From a fairly slow start, the approval procedure has now become quite efficient and projects are approved rapidly. As of June 2009, the

DNA had approved 2,062 projects.[78] The CDM Executive Board had approved 494 projects, of which 110 had had CERs issued by March 2009,[79] representing 44.6 percent of the world total.[80] Priority areas for CDM projects in China are energy efficiency improvement, development and utilization of new and renewable energy, and methane recovery and utilization.[81] The majority of the projects in the pipeline are in renewable energies (1,430), but the projects with the greatest emissions reduction potential are the large HFC-23 chemical reduction projects (see table 8.1).

Another important step for building CDM implementation capacity is being taken by international assistance organizations and bilateral and multilateral donors. Projects are carried out by the UNDP, the World Bank, the Asian Development Bank, and some bilateral donors.[82] This assistance could greatly benefit China and future CDM investments, helping to create an effective system for approval of projects and enhancing awareness of the opportunities offered by the CDM among local stakeholders. This is necessary because the development of the mechanism in general, and in China in particular, has not happened without kinks and criticism.[83] For one, some environmental groups claim many CDM projects are nonadditional and therefore do not contribute to real emissions reductions.

In sum, the CDM can contribute to reducing emissions in China since the country has the potential to generate half of the total worldwide annual CERs.[84] It can also contribute to sustainable development. The CER revenue from CDM projects has been calculated to have a potential annual revenue stream of US$1.51–2.25 billion, based on the price of US$10 per million metric tons of CO_2 equivalents.[85] It is still early for comprehensive evaluations saying whether the CDM is fulfilling its promises in China, but the CDM path does seem like one promising ways for the country to reduce its greenhouse gas emissions.

Concluding Comments: Status and Future Perspectives

China is facing major challenges with regard to future developmental needs, not least in the energy sector. Given these challenges, will it be able to reduce its large greenhouse gas emissions in the near future? We note both negative and positive trends. One side effect of continued economic growth is that energy consumption is now on the rise again and growing faster than GDP after a decline in the late 1990s.[86] In addi-

Table 8.1
Projects Approved by DNA of China (by 12 June 2009)

Type of project	Percentage of projects	Estimated average GHG reduction (tCO_2eq/y)	Percentage of total estimated reduction	Percentage of projects
Afforestation	5	118,520	0.03	0.24
Castoff disposal	1	51,712	0.01	0.05
Cement raw material substitute	2	142,449	0.04	0.10
Chemical pollutants reduction (HFC-23)	12	66,844,322	16.72	0.58
Energy saving and efficiency improvement	378	65,692,794	16.44	18.33
Fuel substitution	30	15,535,659	3.89	1.45
Landfill-burning power generation	1	63,511	0.02	0.05
Manufacture	1	369,202	0.02	0.05
Methane recovery and utilization	137	42,437,761	10.62	6.64
N_2O decomposition	25	23,098,529	5.78	1.21
Renewables	1,455	183,209,717	45.84	70.56
SF_6 recovery and utilization	1	156,465	0.04	0.05
Use of noncarbonated calcium sources in raw mix for cement production	8	1,700,084	0.43	0.39
Others	6	256,844	0.06	0.29
Total	2,062	399,677,569	100	100

Source: Office of the National Coordination Committee on Climate Change 2009a.

Table 8.2
Issuance of CERs in China (by 12 June 2009)

Type of project	Number of projects	Estimated average GHG reduction (tCO$_2$eq/y)	Percentage of emission reductions	Percentage of projects
Chemical pollutants reduction (HFC-23)	11	78,945,870	83.10	10.00
Energy saving and efficiency improvement	9	2,272,451	2.39	8.18
Methane recovery and utilization	8	880,291	0.93	7.27
N$_2$O decomposition	2	7,148,386	7.52	1.82
Renewables	80	5,749,247	6.05	72.73
Total	110	94,996,245	100	100

Source: Office of the National Coordination Committee on Climate Change 2009b.

tion to industrial energy needs, rising standards of living have resulted in greater energy demand in the transport and building sectors. Should today's patterns of energy consumption continue, an increase in greenhouse gas emissions is unavoidable. With continued high prices of oil and gas, cheap coal is bound to be China's main energy source for the foreseeable future.

However, there are also some positive trends. In the long run, the greater political focus on developing alternative energy sources may bring about reductions in greenhouse gas emissions. Energy conservation and energy efficiency are also political priorities for the Chinese leadership. This is a promising development with regard to emissions reductions since China now shows increasing political *willingness* to confront the issue. Also, it is in the national interests of China to diversify its energy consumption and increase energy efficiency for the sake of energy security and thereby also decrease emissions compared to a business-as-usual scenario. The jury is still out regarding China's *ability* to deliver, however. Considering its continued and future heavy dependence on cheap and abundant domestic coal resources, there is little reason to be optimistic regarding future emissions trends. Effective implementation depends on funding, measures to ensure that policy is carried out, and coordination of efforts among the many actors. China's track record has not been impressive in this regard so far.

Will perceived increased vulnerability lead to a more proactive domestic climate policy in China? Climate changes are already taking place in China, according to Chinese experts. There is reason to believe that if this trend intensifies, the climate issue will rise on the domestic political agenda and emerge more as an issue in its own right. That is, China may itself come to see that it is in its own national interest to take the issue more seriously, which is the most important precondition for more forceful action.

Chinese climate policy is made mainly by one commission and a few ministries. The powerful NDRC is responsible for economic development, energy policy and climate change, and the latter is seen largely through the prism of economy and energy. The Ministry of Foreign Affairs stresses the foreign policy nature of the issue. MOST and MEP appear more proactive but also less influential than the NDRC and the MFA. Yet their roles may be strengthened by the growing prominence of non-state actors, especially scientists, and their more activist role in relation to Chinese vulnerability. More generally, there is an increasing number of think tanks and consultants on scientific and economic issues. This means that there are more actors in the policymaking process, thus broadening the basis for decisions taken. China is also increasingly involved in the international scientific process, actively participating in the IPCC and the CDM Executive Board. This may create a better understanding of this issue in China and may also promote greater understanding of Chinese perspectives internationally.

Internationally China has used equity arguments, demanding that developed countries take the lead and provide assistance for developing countries and refusing to take on binding commitments. This position is unlikely to change in the near future. The industrialized states must show greater willingness to curb their own emissions as well as provide considerable assistance before China will change its stance on this. The Obama administration has signaled a more proactive US climate policy, which may bring more political energy into the current negotiations over a new treaty, but expectations should not be too high. Also, if and when the United States takes on commitments, external pressure on China to take on some kind of softer sector-specific commitments or "nationally appropriate" measures will increase.

The UN climate negotiation is the most important one among several arenas for China's climate involvement.[87] China also participates in other types of multilateral, regional, and bilateral cooperation aimed at mitigating climate change, technological development of renewable energies, as well as carbon capture and storage. One important goal for the Asia-Pacific Partnership is that emissions reduction be done without impeding economic growth. Such forums are viewed by China as more "operative" and practical arenas for cooperation on energy technology. In contrast, it considers the UN negotiations the appropriate arena in which to express its opinions on development issues and demonstrate its new role as a leader in the G-77.

Despite some criticism, the CDM is increasingly seen as a useful tool for emissions reductions and sustainable development. Initially skeptical, China has become one of the most active and attractive countries for CDM projects and its project number has increased rapidly in the past few years. An efficient CDM apparatus has been established, and expertise is being further developed throughout the country. Having become the biggest host of CDM projects, after massive interest from foreign governments and enterprises, China has the opportunity to reduce its growing emissions through the CDM, thereby actively participating in global climate change mitigation efforts.

To sum up, we expect no dramatic changes in Chinese climate policy nationally or internationally in the near future; however, there are some indications both at home and abroad that it may gradually become more proactive over the long term.

Notes

1. Allison 1972.

2. CIA World Factbook: China, https://www.cia.gov/library/publications/the -world-factbook/geos/CH.html (accessed 13 June 2009).

3. World Bank 2006.

4. Wen 2003.

5. D. Adam and J. Vidal, "China Overtakes US as World's Biggest CO_2 Emitter," *Guardian Online*, 19 June 2007, http://www.guardian.co.uk/environment/2007/ jun/19/china.usnews.

6. Netherlands Environmental Assessment Agency, "Global CO_2 Emissions: Increase Continued in 2007," http://www.planbureauvoordeleefomgeving.nl/en/ publications/global-co2-emissions-increase-continued-in-2007.

7. China is now first in CO_2 emissions; the United States, second. Netherlands Environmental Assessment Agency, http://www.mnp.nl/en/dossiers/ Climatechange/moreinfo/Chinanowno1inCO2emissionsUSAinsecondposition. html; "Experts Contest CO_2 Emissions Report," *China Climate Change Info Net*, http://www.ccchina.gov.cn/en/NewsInfo.asp?NewsId=8231.

8. International Energy Agency 2004.

9. Chandler et al. 2002.

10. Development Research Center 2004; Sinton et al. 2005; Sugiyama and Oshita 2006.

11. Sinton et al. 2005.

12. International Energy Agency 2004.

13. China to Cut Energy Consumption by 4 percent in 2006, *People's Daily Online*, 5 March 2006, http://english.people.com.cn/200603/05/eng20060305 _248040.html.

14. Sinton et al. 2005.

15. Energy Foundation 2007.

16. National Development and Reform Commission 2005.

17. Energy intensity is energy consumption per unit of GDP.

18. Wen 2007.

19. The Chinese Five-Year Plans (*jihua*) are now called Five-Year Programs (*guihua*), implying that the targets should be considered more as guidelines than mandatory goals (Sugiyama and Oshita 2006). For simplicity's sake, "Plan" will be used in this text.

20. Report on the Work of the Government [full text], *Xinhua Online*, 19 March 2008, http://www.chinadaily.com.cn/china/2008npc/2008-03/19/content _6549177_14.htm.

21. Liu 2009.

22. Heggelund 2007.

23. cnYES, "Nengy uan fa you wang nian nei tong guo ren da chang wei hui shen yi" [Hope That Energy Law Will Be Passed by State Council This Year], http://news.cnyes.com/dspnewsS.asp?rno=7&fi=%5CNEWSBASE%5C2009020 6%5CWEB290&vi=32138&sdt=20090204&edt=20090206&top=50&date =20090206&time=08:58:03&cls=index15_totalnews (accessed 11 June 2009).

24. National Climate Change Coordination Committee 2006.

25. Intergovernmental Panel on Climate Change 2007b.

26. People's Republic of China 2004.

27. Sinton et al. 2005.

28. National Development and Reform Commission 2007.

29. State Environmental Protection Administration 2007.

30. "Wen Jiabao zhu chi hui yi—bu shu ying dui qi hou bian hua he jie neng jian pai gong zuo" [Wen Jiabao Presided over Meeting on Climate Change Mitigation and Energy Savings Work], http://www.china-embassy.org/chn/xw/ t566367.htm (accessed 11 June 2009).

31. Economy 2001.

32. Ibid.; author's interview with SEPA official, November 2006.

33. Economy 1994.

34. "Zhuan jia: Zhongguo qi hou ke neng ji xu bian nuan 2050 nian jiang shang sheng 2.2°C" [Experts: China's Climate Will Most Likely Continue to Warm Up. In 2050 Temperatures Will Rise 2.2 Degrees Celsius], *China Climate Change Info-Net,* 2004, www.ccchina.gov.cn/source/aa/aa2004062402 .htm.

35. Economy 2004.

36. "China Must Cut Emissions to Slow Global Warming: Official," *Xinhua,* 23 November 2007. http://www.chinadaily.com.cn/olympics/2007-11/23/content _6274914.htm.

37. See list of participants Conference of the Parties (COP) Twelfth Session, Nairobi, 6–17 November 2006, http://unfccc.int/resource/docs/2006/cop12/eng/ inf01.pdf.

38. Zhang 2007.

39. Glaser and Saunders 2002.

40. Shambaugh 2002; Glaser and Saunders 2002.

41. Personal communication February 2007. See also Chris Buckley, "China Preparing Plan for Climate Change," 5 February 2007, *Reuters,* http://today .reuters.co.uk/news/articlenews.aspx?type=worldNews&storyid=2007-02 -05T190051Z_01_PEK279914_RTRUKOT_0_TEXT0.xml.

42. Voices of Grassroots, http://www.gvbchina.org/EnglishWeb/ VoicesofGrassroots.htm.

43. Personal communication, February 2007.

44. See for example Heggelund, Andresen, and Sun 2005.

45. Zongwei Shao, "Nation Approves Kyoto Protocol," *China Daily,* 4 September 2002.

46. See Tangen, Heggelund, and Buen 2001.

47. Author's interview with MFA official, Beijing, 2004.

48. Earth Negotiations Bulletin 1997.

49. Chandler et al. 2002; SDPC 1998.

50. Intergovernmental Panel on Climate Change 2007a.

51. Gao 2006; Pew Center 2006.

52. Ministry of Foreign Affairs of the PRC, "Fa yan ren jiu Meiguo ju jue pi zhun Jingdu yi ding shu fa biao ping lun" [The Spokesperson of the MFA Comments on USA's Withdrawal from the Kyoto Protocol], www.fmprc.gov.cn/ chn/9966.html.

53. Authors' interview with officials from the Ministry of Foreign Affairs, Beijing, October 2002.

54. Authors' interview with scientist, Beijing, November 2007.

55. Agrawala and Andresen 2001.

56. Authors' interviews with MFA officials, Beijing, 2004. See more on G-77 and China in Kasa et al. 2008.

57. "Biggest Polluters Back Deep Cuts to Emissions," *Financial Times*, 9 July 2008, http://www.ft.com/cms/s/0/23ee8046-4d64-11dd-8143-000077b07658 ,dwp_uuid=f23403e4-4428-11dd-b151-0000779fd2ac.html?nclick_check=1.

58. Netherlands Environmental Assessment Agency 2008.

59. "About the Asia-Pacific Partnership on Clean Development and Climate," http://www.asiapacificpartnership.org/english/about.aspx (accessed 12 June 2009).

60. Economy 2001.

61. "Wo guo guo ji di wei xian zhu ti gao" [China's International Position Raised Remarkably], *People's Daily*, 30 September 2002. .

62. Heggelund and Backer 2007.

63. People's Republic of China 2004. Summaries in Chinese and English are available at www.ccchina.gov.cn. The full Chinese version was circulated at COP 10.

64. "Jingdu yi ding shu sheng xiao zai ji—Zhongguo jing ji zao yu qi hou ya li" [Kyoto Protocol Soon to Go into Effect—China's Economy Will Encounter Climate Pressure], *China Climate Change Info Net*, www.ccchina.gov.cn/index1 .htm (originally published in *Huanqiu shibao* [Global Times], 27 December 2004).

65. See for example International Energy Agency 2004.

66. Pan 2005.

67. "Wo guo jian chi yi fa zhan zhong guo jia shen fen shu xing Jingdu yi ding shu" [China Will Sustain Developing Country Status in Implementing the Kyoto Protocol], *China Climate Change Info Net*, www.ccchina.gov.cn/index1.htm, and National Climate Change Coordination Committee 2006.

68. Earth Negotiations Bulletin 2006.

69. Skodvin and Andresen 2009.

70. Netherlands Environmental Assessment Agency 2008.

71. Lewis 2007.

72. "CO_2 equivalent" is a measure used to compare the emissions from various greenhouse gases based on their global warming potential, which varies greatly from gas to gas.

73. Wara 2008.

74. Tangen and Heggelund 2003.

75. Office of the National Climate Change Coordination Committee 2005.

76. National Development and Reform Commission 2005.

77. Asian Development Bank 2006; Chinese Firms, WB Ink Deal on Carbon Emission, *China Climate Change Info-Net*, 20 December 2005, www.ccchina .gov.cn/en/NewsInfo.asp?NewsId=4387.

78. Office of the National Climate Change Coordination Committee 2009a.

79. For updated information on the pipeline, registered projects and CER issuance, http://cdm.ccchina.gov.cn/english/.

80. UNEP Risoe CDM Pipeline 2009, http://cdmpipeline.org/publications/ CDMpipeline.xls.

81. Office of the National Climate Change Coordination Committee 2005.

82. Wei et al. 2004.

83. For details on the criticism directed at the CDM, see Haya 2007; Heggelund and Buan 2009; Michaelowa 2008; Victor and Wara 2008; Wara 2008.

84. International Bank for Reconstruction and Development 2004.

85. Asian Development Bank 2006.

86. Sinton et al. 2005.

87. Heggelund and Buan 2009.

References

Agrawala, Shardul, and Steinar Andresen. 2001. US Climate Policy: Evolution and Future Prospects. *Energy and Environment* 12, special issue (2–3).

Allison, Graham. T. 1972. *Essence of Decision: Explaining the Cuban Missile Crisis*. Reading, MA: Addison-Wesley.

Asian Development Bank. 2006. Establishment of the Clean Development Mechanism Fund. People's Republic of China: Technical Assistance Report.

Chandler, William, Roberto Schaeffer, Zhou Dadi, et al. 2002. *Climate Change Mitigation in Developing Countries: Brazil, China, India, Mexico, South Africa, and Turkey*. Arlington, VA: Pew Center on Global Climate Change.

Development Research Center. 2004. *Zhongguo nengyuan fazhan zhanlue yu zhengce yanjiu* [National Energy Strategy and Policy Report 2020]. Beijing: China's Economic Science Press.

Earth Negotiations Bulletin. 1997. Closing plenary. 12 (66): 9. www.iisd.ca/ vol12/.

Earth Negotiations Bulletin. 2006. Summary of the Twelfth Conference of the Parties to the UN Framework Convention on Climate Change and Second meeting of the Parties to the Kyoto Protocol, 6–17 November. 12 (318), 20 November. International Institute for Sustainable Development (IISD). www .iisd.ca/climate/cop12.

Economy, Elizabeth. 1994. *Negotiating the Terrain of Global Climate Change Policy in the Soviet Union and China: Linking International and Domestic Decision-Making Pathways*. Ann Arbor: UMI Dissertation Services.

Economy, Elizabeth. 2001. The Impact of International Regimes on Chinese Foreign Policy-Making: Broadening Perspectives and Policies ... but Only to a Point. In *The Making of Chinese Foreign and Security Policy in the Era of*

Reform, 1978–2000, ed. David M. Lampton. Stanford: Stanford University Press.

Economy, Elizabeth. 2004. *The River Runs Black: The Environmental Challenge to China's Future*. Ithaca: Cornell University Press.

Energy Foundation. 2007. China's motor vehicle fleet is growing at over 20 percent per year. The China Sustainable Energy Program. http://www.efchina .org/FProgram.do?act=list&type=Programs&subType=2&id=0&pageno=1.

Gao, Guangsheng (NDRC). 2006. Policies and Measures of China in Climate Change Mitigation under the Framework of Sustainable Development. Presentation to the Dialogue on Long-Term Cooperative Action to Address Climate Change by Enhancing Implementation of the Convention, Second Workshop, 15–16 November 2006, Nairobi, Kenya. http://unfccc.int/meetings/dialogue/ items/3759.php.

Glaser, Bonnie S., and Philip Saunders. 2002. Chinese Civilian Foreign Policy Research Institutes: Evolving Roles and Increasing Influence. *China Quarterly* 171:597–616.

Haya, B. 2007. Letter to CDM Executive Board On Non-additional Chinese Hydros. International Rivers, http://internationalrivers.org/node/1892 (accessed 1 June 2009).

Heggelund, Gørild. 2007. China's Climate Change Policy: Domestic and International Developments. *Asian Perspective* 31:155–191.

Heggelund, Gørild, Steinar Andresen, and Sun Ying. 2005. Performance of the Global Environmental Facility (GEF) in China: Achievements and Challenges as Seen by the Chinese. *International Environmental Agreements: Politics, Law and Economics* 5:323–348.

Heggelund, Gørild, and Ellen Bruzelius Backer. 2007. China and UN Environmental Policy: Institutional Growth, Learning and Implementation. *International Environmental Agreements: Politics, Law and Economics* 7:415–438.

Heggelund, Gørild, and Inga Fritzen Buan. 2009. China in the Asia-Pacific Partnership—Consequences for UN Climate Change Commitments? *International Environmental Agreements: Politics, Law and Economics* 9:301–317.

Intergovernmental Panel on Climate Change. 2007a. Climate Change 2007: Mitigation of Climate Change. Working Group III to the IPCC Fourth Assessment Report.

Intergovernmental Panel on Climate Change. 2007b. Climate Change 2007: The Physical Science Basis. Summary for Policymakers, Contribution of Working Group I to the Fourth Assessment Report of the IPCC.

International Bank for Reconstruction and Development. 2004. *Clean Development Mechanism in China: Taking a Proactive and Sustainable Approach*. Washington, DC: World Bank.

International Energy Agency. 2004. *World Energy Outlook 2004*. Paris: IEA/ OECD.

Kasa, Sjur, Anne T. Gullhaug, and Gørild Heggelund. 2008. The Group of 77 in International Climate Negotiations: Recent Developments and Future Directions? *International Environmental Agreements: Politics, Law and Economics* 8:113–127.

Lewis, Joanna. 2007. China's Strategic Priorities in International Climate Change Negotiations. *Washington Quarterly* (Winter):155–174.

Liu, Yingling. 2009. *A Chinese Perspective on Climate Change: State of the World 2009.* London: Worldwatch Institute.

Michaelowa, A. 2008. Empirical Analysis of Performance of CDM Projects: Final Report. London: Climate Strategies. http://www.climatestrategies.org/component/reports/category/16/71.html (accessed 1 June 2009).

National Bureau of Statistics of China. 2007. *2007 Zhongguo tongji nianjian* [China Statistical Yearbook 2007]. Beijing: China Statistical Press.

National Climate Change Coordination Committee. 2006. *Qihou bianhua Guojia Pinggu baogao* [China's National Assessment Report on Climate Change]. Beijing: Science Press.

National Development and Reform Commission. 2005. *Jieneng zhnog changqi zhuanxiang guihua* [China Medium and Long-Term Energy Conservation Plan]. Beijing: China Environmental Science Press.

National Development and Reform Commission. 2007. China's National Climate Change Program. 4 June. http://www.ccchina.gov.cn/WebSite/CCChina/UpFile/File188.pdf.

Netherlands Environmental Assessment Agency. 2008. Global CO2 Emissions: Increase Continued in 2007. http://www.planbureauvoordeleefomgeving.nl/en/publications/global-co2-emissions-increase-continued-in-2007.

OECD Statistics Directorate. N.d. Purchasing Power Parities (PPP), Purchasing Power Parities (PPPs) Frequently Asked Questions. http://www.oecd.org/faq/0,3433,en_2649_34357_1799281_1_1_1_1,00.html#1799063.

Office of the National Climate Change Coordination Committee. 2005. Measures for Operation and Management of Clean Development Mechanism Projects in China. http://cdm.ccchina.gov.cn/english/NewsInfo.asp?NewsId=905.

Office of the National Climate Change Coordination Committee. 2007. Clean Development Mechanism in China: Newly Approved Projects by the DNA in China, 12 June. http://cdm.ccchina.gov.cn/WebSite/CDM/UpFile/File1293.pdf.

Office of the National Climate Change Coordination Committee. 2009a. Clean Development Mechanism in China: Newly Approved Projects by the DNA in China. http://cdm.ccchina.gov.cn/WebSite/CDM/UpFile/File2274.pdf.

Office of the National Climate Change Coordination Committee. 2009b. Projects Obtaining Issued CERs (Total 110). http://cdm.ccchina.gov.cn/WebSite/CDM/UpFile/File2191.doc.

Pan, Jiahua. 2005. China and Climate Change: The Role of the Energy Sector. Science and Development Network. www.scidev.net/dossiers/index.cfm?fuseaction=policybrief&dossier=4&policy=64.

People's Republic of China. 2004. *Zhonghua renmin gongheguo Qihoubianhua chushi guojia xinxi tongbao* [Initial National Communication on Climate Change]. Beijing: China Planning Publishing House, October (Zhongguo jihua chubanshe).

Pew Center. 2006. COP 12 Report, Twelfth Session of the Conference of the Parties to the UN Framework Convention on Climate Change and Second Meeting of the Parties to the Kyoto Protocol, 6–17 November, Nairobi, Kenya. www.pewclimate.org/what_s_being_done/in_the_world/cop12/summary.cfm #bus.

Shambaugh, David. 2002. China's International Relations Think Tanks: Evolving Structure and Process. *China Quarterly* 171:575–596.

Sinton, Jonathan E., Rachel E. Stern, Nathaniel T. Aden, and Mark D. Levine, eds. 2005. *Evaluation of China's Energy Strategy Options*. Berkeley, CA: Lawrence Berkeley National Laboratories.

Skodvin, Tora, and Steinar Andresen. 2009. An Agenda for Change in U.S. Climate Policies? Presidential Ambitions and Congressional Powers. *International Environmental Agreements: Politics, Law and Economics* 9:263–280.

State Development and Planning Commission. 1998. *Greenhouse Gas Mitigation from Sustainable Energy and Forestry Action in China*. Beijing: SDPC.

State Environmental Protection Administration. 2007. Wen Jiabao Chaired the First Meeting for the Leading Small Group on Climate Change and Energy Conservation and Emissions Reduction (in Chinese), 10 July. http://www.sepa .gov.cn/hjyw/200707/t20070710_106483.htm#.

Sugiyama, T., and S. Oshita, eds. 2006. *Cooperative Climate: Energy Efficiency Action in East Asia*. Winnipeg: International Institute for Sustainable Development.

Tangen, Kristian, and Gørild Heggelund. 2003. *Will the Clean Development Mechanism be Effectively Implemented in China?* FNI Report 8/2003. Lysaker, Norway: Fridtjof Nansen Institute.

Tangen, Kristian, Gørild Heggelund, and Jørund Buen. 2001. China's Climate Change Positions: At a Turning Point? *Energy and Environment* 12 (2–3):237–252.

Victor, D. G., and M. Wara. 2008. *A Realistic Policy on International Carbon Offsets*. Working Paper #74. Stanford University, Program on Energy and Sustainable Development.

Wara, M. 2008. Measuring the Clean Development Mechanism's Performance and Potential. *UCLA Law Review* 55:1759–1803.

Wei, Lin, Gørild Heggelund, Kristian Tangen, and Li Jun Feng. 2004. *Efficient Implementation of the Clean Development Mechanism in China?* FNI Report 1/2004. Lysaker, Norway: Fridtjof Nansen Institute.

Wen Jiabao. 2003. *Government Working Report, Made to the People's Congress Annual Meeting, March 2003*. Beijing: People Press.

Wen Jiabao. 2007. Report on the Work of the Government [full text], Delivered at the Fifth Session of the Tenth National People's Congress on 5 March 2007 (updated 17 March 2007). http://news.xinhuanet.com/english/2007-03/16/content_5857166.htm.

World Bank. 2006. World Bank's New Partnership Strategy for China Focuses on Economic Integration, Poverty, and Sustainable Development. News Release No. 2006/416/EAP, 23 May. http://web.worldbank.org/WBSITE/EXTERNAL/COUNTRIES/EASTASIAPACIFICEXT/CHINAEXTN/0,contentMDK:20931682~menuPK:318956~pagePK:141137~piPK:141127~theSitePK:318950,00.html.

World Resources Institute. CAIT. http://cait.wri.org/.

Zhang, Haibin. 2007. Zhongguo yu guoji qihou bianhua tanpan [China and the International Climate Change Negotiations]. *International Politics Quarterly* 1:21–36.

9

Conclusion: The Comparative Politics of Climate Change

Kathryn Harrison and Lisa McIntosh Sundstrom

Introduction

As the nations of the world embark on a second, post-Kyoto, effort to collectively address climate change, it is an opportune time to ask what lessons can be learned from experience to date. The case studies in this volume have revealed a diversity of outcomes concerning ratification of the Kyoto Protocol and governments' policy actions to mitigate climate change. Yet while each case exhibits unique developments, we can also identify recurring patterns in configurations of factors that contribute to success or failure. The richness of the individual country cases invites us to compare in some detail the variations across them. We return here to the expectations we introduced in chapter 1, assessing how they have played out in the individual cases and drawing comparisons across the cases for further theoretical insights.

Policymakers' Self-Interest

In chapter 1, we offered two hypotheses concerning the influence of policymakers' own interests. All else being equal, we expected policymakers in democracies to be more willing to ratify and adopt domestic mitigation measures the greater the pressure from domestic voters. In addition, we expected that politicians in all countries, democratic and authoritarian states alike, would face greater opposition, and thus be less willing to ratify and adopt domestic measures, the greater the costs of compliance with the Kyoto Protocol for their citizens.

Electoral Incentives

It is challenging to compare public opinion concerning climate change across countries since polling firms typically operate at the national level, thus limiting comparability of questions and methods across countries. Tables 9.1 and 9.2 report the results of a cross-national survey conducted by World Public Opinion in 2003 and 2005–2006, while table 9.3 reports results from a cross-national survey by Pew. The 2003 survey was done shortly after most countries had made decisions with respect to ratification of the Kyoto Protocol. Although neither Australia nor Japan was included in 2003, the results do indicate much higher levels of concern in Western Europe than in Russia, Canada, and the United States, which ranked last, with less than one-third of respondents considering global

Table 9.1
World Public Opinion Survey, 2003. Approximately 1,000 respondents in each country were asked: "How serious a problem do you consider climate change or global warming due to the Greenhouse Effect to be?"

	Very serious	Somewhat serious	Not very serious	Not at all serious
Italy	63	30	5	1
Germany	54	33	10	2
UK	50	35	9	3
France	46	43	8	1
Russia	43	34	15	1
Canada	40	41	11	5
USA	31	40	13	11

Source: World Public Opinion 2006.

Table 9.2
World Public Opinion Survey, 2005–2006

	Very serious	Somewhat serious	Not very serious	Not at all serious
Japan	75	23	2	—
Germany	73	20	5	1
France	70	24	3	1
UK	70	21	6	2
Italy	68	26	4	1
Russia	59	29	7	1
Canada	57	33	6	3
USA	49	27	12	9

Source: World Public Opinion 2007.

Table 9.3
Approximately 1,000 respondents in each country were asked: "How serious a problem is global warming?"

	Very serious	Somewhat serious	Not too serious	Not a problem	Don't know/ refused
Japan	78	19	2	1	1
Spain	70	25	2	0	3
France	68	27	4	1	0
Sweden	64	25	5	2	4
Germany	60	26	8	4	2
Canada	58	29	8	4	2
Italy	57	35	2	1	6
USA	47	28	13	9	2
Britain	45	37	10	5	3
China	42	46	7	1	4
Russia	40	33	19	6	3

Source: Pew Global Attitudes Project 2007.

warming to be "very serious." Public concern was higher in all countries surveyed in 2006 than 2003 but still consistently higher in Europe, surpassed only by Japan, compared to North America and Russia. Similarly, in 2007 the Pew Global Attitudes Project found the highest fraction of respondents who identified global warming as "very serious" in Japan and various Western European countries, well above the United States, Russia, and China. However, by 2007 concern had increased among Canadian voters and declined among those in the UK.

Consistent with these differences, it is telling that there were larger protests across Europe than in the United States itself (as Schreurs and Tiberghien report in chapter 2) when the Bush administration announced in 2001 that the United States would not ratify the Kyoto Protocol. In member states such as Germany, France, and the UK, even parties on the right are now committed to aggressive measures to address climate change. In the case of Japan, Tiberghien and Schreurs argue in chapter 5 that the Kyoto Protocol took on symbolic significance with voters, not least because it bears the name of a Japanese city, thus rendering it virtually impossible for the government *not* to ratify. In contrast, in Russia, as well as Canada, the United States, and Australia, until recently public opinion was mostly pro-Kyoto, but the public was largely inattentive to the issue of global warming.

In addition to voters' level of concern, typically expressed in response to closed-ended questions, voters' level of attention to climate change is also likely to be important to policymakers. If voters express concern about global warming but are actually more attentive to gasoline prices, politicians understandably would be wary of pursuing aggressive policies to price carbon. We expect voters' level of concern for and attention to climate change generally to go hand in hand, and thus we anticipate that the cross-national differences noted above reflect different levels of both attention and concern. However, within a given country, trends in salience tend to be more pronounced than those in level of concern expressed in response to close-ended questions. We are thus in a position to draw on comparisons over time *within* countries as well as *across* countries.

Here, the most notable case is Australia. As Crowley notes in chapter 7, when asked closed-ended questions in public opinion polls, Australian voters have always supported the Kyoto Protocol and disapproved of the Howard government's handling of the issue of climate change. However, when voters were asked, unprompted, to identify the "most important" issues for the federal government to address, the environment ranked ninth in late 2001, just before the original decision not to ratify. Much had changed by 2005, when voters identified the environment as "the single most important problem facing Australia today."[1] The surge in public attention to climate change coincided with the Australian Labor Party's resurgence of interest in climate change, and thus can account for Australia's belated ratification of the Kyoto Protocol after Labor won a majority in 2007. It is noteworthy, though, that the Howard government did not change its position on the Kyoto Protocol, despite the increase in salience of climate change among voters. We speculate that this reflects that some policy decisions—particularly those that are high-profile and contentious—are difficult for governing parties to retreat from, even when shifts in public opinion would otherwise transform their incentives.

Similar political incentives developed during the 2007 French election campaign, when the emergence of climate change as a salient issue prompted all parties to promise quite dramatic measures to reduce greenhouse gas emissions. In 2009, Nicolas Sarkozy followed through on his commitment to adopt a carbon tax should he be elected president. The effects of an increase in salience were also apparent in Canada. Harrison notes in chapter 6 that a Conservative government elected in 2006 significantly revised its own greenhouse gas reduction targets, though still rejecting compliance with Canada's Kyoto Protocol target, in response to a surge in public attention to climate change after the election.

The Canadian case, however, offers a cautionary tale concerning the fickleness of public attention. The salience of environmental issues, which shot to the top of public opinion polls in Canada in late 2006, had already begun to decline before a federal election was called in the fall of 2008, and that decline was hastened by the spillover of the US economic crisis to Canada in the midst of the election campaign. In response, not only did voters reelect the Conservative government *despite* its weaker positions on climate change compared to the competing parties, but they appear to have done so in part *because* the Conservatives opposed the carbon tax that was the centerpiece of the Liberal Party's platform.

Compliance Costs and Interest Group Pressures
Based on the formal Kyoto targets alone, it is hard to understand the pattern of ratification and nonratification decisions evident in table 1.2. For instance, the European Union ratified the Kyoto Protocol despite having what appears to be the deepest reduction commitment, while Australia initially chose not to ratify despite a relatively lenient target. However, as noted in chapter 1, a country's formal target relative to 1990 emissions is at best a crude measure of the magnitude of effort required to achieve compliance. An alternative measure of the depth of commitment is the degree of reduction below the business-as-usual trajectory for 2010 (the midpoint of the Kyoto compliance period) that each country thought it was undertaking at the time of its ratification decision.[2]

Table 9.4 reorders the data in table 1.2 based on the anticipated cut below the business-as-usual projection. Viewed in these terms, several countries' ratification decisions become clearer. In chapter 4, Henry and Sundstrom demonstrate that it will be relatively easy for Russia to meet its target since economic projections did not anticipate that Russian emissions would return to their 1990 levels (pre–economic collapse) by 2010. Russia not only did not need to do anything to comply but actually stood to gain financially from the sale of any remaining business-as-usual, or "hot air," credits to other countries. In contrast, the United States faced the most demanding target relative to its business-as-usual trajectory. Similarly, although Australia negotiated what seemed like a lenient formal target of +8 percent, dramatic growth in the coal sector implied that Australia still would need to make significant reductions in

Table 9.4
Comparison of Kyoto Targets Relative to Business-as-Usual Trajectory

	Kyoto target	Anticipated reduction relative to business-as-usual emissions in 2010	Ratification
China	N/A	N/A	Yes
Russia	0%	>0%	Yes
EU-15	−8%	~ −3% to −9%[1]	Yes
Japan	−6%	~ −12%[2]	Yes
Canada	−6%	−29%[3]	Yes
Australia	+8%	−14% to −29%[4]	No (2002) Yes (2007)
USA	−7%	−31%[5]	No

1. *Source:* European Environmental Agency 2002a, 2002b.
2. *Source:* Schreurs and Tiberghien, chapter 2, this volume.
3. *Source:* Canada 2002.
4. *Source:* The figures for Australia are, unfortunately, drawn from Australian Greenhouse Office 2006, rather than from data available at the time of Australia's 2002 ratification decision. The reference case emissions projection for 2010 is 53 percent above 1990 (thus entailing a 29 percent reduction), while the *net* emission projection is 25 percent above (thus entailing a 14 percent reduction).
5. *Source:* United States 2002.

its net emissions in order to comply. Critical from Australia's perspective, however, was whether the international community would allow it to claim full credit for ongoing (business-as-usual) reductions in the rate of land clearing (i.e., regardless of the nature of the vegetation being cleared). This issue remained unresolved until late 2002 and thus accounts for the range of reductions depicted in Australia's case in table 9.4 and may also have contributed to the Howard government's rejection of the treaty at that time.

As discussed in chapter 2, an important part of the EU story lay in the emissions trajectories of Germany and the UK. The former experienced significant emissions reductions in the early 1990s as a result of closure of inefficient East German facilities following reunification. The UK, for its part, anticipated that replacement of coal by newly exploited reserves of offshore gas would yield significant emissions reductions by 2010. Neither of these transitions was painless, and in that sense it is noteworthy that both the UK and Germany freely conceded their windfall reductions to the EU bubble rather than extracting financial compensation for them, as did Russia. However, it remains the case that these reductions already had or were about to occur regardless of domestic climate policies. Indeed, building on its windfall reductions, Germany's proposed reduction target accounts for 75 percent of the total EU reduction, and the UK and Germany together account for more than 100 percent of the EU's commitment, thus providing room for other EU states' emissions to grow, in some cases quite dramatically.[3]

Compliance costs are a function not only of the depth of cuts needed, however, but also the marginal costs of making those reductions. Under a perfectly competitive international carbon market, marginal abatement costs would be identical in all countries. In turn, the cost to any given country would simply be proportional to the reduction needed below that country's business-as-usual trajectory. In practice, however, it became apparent early on that a perfect international market was unattainable. First, despite persistent pressure from the umbrella group, the EU did not concede unlimited reliance on international mechanisms until 2002, only after the United States and Australia had indicated their intentions not to ratify the Kyoto Protocol, citing concerns about costs and competitiveness. The absence of binding targets for developing countries not only presented a potential threat to competitiveness for Annex 1 countries but also limited the opportunities for the latter to realize least-cost abatement.[4] To the extent that reliance on international trading was limited, whether by international rules or domestic politics, discussed below, Annex 1 countries would need to make a greater fraction of reductions at home.

Under that scenario, differences in marginal abatement costs in various countries become relevant. All else being equal, countries that are more energy-efficient will have higher abatement costs than those that are less energy-efficient, since the former have already harvested the "low-hanging fruit." An international exercise comparing economic analysis of the Kyoto Protocol using thirteen different models was undertaken in 1998.[5] It projected that, without trading, marginal abatement costs varied from an average of approximately $400 per metric ton for Japan to just over $300 for the EU to roughly $200 for the United States, Canada, Australia, and New Zealand.[6]

While the high marginal abatement costs in Japan and the EU would seem to offset the relatively less demanding targets those jurisdictions received in the Kyoto Protocol (table 9.4), the impact of abatement costs also depends on the nature of each country's economy. Jurisdictions with carbon-intensive economies tend to rely on low-cost fossil fuels for comparative advantage, and thus face relatively greater impacts on competitiveness for a comparable increase in energy prices. The international modeling exercise also estimated GDP losses for different countries or regions under different trading scenarios. Averaging findings across all models yields the conclusion that, with Annex 1 trading only, per capita GDP losses would be roughly twice as high in the United States, Canada, Australia, and New Zealand (all at around $200 per person per year in 2010) than in the EU and Japan (both around $100 per person).[7] In contrast, most models projected financial *gains* for Russia.

Although the business community may not have closely followed academic modeling exercises, the kinds of effects predicted by formal models were nonetheless foremost in the minds of domestic producers, who feared that ratification of the Kyoto Protocol would lead to higher taxes and/or energy prices and a corresponding loss of competitiveness to jurisdictions facing weaker or, in the case of developing countries, no reduction targets. Consistent with both the magnitude of reductions reported in table 9.4 and the economic modeling discussed above, the case studies in this volume show that business opposition was strongest in Canada, Australia, and the United States, where the business community presented a strong and united front against ratification, predicting a loss of tens or even hundreds of thousands of jobs. In contrast, although most Japanese firms expressed concerns about ratification, especially after the United States pulled out of the treaty, industry did not speak with one voice. The business community was further divided in the European Union, where, in stark contrast to the United States, Canada, and Australia, key oil companies, including BP, Royal Dutch Shell, and Austrian OMV, actually supported ratification. The most powerful voices of Russian industry, with the notable exclusion of the oil sector, lobbied *for* ratification.

The evidence concerning electoral interests generally supports our hypotheses. First, countries in which the public was more concerned about climate change at the time of the ratification decision generally were more likely to ratify. We also find that there was stronger and more influential opposition from the business community, where the costs of compliance with the Kyoto Protocol would have been greatest. Thus the combination of strong public and considerable business support facilitated ratification by the EU and Japan, while the public inattention and business opposition is consistent with the United States' nonratification and Australia's initial decision not to ratify. Australia's late ratification, however, suggests that voter support can overcome opposition from the business community. The Canadian case remains puzzling, in that Canada ratified the Protocol despite relatively high costs to the business sector and relatively low public attention. We turn to this case in the next section.

Russia and China also offer interesting exceptions due to the minimal impact of public opinion on government policy. Russia ratified Kyoto despite relatively low levels of public concern because ratification presented no costs and indeed offered potential economic gains for Russia. Public attention thus was not necessary. Similarly, popular opinion has played almost no role in Chinese climate policy since there are no national-level elections. Instead, in these two cases, battles among political leaders and economic and bureaucratic actors have been highly important in shaping policy. Both countries have experienced enormous economic growth over the past decade (albeit China much more dynamically), and their governments are eager to shift from wasteful industrial and public utility practices to more efficient energy use, both to increase profits and to avoid exhausting energy resources that are in ever greater demand from their increasingly affluent (urban) populations. Thus, economic self-interest in energy efficiency drives positive steps to reduce carbon emissions in these cases in particular.

Ideas

Two types of ideas shaped debates on ratification in the case countries: scientific knowledge and normative principles. While there was strong scientific consensus about the contribution of anthropogenic greenhouse gas emissions to climate change, *political* debate about the science did arise in several countries.[8] One of these, the United States, did not ratify the Kyoto Protocol, while two others, Australia and Russia, were late ratifiers.

While the empirical facts of delayed ratification and nonratification suggest that scientific disputes may have played some role in the outcomes, it is difficult to assess the extent to which politicians deliberately overemphasized scientific debate as a reason to avoid emissions reduction programs that could require significant economic sacrifice. It is certainly the case that there was strong agreement among scientists in all of the countries studied. In the Russian case, however, the overwhelming numerical consensus among scientists about climate change was counterbalanced by the fact that the country's most prominent climatologist and a key presidential economic advisor doubted human influence on climate change. These debates appeared less manufactured and more sincere matters of government concern in Russia than in Australia, where skepticism about the science seemed to emerge only after the Howard government had decided that ratification of the Kyoto Protocol was undesirable, and in the United States, where the skeptics often were funded by the fossil fuel industry and there was evidence that opponents pursued a conscious strategy to exaggerate and exploit scientific uncertainty.

Sometimes ideas intervened in the process not because of knowledge disputes but because of the strength of decision makers' commitments to certain norms. In the Russian and Japanese cases, there is evidence that government decision makers were more positively disposed to ratification due to their affinity for particular constitutive norms establishing the identities of their states. In Russia, as described by Henry and Sundstrom in chapter 4, government officials frequently remarked on the need to be part of "the world community," "European politics," or "Western values." Yet the costless nature of Russia's ratification and its calculated bargaining for international side payments undermine the importance of this normative impulse in the ratification decision. In Japan (Tiberghien and Schreurs, chapter 5), the *Kyoto* Protocol had symbolic significance by virtue of its origins in that country, and this seems to have played some role in persuading politicians to ratify, but largely through electoral pressures as a result of Japanese citizens' views on the treaty, rather than in response to politicians' own values. In truth, as authors such as Jeffrey Checkel have pointed out, actors rarely behave out of pure normative impulses or brute strategic calculations; there is usually some combination of logics of appropriateness and consequences involved in actors' decisions.[9]

Canada provides the clearest case of a leader's normative commitment affecting a country's ratification decision. As described by Harrison in chapter 6, the prime minister, Jean Chrétien, in an institutional position of strong decision-making authority, was captivated by the seriousness of global warming as a problem and embraced a norm of multilateralism to resolve foreign policy issues. Despite strong opposition from business, most provincial governments, and even members of his own cabinet, Chrétien personally decided that Canada would ratify the Kyoto Protocol. Here we see a powerful interaction of institutional arrangements with a policymaker's ideas leading to ratification. Yet as will be discussed below, this strong influence of a single decision maker at the level of treaty ratification meant that Canada's commitment to Kyoto was fragile, since successors could just as easily overturn or simply decline to act upon it.

We previously suggested the possibility that politicians with left-wing ideologies may be more receptive to the kinds of economic interventions required to address climate change. Although left and right meant nothing in the Russian and Chinese governments' worldview, in other cases, ideology was a good predictor of governing parties' stances on ratification and action on climate change. This applies to Democrats versus Republicans at the US federal level, Liberals versus Conservatives at the Canadian federal level, Labor versus Conservatives in the UK, Labor versus the Democrats in Australia, the Democratic Party of Japan versus the Liberal Democratic Party, and the general strength of social democratic parties in Europe. However, there was also evidence of ideological divides on the left. For example, disagreements between the trade unionist and environmentalist camps in the Australian Labor Party for many years compromised the party's ability to take a clear stance on policy measures to reduce global warming. And in Canada, the left-wing New Democratic Party opposed carbon taxes both federally and provincially.

Moreover, it is surprising to us that left/right differences have not played a larger role in determining which jurisdictions implement the strongest climate change abatement policies: right-leaning free-market governments did not consistently refuse to take significant policy measures. Indeed, at subnational levels in Canada and the United States, right-wing governments have adopted some of the most aggressive policies on emissions reductions among their peers. In the United States this includes the Schwarzenegger administration in California and the Pataki administration in New York; in Canada, the Campbell government in British Columbia. In Europe, the Christian Democrats in Germany and the UMP under Nicolas Sarkozy in France also have adopted strong positions on climate change. In these cases, an environmentally concerned electorate seems to have pushed conservative governments to embrace more interventionist policies, suggesting that voters' preferences trump politicians' ideologies.

While the influence of values points toward stronger action by industrialized states, in the case of China we see clearly the role that competing norms can play in *hampering* states' participation in international environmental treaties. Chinese negotiators in UN climate negotiations have consistently and strongly argued that China and other developing countries should not be subject to the same pressures to reduce greenhouse gas emissions, since they do not bear historical responsibility for the bulk of worldwide emissions and sharp reductions would necessarily compromise much-needed economic development. As Heggelund, Andresen, and Buan discuss in chapter 8, Chinese negotiators frequently contrast the "'survival emissions' of developing countries with the 'luxury emissions' of developed countries." China, in many ways viewed as the leading state of the developing world, thus exemplifies the continuing challenges hindering adoption of a climate change treaty that commits all states to binding reductions.

Institutions

In chapter 1 we identified three institutional features of interest: expression of voters' preferences, horizontal diffusion or concentration of authority, and vertical diffusion or concentration of authority.

Electoral systems can either give expression to or dampen public concern. In general, since they reflect minority opinions more accurately, electoral systems based on proportional representation permit environmental concern among a minority of voters to have a greater effect on politicians' decisions, especially when the environment may not be a salient issue for the majority of voters. In our set of cases, most of the EU member states and the European Parliament have proportional representation (PR) systems, and this seems to have played a large role in the EU's consistent support for strong policies to combat global warming. In the Japanese case, the introduction of PR in 1994 to elect a significant fraction of members of parliament has meant that politicians (particularly urban backbenchers) now have stronger incentives to build alliances with issue-based social movements and NGOs, including pro-Kyoto Protocol environmental groups.

In two others cases, however, PR systems did not have the same effect. In Australia, the Senate (upper house) is elected by a proportional representation system (single transferable vote) and as a result there are Green Party senators. However, the Senate cannot introduce appropriation bills and the lower house is the confidence chamber, which means that in practice the Senate does not initiate most Australian legislation. In Russia, although half of its legislative seats at the time of the ratification debate were elected by proportional representation (by 2007, the system had changed to all PR seats), the State Duma is a weak body compared to the president, especially in international treaty matters, and pro-presidential parties dominate the legislature. The Australian and Russian cases demonstrate that electoral systems can only have an impact to the extent that the legislature to which they apply has real influence.

In contrast, first-past-the-post electoral systems demand that electoral candidates win more votes than all other candidates in order to win any representation at all in a particular district. These systems reward appeals to the broad majority of voters. Majoritarian electoral systems, as in Canada and the United States, thus demand that concern about global warming is highly salient for a significant share of voters before politicians will stake their political campaigns on the issue, a hurdle that has been difficult to clear in both countries.

The case studies reveal interactions between the horizontal concentration of authority with both ideas and electoral incentives. Despite Russia and Canada's highly dissimilar political systems in most respects, the two systems are the most similar among our cases with regard to concentration of authority. In both cases, the head of government (Chrétien in Canada and Putin in Russia) was able to make a ratification decision effectively unilaterally. In Russia's strongly centralized, superpresidential political system, ratification was essentially up to the president to decide alone. Because Jean Chrétien was about to retire from political life and thus may have been less sensitive to electoral implications of his decisions than is typically the case for a Canadian prime minister, the two leaders' circumstances were unusually similar. When there are few actors who can veto a leader's decision, individual leaders' views can be influential even in the face of apparent economic or electoral interests.[10]

While the two cases of concentrated authority included here both ended with a positive ratification decision, the opposite outcome can occur just as easily. Made at another time or by another leader, these decisions could have been different. This is abundantly clear from the Canadian case, in which Chrétien's eventual successor, Conservative leader Stephen Harper, declared soon after assuming office that his government would not even try to comply with Canada's Kyoto Protocol target. In the case of Russia, had President Putin paid more heed to the models provided by climatologists and economic advisors critical of Kyoto, he could easily have decided not to ratify.

Interaction between horizontal diffusion of authority and electoral incentives is illustrated most clearly by the US case. In contrast to the concentration of authority in Canada's parliamentary system, the US system of checks and balances affords organized interests multiple veto points with which to block policy change. Business and labor were able to express their opposition to the Kyoto Protocol at multiple access points and thus to preclude ratification by the Senate, despite support for ratification from President Clinton and Vice President Gore. A decade later, the same interests remain a formidable obstacle to passage of climate change legislation under President Obama.

Vertical diffusion of authority through federalism or multilevel governance had complex patterns of influence on ratification. In the case of the EU, Schreurs and Tiberghien argue in chapter 2 that multilevel governance was critical to the EU's leadership role, as key member states provided leadership to laggards, and in turn central institutions, especially the European Parliament and European Commissions, reinforced that resolve. In the US case, Harrison in chapter 3 describes a similar dynamic at the subnational level in recent years, as states such as California and New York have shown leadership, in so doing prompting other states to follow their lead. However, the United States has not seen the same sort of dynamic between states and the national government as in the EU, given the US federal government's pattern of inaction to date. In Canada, federalism has for the most part played an obstructive role, as most provincial governments sought to block ratification and federal policy initiatives, though that changed to some degree with a surge in public attention to the environment in 2006.

But why should a similar institution have such different effects in different settings? We identify three factors. First, federal institutions interact with public opinion. In the EU, public pressure pushed key member states, most notably Germany, to demonstrate early leadership by committing to unilateral greenhouse gas reduction targets. When the EU later negotiated its bubble agreement, fellow member states held those leaders to their prior commitments, and that facilitated agreement by all fifteen member states, not least because deep cuts by some allowed others to continue to increase their emissions.[11] Moreover, shifts in public opinion have prompted new leaders, including most recently France, to emerge over time. In the United States, it has been wealthy states (which tend, not coincidentally, to be relatively "green") that have led the charge. And unilateral actions by Canadian provincial governments emerged only after a shift in public attention to climate change in 2006.

Second, the rules of the game can be quite different in different federations. In the case of the EU, regulatory decisions at the EU level are made by a qualified majority vote. Although a requirement for consensus on taxation effectively precludes a Europe-wide carbon tax, it was possible to gain sufficient votes under the qualified majority rule to establish the European Emissions Trading Scheme. In contrast, as owners of most of Canada's vast land mass, provincial governments also control most of the natural resources in question when it comes to climate change. While the provinces do not formally exercise a veto, the combination of their resource ownership and the weak federal treaty power has put the Canadian federal government in a weaker position than the European Union.

Third and perhaps most important, the distribution of costs was very different among these federal or quasi-federal systems. As noted above, the two largest players in the EU, Germany and the UK, had experienced windfall emissions reductions and thus were in a position to embrace proposals for relatively deep cuts in EU emissions. Similarly, two of the most populous states in the United States, California and New York, do not have heavily carbon-intensive economies, and it is probably no coincidence that these two have shown the greatest leadership. In contrast, in Canada, two of the most economically important and thus politically influential provinces, Alberta and Ontario, are keen to protect carbon-intensive local industries—oil (Alberta) and automobile manufacturing (Ontario)—and thus sought to block ratification. Although after a change in government and shift in public opinion Ontario now supports more aggressive action, and indeed has committed to emissions trading with California and other US states through the Western Climate Initiative, the Alberta government continues to project emissions growth for decades to come as it develops its oil sands reserves.

International Influences

International factors continued to interact with domestic interests and ideas even after the Kyoto treaty was negotiated among the state parties. There are three basic international factors that affected the balance of domestic interests—and thus politicians' incentives—for or against Kyoto ratification. The first was ongoing diplomatic bargaining among governments that influenced the "price" of ratification. This became particularly intense once the United States announced that it would not ratify the Kyoto Protocol and Russia and Japan's ratification suddenly became indispensable. In the Russian case, such bargaining was particularly important to the outcome, given the lack of domestic public pressure for ratification and the withdrawal of the largest potential international buyer of Russian emissions credits. Although never confirmed officially by either side, EU approval of Russia's WTO bid came at roughly the same time as the Russian government finally decided to ratify, suggesting that WTO approval was granted as a side payment to Russia to induce its positive ratification decision. Similarly, as Tiberghien and Schreurs in chapter 5 and Harrison in chapter 6 describe, once the United States had abandoned ratification, Japan and Canada were able to extract more advantageous conditions with regard to using forest sinks to offset carbon emissions and the extent to which international flexibility mechanisms could be used to reduce parties' emissions totals. The treaty terms ratified by these countries thus were considerably more generous than the ones the United States rejected.

The second factor was moral pressure from transnational actors, both governmental and nongovernmental, in support of or against ratification. Efforts by foreign states were especially strong on the late ratifiers, Japan, Canada, and then Russia, following the United States' announcement that it would not ratify. The leaders of Japan and Russia faced enormous pressure from the leaders of countries that had ratified—especially European countries—as well as pressure from the US presidential administration, urging them not to ratify. These pressures may have had some effect on leaders' decision-making processes, but since such pressure came strongly from both the United States and Europe, it was fairly balanced in both encouraging and discouraging ratification.

In addition, a "boomerang pattern" of sorts took place.[12] Transnational environmental NGO networks such as Greenpeace and World Wildlife Fund worked with their partners in states that had not ratified in order to support local NGOs in their campaigns to urge ratification. In an interesting twist, NGOs in the major nonratifier—the United States—worked especially hard following the US rejection of Kyoto to ensure that the treaty would survive nonetheless. The Environmental Defense Fund launched a special campaign focused on Russia's ratification, working closely with Russian environmental scientists and activists, as soon as the United States had backed out. However, the vigorous activity of NGO networks to push for ratification is unlikely to have had much effect on the ultimate pro-ratification outcome, given the lack of contact between President Putin and the NGO activists (when the decision was his alone) and the low level of public awareness of the Kyoto Protocol in Russia. Probably more influential was cooperation among Russian and Western scholars—climate scientists and environmental economists—who were able to allay fears planted by the president's chief economic advisor, Andrei Illarionov, that ratification of the Kyoto Protocol would hamper Russian economic growth.

While transnational networks among NGOs advanced normative arguments in favor of ratification and domestic action to bolster the position of domestic environmentalists, a third factor of international economic ties was a source of self-interested arguments against ratification. Business in countries that had accepted more demanding targets argued that they would not be able to compete with their counterparts in countries that either had less onerous targets or no commitments at all (in the case of developing countries). This was the chief reason for withdrawal by the United States and, initially, Australia. Then once the United States had withdrawn, the governments of other countries—particularly Canada and Japan—became even more concerned that they would not be able to compete with their chief trading partner, the United States.

Finally, there is a fourth international factor of changing international environmental norms that made it possible for states to commit to a treaty on emissions reductions to combat global warming at all, but likely does not explain varying state choices concerning ratification. Steven Bernstein has argued that "liberal environmentalism"—a package of supportive causal and principled norms include the polluter-pays principle, market-based approaches such as emissions trading, and especially the concept of "sustainable development"—facilitated international agreement on the Kyoto Protocol by allowing states to reconcile their commitments to free trade with their aspirations for environmental conservation.[13] While Bernstein makes a compelling case that liberal environmentalism shaped the design of the Kyoto Protocol, particularly the inclusion of international trading mechanisms, the chapters on the United States and Canada suggest that the academic idea of international trading did not resonate with domestic voters. Members of the US Congress were highly critical of the idea of international trading, prompting the White House to hide the extent to which the United States would need to rely on the Protocol's international mechanisms. Similarly, the Liberal government in Canada avoided revealing the large fraction of reductions that would need to be obtained through international mechanisms, while their Conservative successors simply announced that they would not "play with taxpayers money" by participating in international emissions trading. Moreover, the "win-win" promise of sustainable development could not be sustained in either Canada or the United States, as policymakers confronted very real tradeoffs between winners and losers, with the latter especially vocal and adamantly opposed to ratification and adoption of domestic abatement measures.

Overall, international factors were mixed in the direction and extent of their influence on ratification and domestic policy decisions. The simple presence of an international agreement to cut emissions largely resolved the basic collective action problem typically involved in global environmental issues. The Kyoto Protocol's existence spurred some governments to undertake emissions reductions because there was some reassurance that other countries would also act. Transnational networks mostly in favor of the Kyoto Protocol nudged governments further in some of the later ratifiers, but their influence was limited. On the opposite side, the presence of competitive, closely interwoven international trade markets was a significant factor for many countries. This ultimately led to the withdrawal of the country then responsible for the largest share of global emissions, and to persistent implementation challenges even among countries that chose to ratify, an issue to which we now turn.

Comparison of Outcomes: Ratification versus Domestic Mitigation Policies

The hypotheses introduced in chapter 1 do not distinguish between the two outcomes of interest. We anticipated that, all else being equal, greater public pressure, lower compliance costs, stronger influence of norms, and electoral systems that provide for greater representation of minority interests would facilitate both ratification of the Kyoto Protocol and adoption of domestic policies to abate greenhouse gas emissions. In this section we consider whether these two outcomes in fact go hand in hand.

Any analysis of domestic climate policies is necessarily preliminary since even the "greenest" jurisdiction considered in this volume, the EU, is still in the process of devising and implementing policies to ensure compliance with its Kyoto Protocol target by the commitment period, 2008–2012. This is most clearly the case for Australia, which only ratified in late 2007 after a change in government.

One way to compare policy stringency is to compare policy impacts, that is, trends in greenhouse gas emissions. Table 9.5 compares emissions trends from 1990 to 2005 among the jurisdictions covered in this issue. While there is tremendous variation in performance, from a 34 percent decline in emissions in Russia to a 25 percent increase in Canada, the variation in population growth evident in the next column suggests that emissions trends reflect more than policy efficacy. Canada, the

United States, and Australia have experienced much greater increases in emissions in large part because they have experienced much greater population growth than other jurisdictions. Indeed, when one compares trends in per capita emissions, it is striking that the only country to see a decline other than the three that experienced "windfall" reductions (Germany, the UK, and Russia) is the United States, which has been vilified for its decision not to ratify the Kyoto Protocol. With the exception of Germany and the UK, the rest of the EU countries have experienced increases in per capita emissions comparable to those of Canada and Australia.

The figures in table 9.5 suggest that few, if any, countries had adopted effective climate policies as of 2005. One might argue, however, that it is simply too soon to assess impacts on emissions since most parties to the Kyoto Protocol only became serious about devising policies to reduce their emissions after ratification. Another means of comparing climate policies is to consider the range of policy instruments various jurisdictions have adopted to date, though such a comparison is necessarily preliminary in light of ongoing policy development in all jurisdictions. The degree to which different jurisdictions have employed instruments ranging from politically less challenging planning and voluntary mea-

Table 9.5
Comparison of Greenhouse Gas Emission Trends

Country	Emissions growth (without LULUCF) 1990 to 2005[1]	Population growth, 1990 to 2005[2]	Increase in emissions (without LULUCF) per capita, 1990 to 2005
Australia	+24.2%	+19%	+4.5%
Canada	+24.7%	+17%	+7.0%
China[3]	+31.9%	+10%	+19.4%
Japan	+6.9%	+3%	+3.6%
Russia	−33.7%	−4%	−31.3%
United States	+18.6%	+18%	−0.4%
EU-15	−1.7%	+5%	−6.7%
Germany	−18.3%	+4%	−21.4%
UK	−15.3%	+5%	−19.4%
Rest of EU	+12.1%	+5.9	+5.8%

1. *Source:* UNFCC, http://unfccc.int/ghg_emissions_data/items/3954.php.
2. *Source:* US Census Bureau. http://www.census.gov/ipc/www/idbrank.html.
3. *Source:* CAIT, http://cait.wri.org/cait.php?page=yearly&mode=view. Data for China is from 2000.

sures through more contested but also more effective measures, such as regulation and taxation, is summarized in table 9.6. (The table includes information only through the end of 2007 for Australia, and thus we treat the latter as a nonratifier in the following analysis.)

Perhaps not surprisingly, the one Annex 1 jurisdiction that did not ratify the Kyoto Protocol, the United States, has not made very aggressive efforts to date to control or offset greenhouse gas emissions. Under both the Clinton and Bush administrations, the United States relied on a mix of federal spending for research, subsidies for business, and voluntary programs. The election of the Barack Obama in November 2008 ushered in an era of greater openness to regulatory approaches in US climate policy. However, as of late 2009, the federal government had yet to adopt any regulations or taxes in order to reduce greenhouse gas emissions. That said, many state governments, led most notably by California, have moved ahead with their own climate abatement programs.[14]

In contrast to the United States, the Howard government in Australia committed to meeting Australia's Kyoto Protocol target, even though it

Table 9.6
National Governments' Reliance on Alternative Policy Instruments

	China	USA[1]	Australia	Russia	Canada	Japan	EU
Recipient of foreign investment	Yes	No	No	Yes	No	No	No
Plan to meet Kyoto target	N/A	No	Yes	Yes	· No	Yes	Yes
Voluntary programs		Yes	Yes	Yes	Yes	Yes	Yes
Spending on domestic programs		Yes	Yes	No	Yes	Yes	Yes
Spending on international mechanisms	No	No[2]	No	No	No	Yes	Yes
Regulation	No	No	No	No	No	No	Yes
Taxes	No	No	No	No	No	No	Yes

1. Federal level only.
2. As nonratifiers, the US and Australia are not eligible for Joint Implementation, the Clean Development Mechanism, and international trading.

rejected ratification of the Kyoto Protocol. Crowley argued in chapter 7 that that commitment is largely symbolic, resting heavily on business-as-usual reductions in land use clearing and "no regrets" energy efficiency measures (i.e., those that pay for themselves). When it comes to control of greenhouse gas emissions, as distinct from land use clearing, Australia's federal government, like that of the United States, has relied exclusively on expenditures and voluntary programs.

While the relatively weak domestic programs of these two jurisdictions are consistent with their status as nonratifiers, more striking is the degree of variation in domestic programs among the countries that ratified. Russia and China represent special cases—China because it did not have to meet any emissions targets as a developing country, Russia because that country received such a generous target in the Kyoto Protocol that it does not have to undertake mitigation measures in order to comply. However, the fact that it has largely done so would seem to reinforce the argument that Russia's ratification was motivated by material interests rather than international or domestic norms. The president signed a climate "doctrine" document in December 2009 that focused mostly on energy efficiency and adaptation to climate change. A significant unresolved question in the Russian case is the extent to which it will take advantage of Joint Implementation projects, which would have other Annex 1 parties pay to modernize and increase the profitability of the Russian oil and gas industries and energy grid. By early 2010 the government was eligible to participate in both Track 1 and Track 2 Joint Implementation programs, but no Russian projects had yet been completed and verified.

Among Canada, Japan, and the EU, one might have expected differences in the aggressiveness of domestic policies reflecting more or less demanding targets in the Kyoto Protocol. However, the variation observed is inconsistent with that. With the United States no longer a party to the treaty, Canada faces the most demanding reduction target, yet of these three jurisdictions it is the one that has done the *least* to contain its emissions. Despite three aborted plans since ratification, the Canadian federal government has relied to date exclusively on voluntary programs and subsidies to business (for instance, for bio-fuels) and consumers (for home energy efficiency improvements). Although regulations have been promised by a succession of three governments, they have yet to materialize. The current Conservative federal government promises only to end Canada's emissions *growth* by 2010, by which time its emissions are expected to be a third or more above its Kyoto target.

In contrast, the EU has established a Europe-wide cap-and-trade program. Several EU countries are also relying on the Kyoto international mechanisms. Japan lies between these two poles, with extensive reliance on international mechanisms and spending, but to date only voluntary agreements with industry concerning greenhouse gas emissions and a voluntary challenge to citizens to reduce their energy use.

Canada, Japan, and the EU converged with respect to ratification yet have diverged with respect to domestic abatement policies. How can one account for this difference? One possibility is that some countries, most obviously Canada, symbolically ratified but simply never intended to comply. Harrison argues in chapter 6 that while there is reason to doubt whether all Cabinet members who supported Canada's ratification believed that Canada would fully comply with its Kyoto target, they did ratify with good intentions of delivering significant emissions reductions via a host of programs that in the end never materialized. We thus focus on three other explanations.

The first is that key factors can change between the time of ratification and the later time when concrete policy options are debated. This is most pertinent in the case of Canada, where a change in the governing party resulted in a significant shift in climate policy. Although previous Liberal governments were reluctant to regulate, they had planned extensive reliance on the Kyoto Protocol's international mechanisms in an attempt to meet Canada's emissions reduction target. In contrast, when the Conservative Party won the 2006 election (for reasons unrelated to their positions on climate change),[15] they simply announced that Canada "could not" comply and stopped even trying.

A second explanation for variation in domestic policies of ratifying countries lies in differences between the enterprises of ratification and adoption of domestic abatement policies. In most jurisdictions, the decision to ratify received a great deal of attention, from the legislature, the media, and the public. However, the black-and-white question of ratification then gave way to technical questions, cost–benefit analyses, and complicated emissions projection scenarios. As these efforts to devise concrete policies to deliver emissions reductions fade from the limelight, good intentions confront persistent interest-group opposition. Moreover, while voters tend to be strongly supportive of the *idea* of compliance with international environmental treaties, they can simultaneously resist the reality of higher taxes or energy prices, as French President Nicolas Sarkozy is discovering as he follows through on his commitment to a carbon tax. The political incentives thus can be very different between ratification and domestic implementation of that international commitment. While this is true in all jurisdictions, as evidenced by considerable foot-dragging even in the EU, the implications tend to be greatest where the costs of compliance are highest, thus provoking stronger interest-group and voter backlash.

An important implication of this is that ideational commitments to ratification are easier than sustained implementation. This was evident in both the Canadian and Japanese cases. Chrétien's normative commitment was sufficient to carry the question of ratification but insufficient to bind his successors as they confronted continuing institutional and interest-group obstacles. Similarly, Tiberghien and Schreurs find in chapter 5 that the symbolism of the Kyoto Protocol rendered it almost impossible for Japanese politicians not to ratify, but that symbols alone cannot reduce emissions.

Third, we find that institutions can have different effects at different stages in the process from international negotiation to domestic implementation. In Canada's case, provincial governments who opposed the Kyoto Protocol were not in a position to block ratification, but given their ownership of key natural resources, they are in a position to obstruct implementation of that international commitment. Moreover, as discussed in chapter 1, although it may be more difficult to get agreement on action in systems with either horizontal or vertical diffusion of authority, when that agreement is achieved, it often takes the form of contractual agreements that bind successors. Thus, as a result of the complex negotiations of EU burden sharing and ongoing negotiation concerning abatement strategies, the European Commission has been granted authority to approve or disapprove member states' abatement plans, including their allocation of carbon credits for the European emissions trading system. The price of carbon crashed temporarily in 2006 due to a glut of credits on the market created by member states' excessive generosity in the first round. However, the Commission is playing a stronger role in rejecting member states' proposed credit allocations in the second round, which is expected to result in real emissions reductions and has already resulted in a higher price for carbon. In effect, the Commission is in a position to play an "enforcer" role when member states attempt to backslide.

In contrast, in majoritarian parliamentary systems such as Canada's, it was relatively easy for the Conservative government to dismantle implementation plans made by previous Liberal governments. Similarly, the Russian president had incentives to ratify Kyoto for reasons that had little to do with climate policy itself and much to do with receiving side payments on other issues of international negotiation. Since ratification was a unilateral decision that did not need to be negotiated with other branches of government or subnational units, the approach to implementation was unsettled prior to ratification and has been extremely slow to proceed following ratification.

Conclusions

In 2009, John Ashton, the British special envoy on climate change, reflected, "In Kyoto we made a lot of promises to each other, but we hadn't done the domestic politics."[16] As the Kyoto Protocol compliance period draws to a close and nations of the world look toward a post-Kyoto regime, it is thus timely to consider what lessons can be drawn from examination of the domestic politics of climate change.

Our exploration of climate policy using the theoretical lens of comparative politics yields several insights. First, even in responding to moral imperatives to conserve the planet's resources and protect future generations, costs still matter a great deal. The mere fact of an international treaty is a necessary step toward equalizing costs to different countries given conditions of both economic and environmental interdependence. However, the Kyoto Protocol equalized costs crudely at best. The commitment by industrialized countries to demonstrate leadership in the first round, while morally laudable, raised the issue of weakened competitiveness—an objection voiced loud and clear by domestic producers.[17] Second, Annex 1 parties to the treaty took on commitments of varying depth. Countries that had committed to deeper reductions faced greater domestic opposition from business and industrial sectors, which threatened higher prices, loss of jobs, and reduced economic growth. While it is tempting to paint the United States as an international outlaw for its withdrawal from the Kyoto Protocol, economic models suggest that the treaty would have imposed higher costs on the United States than on other jurisdictions. This suggests that in the international climate treaty that follows the Kyoto Protocol, it will be critical to find ways both to better equalize costs among Annex 1 countries and to secure a commitment from developing countries to limit growth of (though not necessarily to reduce) their emissions.

The magnitude of compliance costs and resulting domestic political opposition cannot, however, explain why Japan, Canada, Australia, and the EU would ratify the Kyoto Protocol. The case of Canada demonstrates that under the right institutional conditions, leaders' normative commitments can carry the day, despite considerable political opposition. In the cases of Japan, the EU, and Australia, it was voters', rather than policymakers', normative commitments that ensured a positive outcome. Consistent with Vogel's earlier work,[18] these cases demonstrate that when voters feel strongly enough, politicians can and do rise to the challenge.

However, the magnitude of that challenge also depends on political institutions in several ways. First, proportional electoral systems give greater expression to environmentally motivated voters' concerns than first-past-the-post systems, thus amplifying electoral incentives for policymakers, especially though Green parties. Schreurs and Tiberghien argue in chapter 2 that Green Party representatives in key EU member states and in the European Parliament played a key role in promoting EU leadership on climate change. Moreover, it is likely that the existence of Green parties in turn alerts other, less green voters to their latent environmental concerns.

Second, diffusion of authority can either facilitate or obstruct action on climate change, depending on interaction with other factors. Schreurs and Tiberghien report that a competitive dynamic emerged among EU member states. Similarly, federalism has been a positive force in the United States as well, where leadership by large green states has provided the necessary reassurance for others to follow suit. However, in both cases it was fortuitous that the largest and most influential players were relatively green. In contrast, federalism has for the most part been a negative force in Canada, where provincial governments control key natural resources and closely guard local industries that rely on them. The separation of powers, a form of horizontal diffusion of authority in the US presidential system, also played a critical role in the US nonratification and federal policy inaction to date.

Third, there is evidence of the importance of institutional lock-in effects in the EU. Although pressure from voters prompted ratification in both Japan and the EU, the EU has made significantly greater progress in adopting mitigation policies, in large part because the formal nature of EU compromises concerning burden sharing and various policy directives are enforced by the European Commission. In contrast, detailed emissions standards for particular industries apparently did not have the same symbolic significance as did ratification of the Kyoto Protocol for Japanese voters.

It is difficult to derive practical lessons from these various institutional effects, since in the time frame during which actions are urgently needed to address global warming, institutional reform is unlikely to be an option. Climate policy thus will remain more of an uphill battle for some jurisdictions than others.

While institutions may deter action, there are two possible routes to action to address climate change. The first is policymakers acting on their own values, despite attendant political risks. While the cases in this volume suggest that policymakers have enjoyed some success, in the absence of electoral support it has been difficult to sustain that commitment. In the United States, the lack of public attention to climate change, combined with the economic crisis, suggests that the Democratic leadership's apparent desire to follow their "good policy motives" could well be tested. The second and more sustainable route is activism to persuade voters to place the environment higher on their lists of policy priorities. In the end, the cases in this volume demonstrate that it is voters' sustained normative commitments to the problem of climate change that ultimately matter; arguably they are the only thing that ever has.

Notes

1. See Roy Morgan polls 3073, 3269, 3398, 3465 (http://www.roymorgan.com/news/polls/polls.cfm), which reveal that the environment ranked between sixth and ninth between June 1992 and October 2001 when respondents were asked to identify "the three most important things the federal government should be doing something about." Thereafter the question does not seem to have been asked in the same form, and a new question was introduced in 2005 asking for "the [single] most important problem facing Australia today." The environment ranked first and second in September and November 2005, respectively (polls 3895 and 3293). A poll by Australia National University still had the environment as the public's top priority in April 2008, although the economy edged ahead by the summer (Australian National University/Social Research Centre 2008).

2. There is a separate question of what countries thought they were undertaking at the time of the Kyoto *negotiations*. In some cases, there is a significant different between projections in 1997 and 2001–2002. Table 9.4 focuses on the latter because it is most relevant to one of our dependent variables, the decision to ratify.

3. A 21 percent reduction of Germany's 1990 emissions yields 257.5 MT, while a 12.5 percent reduction in UK baseline emissions yields 97 MT. Together these exceed the EU-15's commitment of 341.2 MT.

4. Although the Clean Development Mechanism represented a step in that direction, the US administration's analysis of compliance costs assumed that as a result of extensive transaction costs the Clean Development Mechanism would only realize 20 percent of the trading opportunities that would have materialized had developing countries accepted binding targets. It is noteworthy that the United States was not proposing that developing countries' emissions be capped at current levels but rather than they be limited to a reasonable growth trajectory, thus creating opportunities for trading.

5. Weyant and Hill 1999.

6. Averaged based on figures provided in figure 8 of Weyant and Hill, assuming no trading. Note that Canada, Australia, and New Zealand were modeled as a single region.

7. These estimates are based on averages drawn from data in figure 9 in Weyant and Hill 1999.

8. Dessler and Parson 2006, 136.

9. Checkel 2001.

10. Lantis 2006 makes a similar point, although he argues specifically that government leaders who take a treaty home for ratification from international negotiations are more likely to achieve a successful ratification outcome the more centralized power is in the *electoral* system (43).

11. Ringius 1999. See also Cass 2006 on the history of national commitments prior to the Kyoto Protocol.

12. Keck and Sikkink 1998.

13. Bernstein 2001, 2002.

14. Rabe 2004.

15. The central issue in the election was a scandal concerning the Liberals' use of sponsorship funds in Quebec.

16. Elisabeth Rosenthal, "Obama's Backing Raises Hopes for Climate Pact," *New York Times*, 1 March 2009.

17. Migration of industry from industrialized to developing countries would also tend to undermine the benefits of reductions by industrialized countries. However, the question of "leakage" is a separate issue politically from the magnitude of costs.

18. Vogel 1993.

References

Australian Greenhouse Office. 2006. *Tracking to the Kyoto Target 2006*. Canberra: Commonwealth of Australia.

Australian National University/Social Research Centre. 2008. Public Opinion towards Governance: Results from the Inaugural ANU Poll. April. http://www .anu.edu.au/anupoll/content/publications/report/governance_april_2008/ (accessed 30 September 2008).

Bernstein, Steven. 2001. *The Compromise of Liberal Environmentalism.* New York: Columbia University Press.

Bernstein, Steven. 2002. International Institutions and the Framing of Domestic Policies: The Kyoto Protocol and Canada's Response to Climate Change. *Policy Sciences* 35:203–236.

Canada. 2002. *Climate Change Plan for Canada.* Ottawa: Government of Canada.

Cass, Loren R. 2006. *The Failures of American and European Climate Policy: International Norms, Domestic Politics, and Unachievable Commitments.* NY: SUNY Press.

Checkel, Jeffrey T. 2001. Why Comply? Social Learning and European Identity Change. *International Organization* 55:553–588.

Dessler, Andrew E., and Edward A. Parson. 2006. *The Science and Politics of Global Climate Change.* New York: Cambridge University Press.

European Environmental Agency. 2002a. *Greenhouse Gas Emission Trends and Projections in Europe.* Copenhagen: EEA.

European Environment Agency. 2002b. *Analysis and Comparison of National and EU-Wide Projections of Greenhouse Gas Emissions.* Copenhagen: EEA.

Keck, Margaret, and Kathryn Sikkink. 1998. *Activists beyond Borders: Advocacy Networks in International Politics.* Ithaca: Cornell University Press.

Lantis, Jeffrey S. 2006. The Life and Death of International Treaties: Double-Edged Diplomacy and the Politics of Ratification in Comparative Perspective. *International Politics* 43:24–52.

Pew Global Attitudes Project. 2007. Global Unease with Major World Powers. 27 June. http://pewglobal.org/reports/display.php?ReportID=256.

Rabe, Barry. 2004. *Statehouse and Greenhouse: The Emerging Politics of American Climate Change Policy.* Washington, DC: Brookings.

Ringius, Lasse. 1999. Differentiation, Leaders, and Fairness: Negotiating Climate Commitments in the European Community. *International Negotiation* 4:133–166.

United States. 2002. Climate Action Report. Washington, DC: US Department of State.

United States. 2007. U.S. Climate Action Report 2006 (April 2007 draft). Washington, DC: US Department of State.

Vogel, David. 1993. Representing Diffuse Interests in Environmental Policy-making. In *Do Institutions Matter? Government Capabilities in the United States and Beyond,* ed. R. Kent Weaver and Bert A. Rockman. Washington, DC: Brookings.

Weyant, John P., and Jennifer Hill. 1999. Introduction and Overview. *The Energy Journal*. Special issue: The Costs of the Kyoto Protocol: A Multi-Model Evaluation.

World Public Opinion. 2006. GlobeScan Poll: Global Views on Climate Change Questionnaire and Methodology. April. http://www.worldpublicopinion.org/pipa/pdf/apr06/ClimateChange_Apr06_quaire.pdf.

World Public Opinion. 2007. Poll Finds Worldwide Agreement That Climate Change Is a Threat. 13 March. http://www.worldpublicopinion.org/pipa/articles/btenvironmentra/329.php?lb=bte&pnt=329&nid=&id=.

Contributors

Steinar Andresen is a senior research fellow at the Fridtjof Nansen Institute in Norway. He has published extensively on global environmental politics and climate changes in journals such as *Global Environmental Politics, Global Environmental Change,* and *International Environmental Agreements.*

Inga Fritzen Buan is a researcher with the Fridtjof Nansen Institute in Norway, where she currently is the primary researcher on Chinese energy and climate politics. Her academic background is in human geography and Chinese language and culture studies. She has published articles and commentaries on Chinese climate policy.

Kate Crowley is an associate professor and head of the School of Government at the University of Tasmania. She has published widely on environmental politics and policy in journals such as the *Journal of Environmental Policy and Planning, Environmental Politics, Local Environment,* and the *Australian Journal of Political Science.* She is coeditor of *Australian Environmental Policy: Studies in Decline and Devolution* (1999) and chair of the Tasmanian Premier's Climate Action Council.

Kathryn Harrison is professor of political science at the University of British Columbia. She is the author of *Passing the Buck: Federalism and Canadian Environmental Policy* (1996), coauthor of *Risk, Science, and Politics: Regulation of Toxic Substances in Canada and the United States* (1994), coeditor of *Managing the Environmental Union* (2000), and editor of *Racing to the Bottom? Provincial Interdependence in the Canadian Federation* (2006). She has published recent articles in the *Canadian Journal of Economics,* the *Journal of Policy Analysis and Management,* the *Canadian Journal of Political Science,* and *Governance.*

Gørild Heggelund is currently senior climate change advisor with the United Nations Development Programme in Beijing. As a specialist on Chinese energy and environmental policy, Dr. Heggelund is the author of *Environment and Resettlement Politics in China* (2004), and has published extensively in journals such as *International Environmental Agreements, Asian Perspective,* and *Development and Change.*

Laura A. Henry is an associate professor in the Department of Government and Legal Studies at Bowdoin College. Her research has focused on the Russian environmental movement. She is the author of the book *Red to Green: Environmental Activism in Post-Soviet Russia* (Cornell University Press, forthcoming) and coeditor of the volume *Russian Civil Society: A Critical Assessment* (M. E. Sharpe, 2006).

Miranda A. Schreurs   is director of the Environmental Policy Research Institute and Professor of Comparative Politics at the Free University of Berlin. Prior to this she was associate professor in the Department of Government and Politics, University of Maryland. She is author of *Environmental Politics in Japan, Germany, and the United States* (2002), coauthor of the *Historical Dictionary of the Green Movement*, 2nd edition (2007), and coeditor of *The Environmental Dimension of Asian Security: Conflict and Cooperation in Energy, Resources, and Pollution* (2007).

Lisa McIntosh Sundstrom   is an associate professor of political science at the University of British Columbia. Her publications include *Funding Civil Society: Transnational Actors and NGO Development in Russia* (Stanford University Press, 2006) and articles in the journals *International Organization, Demokratizatsiya,* and *Canadian Foreign Policy.*

Yves Tiberghien   is an associate professor of political science at the University of British Columbia and a faculty associate at the Center for European Studies of the Institut d'Études Politiques, Paris. He is author of *Entrepreneurial States: Reforming Corporate Governance in France, Japan, and Korea* (Cornell University Press, 2007). He is currently working on a book on the global governance of genetically modified organisms as well as another on global institutional reforms led by the EU, Japan, and Canada.

American and Comparative Environmental Policy

Sheldon Kamieniecki and Michael E. Kraft, series editors

Steven Cohen, Sheldon Kamieniecki, and Matthew A. Cahn, *Strategic Planning in Environmental Regulation: A Policy Approach That Works*

Michael E. Kraft and Sheldon Kamieniecki, editors, *Business and Environmental Policy: Corporate Interests in the American Political System*

Joseph F. C. DiMento and Pamela Doughman, editors, *Climate Change: What It Means for Us, Our Children, and Our Grandchildren*

Christopher McGrory Klyza and David J. Sousa, *American Environmental Policy, 1990–2006: Beyond Gridlock*

John M. Whiteley, Helen Ingram, and Richard Perry, editors, *Water, Place, and Equity*

Judith A. Layzer, *Natural Experiments: Ecosystem-Based Management and the Environment*

Daniel A. Mazmanian and Michael E. Kraft, editors, *Toward Sustainable Communities: Transition and Transformations in Environmental Policy*, second edition

Henrik Selin and Stacy D. VanDeveer, editors, *Changing Climates in North American Politics: Institutions, Policymaking, and Multilevel Governance*

Megan Mullin, *Governing the Tap: Special District Governance and the New Local Politics of Water*

David M. Driesen, editor, *Economic Thought and U.S. Climate Change Policy*

Kathryn Harrison and Lisa McIntosh Sundstrom, editors, *Global Commons, Domestic Decisions: The Comparative Politics of Climate Change*

Index